DATE DUE

TWAYNE'S WORLD LEADERS SERIES

Pope Pius IX

TWLS 81

POPE PIUS IX:
Crusader In A Secular Age

By FRANK J. COPPA

St. John's University

TWAYNE PUBLISHERS

A DIVISION OF G. K. HALL & CO., BOSTON

262.13
P688zC
IX

Copyright © 1979 by G. K. Hall & Co.

Published in 1979 by Twayne Publishers,
A Division of G. K. Hall & Co.
All Rights Reserved

Printed on permanent/durable acid-free paper and bound
in the United States of America

First Printing

Library of Congress Cataloging in Publication Data

Coppa, Frank J.
Pope Pius IX.

(Twayne's world leaders series; TWLS 81)
Bibliography: p. 225-59
Includes index
1. Pius IX, Pope, 1792-1878. 2. Popes—Biography.
I. Title.
BX1373.C67   262'.13'0924   [B]   79-13451
ISBN 0-8057-7727-X

To my wife, Rosina
and daughters,
Francesca and Melina.

Contents

About the Author
Preface
Chronology
Introduction

1. Giovanni Maria Mastai-Ferretti: The Youth and the Man	19
2. The Long Apprenticeship: Mastai-Ferretti as Bishop	32
3. The New Pope	43
4. The Failure of Reformism	57
5. Toward Revolution	71
6. Revolution and Flight	84
7. Restoration	98
8. The Conservative Pope	112
9. Pio Nono and Cardinal Antonelli Confront Italian Unification	126
10. The Syllabus of Errors	140
11. The Vatican Council	154
12. The Collapse of the Temporal Power and the Roman Question	169
13. The *Kulturkampf*	181
14. Conclusion	193
Notes and References	199
Selected Bibliography	225
Index	259

About the Author

Frank J. Coppa is Professor of History at St. John's University, New York, as well as an Associate in the Columbia Seminar on Studies on Modern Italy. Educated at Brooklyn College and the Catholic University of America, Dr. Coppa is the author of *Planning, Protectionism and Politics in Liberal Italy: Economics and Politics in the Giolittian Age* (Washington, D.C.: Catholic University Press, 1971) and *Camillo di Cavour* (New York: Twayne Publishers, Inc., 1973). He has served as co-editor of *From Vienna to Vietnam: War and Peace in the Modern World* (Dubuque: Brown, 1969), *Cities in Transition: From the Ancient World to Urban America* (Chicago: Nelson-Hall, 1974), and *The Immigrant Experience in America* (Boston: Twayne Publishers, 1976) and has edited as well as contributed to the volume *Religion in the Making of Western Man* (New York: St. John's University Press, 1974).

Preface

Although this work is entitled *Pius IX*, the reader will not find within these pages a detailed account of the life of a Pope who ruled almost twenty-five years, pontificated for almost thirty-three, and whose lifetime spanned and influenced the entire *Risorgimento*. The field of his activity was so vast, the range of his responses so broad, and the consequences of his actions so far-reaching that any definitive study would require a multi-volume work, each many times the pages found within this single volume.

Alberto Serafini commenced such a broad study but unfortunately produced only one volume before his death. Nonetheless his *Pio IX*, which accounts for the life of Giovanni Maria Mastai-Ferretti up to 1846, prior to his accession to the papal throne, has almost 2,000 pages. Giacomo Martina, who has assumed the responsibility of completing the study, has to date produced one volume (566 pages), which examines the years from 1846 to 1850, and plans another two or three volumes to complete the biography. Very clearly the present work cannot duplicate their efforts nor is it a study of the Church in the age of Pio Nono such as produced by Roger Aubert.

The aims of this book are rather more modest. It will hopefully provide a broad yet scholarly survey of the life and times of Pius while objectively assessing his impact upon the *Risorgimento*, Italy, and the Church.

To date objectivity has not been the hallmark of studies of Pio Nono; indeed it has been the exception rather than the rule. In Italy the controversy surrounding this pope remains very much alive, with some contemporaries showing the same hatred that inspired a group of Romans in 1881 to attempt to throw his coffin into the Tiber as it was being moved from St. Peter's to its final resting place in the Basilica of San Lorenzo. Abroad, as well as at home, controversy still surrounds the longest-reigning Pope. The recent work of the Swiss-German priest August Hasler entitled *Pius IX: Papal Infallibility and the First Vatican Council* claims that Pius all but rigged the Assembly and goes so far as to suggest that by the time of the Council the Pope was no longer sane.

The polemical nature of much of the secondary literature, which is either apologetic or antagonistic in tone, explains why I have attempted, whenever possible, to rely upon primary sources. However, the reader will find a broad range of works included within the Selected Bibliography.

During the course of my research I had occasion to use the facilities of a number of archives and libraries and am particularly indebted to Monsignor Martino Giusti, Prefect of the *Archivio Segreto Vaticano*, and Monsignor Hermann Hoberg, Vice-Prefect, who permitted me to utilize the archive in the afternoons as well as in the morning, when it was open to the general scholarly community. The Directors of the *Archivio di Stato* and the *Archivio Centrale* were most helpful, as was Cipriana Scelba, Director of the American Commission for Cultural Exchange with Italy, who graciously provided me with a number of letters of introduction. Likewise I am indebted to the chief librarian of the Library of the Chamber of Deputies. I should like to thank Emilia Morelli, Director of the Instituto per la Storia del Risorgimento and editor of the *Rassegna Storica del Risorgimento*, for her suggestions.

I wish also to express my appreciation to the Reverend Robert Trisco, editor of the *Catholic Historical Review*, who has long provided support and encouragement. I should also like to thank Reverend Joseph Moody, President of the American Catholic Historical Association, who has given generously of his time and knowledge. I am grateful to Professor John K. Zeender of the Catholic University of America for reading the chapter on the *Kulturkampf* and Professor Hans Trefousse of Brooklyn College for reading the Introduction. Finally, I should like to thank my wife for her moral support and understanding. The shortcomings of this work are, of course, my own.

The research for this work was in part supported by a grant from the National Endowment for the Humanities, which permitted me to return to Rome to work in the Vatican Archive, and by a Research Leave provided by St. John's University.

Chronology

1792	Giovanni Maria Mastai-Ferretti born in Senigallia.
1802–1809	Giovanni studies at the College of Volterra in Tuscany.
1819	Giovanni ordained a priest.
1819–1823	Giovanni spends his years at the Roman orphanage of the "Tata Giovanni."
1823–1825	He accompanies Monsignor Giovanni Muzi, apostolic delegate to Chile and Peru, in his visit to South America.
1825	Giovanni returns to Italy.
1825–1827	He serves as director of the Roman hospice of San Michele.
1827–1832	Serves as Archbishop of Spoleto.
1832–1846	Serves as Bishop of Imola.
1840	He is made a cardinal.
1846	He is elected Pope and takes the name Pius IX, in deference to the memory of Pius VII. Grants an amnesty.
1847	The new Pope grants a limited liberty of the press, a *Consulta di Stato*, Civic Guard, and a Council of Ministers.
1848	Constitution of Papal State published. Pius flees his capital following a revolutionary outburst.
1849	The establishment of a Roman Republic leads Pius to ask for the intervention of the Catholic powers to restore his temporal authority.
1850	The Pope and Cardinal Antonelli reenter Rome. The reestablishment of the Catholic hierarchy in England.
1853	The reestablishment of the Catholic hierarchy in Holland.
1854	The proclamation of the Immaculate Conception of Mary.
1855	Austria signs a concordat that is favorable to Church.
1857	The Pope visits his northern provinces.
1860	Battle of Castelfidardo results in the defeat of the papal forces. Pius issues a bull of excommunication which collectively

	condemns all those who conspired to deprive the Pope of his possessions.
1861	The Kingdom of Italy proclaimed.
1864	Pius responds to the September Convention by issuing the encyclical *Quanta cura*, to which is attached the Syllabus of Errors.
1868	The Papal Bull *Aeterni patris* convokes the Ecumenical Council.
1869	The opening of the Vatican Council.
1870	The proclamation of Papal infallibility. The loss of Rome to the Italians; Pius proclaims himself a "prisoner in the Vatican."
1871	The twenty-fifth anniversary of Pius's election as Pope, his jubilee.
1875	Pius's encyclical *Quod nunquam* condemns the *Kulturkampf* in Germany.
1876	Death of Cardinal Antonelli, Pius's Secretary of State since 1849.
1877	Pius's golden episcopal jubilee celebrates his fifty years service as a bishop.
1878	Death of Pius IX.

Introduction

Pope Pius IX is one of the central figures of the nineteenth century. As ruler of the Papal States he was important in Italian and European affairs and as head of the universal Church he was a personality of worldwide importance. To millions of Catholics he was the greatest figure of the age while to others he was the most conspicuous. "Pius IX is, at this day, the only representative of exclusive moral force upon the earth," wrote a contemporary shortly after his accession; "it is by moral force alone that he has conquered his throne and his people, and we shall see, hereafter, this irresistible moral force conduct him without treasure and without armies, to the victory of all Italy. . . ."[1] Certainly critical events filled his pontificate and closely bound his life with developments in the three decades after the revolutionary upheaval of 1848.

The larger history of these thirty years was in part shaped by this Pope, who had an even greater influence upon his 200 million spiritual subjects. Elected Pope in 1846, he was destined to sit in the Papal chair longer than any of his predecessors. His devotion to Mary led to the proclamation of the Immaculate Conception on December 8, 1854, while his determination to protect the prerogatives of the Bishop of Rome led to an increasing centralization in the Church which culminated with the proclamation of the dogma of papal infallibility in July 1870. Thus as Rome was in the process of losing its temporal power and could persuade no state to uphold its cause, the papacy under Pius IX was to exercise over believing Catholics a power more absolute than ever.

During his first two years as Pope, Pius seemed to depart from the conservative course of his predecessors, and many of his policies appeared to be in marked contrast to those of Gregory XVI, whom he succeeded. Indeed Pius was hailed as the envoy sent by God to conclude the great business of the nineteenth century, the reconciliation of religion and liberty. Popular demonstrations in his favor were held from the Alps to Sicily. The enthusiasm he generated transcended Italy and even the Catholic world of Europe, reaching the

United States, where a series of demonstrations were held in his honor.[2]

The liberal reforms initiated by Pius won him the approval of his subjects, the goodwill of most Italians, and the respect of Catholics and non-Catholics alike. In London, Paris, Madrid, Brussels, Florence, and even Constantinople the press with unanimous cordiality extolled the merits of the new Pope. The constitutional states of Europe, including Protestant England, supported his endeavors. "The present Pope has begun to enter upon a system of administrative improvements in his dominions," wrote Lord Palmerston, "and it appears to Her Majesty's Government that his proceedings in these matters are upon general principle highly praiseworthy, and deserving of encouragement from all those who take an interest in the welfare of the people of Italy."[3]

Giuseppe Mazzini, the organizer of Young Italy and the prophet of Italian unification, from his exile studied the Holy Father's innovations with immense hope and believed that they might translate into reality the instinct which vibrated from one end of the peninsula to the other.[4] From America Giuseppe Garibaldi, the future conqueror of the Italian South, looked upon Pius as the man provided by providence to restore independence to the country of Caesar. "If these hands used to fighting, would be acceptable to his Holiness, we would most thankfully dedicate them to the service of him who deserves so well of the Church and of our Fatherland," he wrote to the papal nuncio in Uruguay. "Joyful indeed, we, and our companions, in whose name we write, shall be, if allowed to shed our blood in defense of Pius IX's work of redemption."[5]

The Austrian Chancellor, Prince Klemens von Metternich, was one of the few who early warned of the grave consequences of the Pope's actions, which he frankly disapproved. "Born and raised in a liberal family, he has been formed in a bad school: a good priest but one who has never turned his mind to affairs of government," he wrote in 1847. "Warm hearted, with little imagination, he has since his election to the Papacy, allowed himself to be drawn into a net from which he is no longer able to escape and if events pursue their natural course he will get himself chased out of Rome."[6] Metternich's words were prophetic; for at the end of 1848 Pius was forced to flee his capital while his subjects, under the inspiration of radical leadership, terminated the temporal power and proclaimed a Republic.

Following the intervention of the powers and the collapse of the Republic, Pius was seen to pursue a new course, condemning

Introduction

liberalism as a dangerous delusion. The Pope now emerged as one of the protagonists of the great ideological conflict of the nineteenth century, convinced that the excesses of liberalism and nationalism violated Christian morality and threatened the temporal power. Well disposed toward the contributions of science and technology, Pius was critical of positivism, which he claimed sought to destroy the world of faith by fact, and he denounced economic liberalism as selfishness disguised as science. He, more than anyone else, expressed the opposition of the Church toward these doctrines in a series of pronouncements and above all the encyclical *Quanta cura* and its accompanying Syllabus of Errors.

Critics of the course pursued by the Catholic Church in the nineteenth century inevitably find themselves opposed to the political and ecclesiastical decisions made by Pio Nono. Recently this has been clearly seen in the works of the Swiss-born theologian and priest Hans Küng, who has delved into the hierarchical structure of the Church and challenged the doctrine of papal infallibility in his book *Infallible?: An Inquiry*. In this and other works Küng has questioned the basis of infallibility, which has a long tradition in the Church but was only explicitly defined, with the support of Pope Pius IX, in 1870. The petrine office, clothed with the mantle of infallibility provided by Pio Nono, has evoked fears and anxieties that continue to haunt some Protestants, who view it as a major obstacle to Christian unity.

Despite the crucial role played by Pius in the history of the nineteenth century and the evolution of the Church, studies of him have been more polemical than historical, generating more heat than light. During his own lifetime he was exalted as a "saint" and "the conqueror of all hearts" by some and accused of being a "vain autocrat" and the "enemy of the Italian people" by others. All sorts of charges were launched against him, including the one that he had earlier joined the Freemasons. Still others claimed that he was the puppet of the reactionaries and above all the Cardinal Secretary of State, Giacomo Antonelli, who was depicted as the guiding evil genius of the counter-*Risorgimento*, with the amiable Pius portrayed as his helpless follower.

The exact responsibility of Pius for the momentous events of his pontificate remains uncertain. There are still those who pose the problem, at least on the political plane, as it was presented in Pius's time: should the Pope be considered a traitor to the Italian cause, was he betrayed, or was he simply lacking in good political sense and thus was the cause of his own catastrophe? Carlo Cattaneo in his *Consid-*

erations on Italian Matters (1850-1855) concluded that Pius was created by others, but undid himself. Pius was a fairy tale imagined to instruct the people a truth. Pius IX was a poem.[7]

Very early a historiography developed which depicted Pius as the good shepherd, determined to do all he could for his flock, but finding his kindness reciprocated by ingratitude, persecution, and exile. Nonetheless he was seen to overcome all these iniquities by sanctity and supernatural assistance. Within some of these works Papa Mastai was presented as the "Saint of God" who could do no wrong.

This interpretation was almost immediately opposed by an equally simplistic one developed by national and radical elements which accused Pius of having encouraged and then betrayed the national cause. Many liberal historians found it difficult if not impossible to write objectively of the figure they held responsible for the failure of the anti-Austrian crusade of 1848. They were incensed that he had turned his back on the liberal program of the first two years of his pontificate, issuing the Syllabus of Errors and the dogma of papal infallibility and marshaling the forces of the counter-*Risorgimento* against Italian unification and the progressive ideologies of the day. Indeed from the time of the restoration of 1849 to the Pope's death in 1878 those in the liberal camp considered Pius their greatest ideological foe. Some, in fact, called for a struggle to preserve their "progressive" culture from the "medieval" approach of the papacy. In Piedmont first and later the Kingdom of Italy, this led to a bitter Church-State conflict; in Germany the ensuing conflict was appropriately termed the *Kulturkampf,* or struggle for culture.

Neither of the extremes served the cause of truth or sound scholarship. The fact that the Vatican Archives remained closed for this important period contributed to the confusion. Father Pietro Pirri, who was granted limited access to the papers of Pio Nono, did shed some light on the personality of this polemical figure and the nature of the counter-*Risorgimento.* However, many issues remained unresolved. An adequate biography of Pio Nono had perforce to await the opening of the Vatican Archives for the pontificate.

The opening of Pius's papers in 1967, the collection of material by the commission favoring his beatification, the founding of a journal dealing with the life of the Church during his time, and the renewed interest in the age of Vatican I, following the calling of Vatican II, have all contributed to make a new biography of Pius not only desirable but possible. Giacomo Martina has planned a three-volume

Introduction

study in Italian, continuing where Alberto Serafini's scholarly study of Mastai-Ferretti, before his election, left off. To date, only the first volume, *Pio IX (1846-1850),* has appeared, but two more are projected, and Martina may rewrite the Serafini volume. The present study is far less ambitious. Nonetheless it seeks to provide for the English reader an objective account of the life and times of Pope Pius IX, the most controversial as well as the most important Pope in the nineteenth century.

CHAPTER 1

Giovanni Maria Mastai-Ferretti: The Youth and the Man

THE afternoon of September 19, 1870, as the Italian forces camped outside Rome prepared for their entry into the Eternal City, Pope Pius IX left the Vatican Palace for the summit of the Lateran Hill. There he entered the building which houses the Santa Scala, or Holy Stairs, which according to tradition were taken from the hall in which Pontius Pilate sat in judgment of Jesus, and which he descended following his condemnation to death. The Pope-King, like other penitents and suppliants, climbed the twenty-seven steps on his knees, pausing on each to pray. Distraught by the impending invasion of his capital which would deprive him of the remnant of his state and destroy the temporal power, Pius, as in other times of crisis, resorted to prayer and trusted in the will of God. This had enabled him to cope with the Garibaldian incursions into his state in the 1860s, the Piedmontese invasion of 1860, which resulted in the loss of his richest provinces, and the revolutionary whirlwind of 1848, which forced him to flee his capital and state.

Giovanni Maria Mastai-Ferretti had overcome personal as well as political problems through prayer and faith in God's mercy from the onset of his *malattia di nervi,* or nervous malady, diagnosed as epilepsy, which troubled his childhood and threatened to prevent his entry into the priesthood, to the troubles and embarrassment caused him by members of his family: including brothers, sisters, and nephews. Prayer had formed an important part of his life since his earliest years in Senigallia, a small city in the Marches on the Adriatic coast, not far from Ancona.

Giovanni Maria was born the ninth and last child of Count Girolamo Mastai-Ferretti and the former Caterina Solazzi in 1792, in the Palazzo Mastai, which had been inhabited by the family since the end of the sixteenth century.[1] Born of a noble but far from wealthy provincial family between Saturday, May 12, and Sunday, May 13, Giovanni always considered the thirteenth his birthday, on the assumption that he entered the world shortly after midnight. It was from his mother that he inherited his smiling expression and derived his religious outlook. The fact that his mother was devoted to Mary, mother of Jesus, is reflected in the fact that five of the children were given the name: his sisters Maria Virginia, Maria Teresa, Maria Isabella, and Maria Tecla, as well as Giovanni Maria.

The Mastai family, which belonged to the lower nobility and had played a prominent role in the Papal States for centuries, was bound to be affected by the French revolutionary wars which erupted in the year of Giovanni's birth. Aware of his nobility, which he considered a gift of God, Giovanni later was wont to relate that even though Christ had been born humbly in a stall, he had a long genealogy as a descendant of princes and kings.[2] Giovanni's father served as gonfalonier of Senigallia seven times; his uncle Andrea, who was also his godfather, was Bishop of Pesaro; his father's other brother Paolino[3] was a canon of St. Peter's and was closely tied to the Roman court. Another uncle, Gabriele, Canon of Senigallia, had died earlier in Pisa in 1778.

Ecclesiastical life in his father's family was something of a tradition for more than a century, and the Mastai-Ferretti were dedicated to the existing order in the peninsula and to the government of the Pope in particular. This did not prevent the future Pope's brother Giuseppe, who was ten years older than Giovanni, from joining Joachim Murat's army as a lieutenant, or his father from taking part in the Caesarean Magistrate of Senigallia in the Napoleonic period.[4] They, like so many others, could not ignore the French incursion into the peninsula in 1796 and the unprecedented conquests of Napoleon which shattered the old regime in Italy.

The Napoleonic victories in northern Italy against the Austrians and Piedmontese encouraged the Papal Legations of Bologna and Ferrara to secede and join Modena in the Cispadane Republic, which later merged with the Duchies of Milan and Mantua to form the Cisalpine Republic. This brought Napoleon into open conflict with the aged Pope Pius VI (Giovanni Angelo Braschi), but the latter, faced by a full-scale invasion early in 1797, agreed to the Peace of Tolentino. Under its terms the Pope was forced to recognize the earlier loss of Avignon to France, surrender the citadel and port of Ancona to the French army, renounce his claims to Bologna, Ravenna, and Ferrara, and agree to pay an indemnity of some 30 million French *livres* and send hundreds of art objects to France. Among the prayers that the Countess Mastai had Giovanni recite every evening were those to give the Pope courage and his persecutors repentence.[5]

Napoleon left the Pope with a truncated state, but prophesied that it could not continue to exist for long in this form and would collapse of its own weight. The Directory in Paris and the republicans of the Cisalpine state, however, were not prepared to wait and preferred to precipitate matters. The shooting of a French general in Rome provided the pretext for intervention as General Louis Alexandre Berthier's forces marched over the Apennines and on February 11 entered the capital and occupied the Castel Sant' Angelo. Despite the apathy of the Romans, French connivance led to the formation of a Roman Republic, the deposition of the temporal power, and on February 17, 1798, the eighty-year-old Pontiff was ordered to leave his capital within three days. The moribund Pius VI was dragged to France and died a virtual prisoner at the end of August. The Roman Republic which replaced his government proved to be shortlived as the Russo-Austrian forces of the second coalition led by Marshal Alexander Suvorov penetrated northern Italy, provoking the flight of the French forces that had created and bolstered the satellite republics.

In March 1800, after a difficult conclave held in Venice, the fifty-nine-year-old Gregorio Luigi Barnaba Chairamonti, the Cardinal Archbishop of Imola, was elected Pope and assumed the name Pius VII. Napoleon, who was the real master of France since the coup d'etat of November 1799, sought an accommodation with the Church and realized that Chiaramonti, whose diocese fell in the Cisalpine Republic, had endeavored to reconcile the Church with the revolution. The way was thus paved for an improvement in relations between the new Pope, who entered Rome in July 1800, and Napoleon, who defeated the main Habsburg army at Marengo just a month earlier. Within a year Pius had concluded a concordat with the French that assured him possession of his territory, without, however, receiving the Legations and the territory ceded to the French at Tolentino.

During these troubled years Giovanni Mastai-Ferretti, the youngest in the family, was sheltered from the turmoil in his father's house, where much of his early education was provided by his mother. Likewise the religious tone of the household was set by Caterina, who remained devoted to Mary and often took her youngest son to the

Church of the Servite Fathers to pray before her statue. Later the children were instructed by a young priest who provided them with an elementary education and prepared Giovanni for the sacrament of Communion. Giovanni apparently received this sacrament in 1802, and not in 1803 as is commonly believed.[6] He was then in his tenth year and this attests a considerable mental and spiritual development because even in the Papal States at that time it was not the custom to admit children to the communion table before they reached their twelfth or thirteenth birthday.[7]

In 1803, when Giovanni was just over eleven years old, he was sent to Saint Michael's School in the mountain town of Volterra in Tuscany, run by the Scolopi Fathers. It was selected because it enjoyed a good reputation and the countess was apparently aware of the fact that the founder of the institution had dedicated it to the mother of Jesus. The Congregation of the Scolopi was devoted to Mary, and her veneration was inculcated in their students as well. At the school Giovanni distinguished himself in mathematics and the physical sciences, displaying considerable powers of reflection and observation.

While at Volterra the young Mastai learned that Pope Pius VII had passed through Tuscany on his way to Paris to crown Napoleon emperor in 1804.[8] The next year word reached him that Napoleon had established a Kingdom of Italy and had taken the crown for himself. Rumor also had it that relations between the Pope and the emperor were far from cordial, but Mastai had problems of his own to confront. While at St. Michael's his health remained delicate and he was subject to seizures which cast a shadow over his future.

In 1809 the seventeen-year-old Giovanni received the first ecclesiastical tonsure at the hands of the local bishop, Monsignor Giuseppe Gaetano Incontri. This step was not indicative of any vocation for at the time Giovanni had no intention of entering the priesthood, but rather reflected his parents' concern for his future and this tonsure made him eligible eventually to administer one of the benefices controlled by his family.

Giovanni's six years at the college in Volterra came to an end in October 1809 after he experienced what was diagnosed as an epileptic seizure and was personally escorted home by Father Bacci of the Scolopi Order. Whether it was actual epilepsy or some nervous disorder with similar symptoms is not certain. What is clear is that the priests of St. Michael were not prepared to assume the grave responsibility of caring for Giovanni, and the seventeen-year-old was not able to continue his studies there. Some three years later, when he was called upon to take part in the Guard of Honor of the Kingdom of Italy, he was exempted from the conscription list because he was deemed subject to epilepsy.[9]

It has been suggested that soon after Caterina took her son to the Shrine of the Madonna of Loreto to pray for his recovery in 1809, the decision was made that he dedicate himself to the Church. This cannot be substantiated, however, and indeed the young Mastai's correspondence indicates that he had not yet found a vocation. He was desirous of continuing his education and could not do so in Senigallia, which offered no university courses. The fact that his health was still poor, that the financial resources of the family were limited, and that he had to be closely watched all contributed to his mother's decision to send him to Rome, where he might study under the watchful eye of his uncle Paolino, who might also assist in his support.

Conditions in Rome were not conducive for the quiet philosophical studies the countess sought for her nervous and depressed son. Pope Pius VII had earned the displeasure of Napoleon for his refusal to declare invalid the marriage of his brother to an American Protestant,[10] his unwillingness to close his ports to English vessels and expel all enemies of France from Rome,[11] and his unwillingness to declare war upon Great Britain. At the beginning of 1808 French troops entered the City on the Tiber and the Pope shut himself in the Quirinale Palace, declaring himself a prisoner in his capital as long as the French remained. In May an Imperial Decree united the Papal States to the French Empire and declared Rome an Imperial Free City.[12] In early June Papal insignias were removed throughout Rome, including the Castel Sant' Angelo, and replaced by the imperial coat of arms. The Pope, cardinals, ecclesiastics, and those faithful to the Holy See found themselves in a difficult position.[13] Pius responded by the publication of his bull of excommunication *Cum memoranda illa die*, which was affixed to the walls of Santa Maria Maggiore and San Giovanni in Laterano. In turn Napoleon had the Pontiff removed from his apartments and deported.

The Mastai family was viewed with some suspicion by the French and their allies both in Rome and in the provinces. His uncle Andrea was arrested for his failure to take an oath of loyalty to the Kingdom of Italy and, after being banished to Mantua, was confined in Vigevano, where he remained while the Kingdom survived. In 1810 both Giovanni and his uncle Paolino were forced out of Rome and returned to Senigallia. Only the disastrous Russian campaign and the success of the sixth coalition against Napoleon provided the basis for the restoration of the Pope's freedom and temporal possessions and better days for the Mastai-Ferretti.

These were difficult years for Giovanni, whose physical and mental health did not permit him to concentrate seriously upon his studies. His anguish is reflected in his spiritual exercises and personal assessment of April 1810, the oldest and in many ways the most revealing autobiographical statement he preserved. In it he wrote that he was troubled by his propensity to anger and his submission to the sin of pride reflected in his self preoccupation and his great ambition. At the same time he showed a great desire to preserve his chastity and to do so determined to flee from occasions of sin, shun dangerous company, avoid impure thoughts, and lower his eyes rather than satisfy his desire to look at certain objects. Although the reflections of a layman, and labeled as such, he saw the need to instruct himself in doing the divine will, if God gave him the strength and health to do so. The question of health was paramount, for Giovanni continued to suffer from depression and epilepsy, and as late as April 1814 he suffered from a severe attack of his malady which left him weak and confused.[14]

In May 1814 Pope Pius learned that he was free to return to Rome and set out for the Eternal City. On impulse Giovanni joined a group from Senigallia that decided to venture to Rome to join the throngs welcoming the Pope home. Years later he recalled that when Pius VII went to the Basilica of St. Peter, a King of Sardinia, the saintly Carlo Emanuele IV, was there to greet him.[15] Giovanni did not know how long he would remain in Rome, but, having an uncle employed by the papal government, he thought he might be of help in securing a post for himself—although he admitted that nothing had been decided yet. After a year in Rome, the summer of 1815, he let friends know that he was considering entering the Pope's Noble Guard and petitioned its commander, Prince Altieri, through an intermediary. Although it has been alleged that he was denied entry because of his epilepsy, the correspondence tells another story. It reveals that, by November 1815, he had second thoughts about having secured a place for himself in the Guard that was being formed. This leads one to believe that, having secured admission, he abandoned the idea by the end of 1815.[16]

The decision to enter the priesthood was the resolution of a spiritual crisis that flowed from November 1815 to February 1816 and was taken after long and pondered thought and after he had sought the advice of a number of counselors. One text of the Roman Process for the beatification of Pius has placed the decision at the beginning of February when, hearing Mass at the Chiesa della Morte in via Giulia, he resolved to don the clerical vestment and become a priest if he could overcome the obstacle of his epilepsy. However, by the end of 1815 he was already referring to himself as a cleric and was determined to pursue a life in conformity with the state he had embraced. "My health has made me more fully aware," he wrote a friend in April 1816, "that there is no happiness in this world, which is a place that man must prepare himself for it."[17]

Although Giovanni had resolved to concentrate upon the next life rather than indulge in the pleasures of the world, he decided to do so in Rome rather than Senigallia. He preferred the capital with its variety of events and social contacts to his quiet native city which came to life only at the time of the great fair. In a number of letters he indicated that he found Senigallia depressing and believed it contributed to his infirmity while the Eternal City, with its movement, variety, and distractions served to lift his spirit. It was in Rome, too, that he found the spiritual solace that helped him overcome the melancholy and depression that afflicted his earlier years and contributed to his physical malady. With the passage of time the jovial, ebullient, and very social personality, which masked but did not eradicate a prevailing pessimism, emerged and would remain with Giovanni throughout his long life. By the summer of 1816 he felt sufficiently well to visit Naples, which he had desired to see for some time.

In Rome one of Pius VII's first official acts was the restoration of the Jesuits. These teachers asked for a number of volunteer catechists and Mastai, who was continuing his theological studies under the direction of Giuseppe Graziosi at the Seminary of Saint Appinarius, philosophical studies at the Collegio Romano under the direction of the Abbe Conti, and juridical studies under the lawyer Capogrossi at the Università Romana, answered their call. Due to his health and the political difficulties of the period his study was superficial, especially in history and canon law, but less so in sacred scripture.[18] During this time Mastai also devoted considerable time to the orphanage of the *Ospizio* "Tata Giovanni" in Via Giulia in the quarter of the carpenters, along the Tiber. This asylum, founded some thirty years earlier by the mason Giovanni Borgi, provided refuge and education for more than 100 homeless boys who called their protector Tata Giovanni, or Father John.

Mastai assisted the boys of the asylum with religious instruction as well as elementary education. However, he was still afflicted with the symptoms of epilepsy and one day experienced a seizure outside the orphanage. During the course of his retreat just before Christmas 1817, Giovanni indicated that his ceaseless prayer would be that he could be included among God's sacred ministers.[19] He despaired that the ecclesiastical career he had now set his heart upon would be denied him. Although interested in news from home, he was not in the least disposed to abandon his goal.[20] Pius VII, who heard of his plight, invited Mastai to pay him a visit and was supportive of his vocation.

In September 1818, Monsignor Carlo Odescalchi enlisted his support as a special catechist during a missionary tour which he and Bishop Vincenzo Strambi of Macerata were about to make in Senigallia and along the northern coast of the Adriatic.[21] Upon their return Monsignor Odescalchi, who noted the young catechist's success both with adults and children, recommended that Mastai be admitted to Holy Orders. Likewise Cardinal Fabrizio Testaferrata, Bishop of Senigallia, who was questioned by Monsignor Cristaldi about the opportuneness of providing Mastai with a dispensation for his illness, reacted positively. He and others testified to the fact that of late Giovanni no longer suffered the frequent seizures that had troubled him for some nine years and urged the Pope to permit Mastai to realize the ecclesiastic vocation he longed for. The Pope gave his consent so that Mastai became subdeacon in December 1818 and deacon in March of the following year.

The twenty-seven-year-old Mastai was ordained a priest on Holy Saturday, April 10, 1819, in the chapel of the Doria Panfili Palace on the Corso. Owing to the apprehensions of his physicians that the epileptic attacks would return, as well as to the concern of Pope Pius VII, who had granted the dispensation to permit his ordination, it was stipulated as a precautionary measure that the young priest should have another priest or deacon in attendance whenever he offered Mass. Later this restriction was removed. On Easter Sunday, April 11, 1819, Mastai celebrated his first Mass, assisted by his uncle Paolino in the presence of the orphans of the "Tata Giovanni" and relatives and friends in the Church of S. Anna dei Falegnami.[22] Shortly thereafter he wrote to the Bishop of Senigallia, Cardinal Testaferrata, that he was extremely happy in the new state to which he had been called and asked nothing more than to be given the grace to fulfill his obligations. He had, he continued, a good deal to be thankful for, noting particularly the miraculous improvement in his health. He attributed this to the protection of the Blessed Virgin, to whom he was devoted and to whom his mother had consecrated him as an infant.[23]

Initiated into Jesuit spirituality by Carlo Odescalchi, for at least three years, from 1819 to 1821, Mastai considered joining the Order. However, he never forgot what a "saintly Bishop," most likely his uncle Andrea Mastai, Bishop of Pesaro, had told him: that it was more worthy in the sight of God to overcome adversities by combatting them in the world as a secular priest rather than overcoming them by fleeing from them and withdrawing to a convent.[24] He thus spent his first years as a priest assigned to the "Tata Giovanni," where he had earlier done volunteer work, first as assistant to the director and later as director. While there he preached on a number of subjects, drawing inspiration from the various feast days and the Gospels.[25] In many ways the years he lived there, from February 1818 to July 1823, were the happiest of his life.

This period of tranquility came to an end in 1823, in part due to a remark that Mastai made to one of the priests that frequented the "Tata Giovanni" as a confessor, Pietro Ostini, and who had recently been invited by Cardinal Ercole Consalvi to go to Chile on an important Church mission. When Mastai heard of the plans, he responded, "Lucky you, how I would like to come along."[26] Father Ostini, delighted at the prospect of having his friend join him, immediately took steps to secure his inclusion by speaking first to the secretary of state and then to Monsignor Giovanni Muzi, secretary to the nuncio at Vienna and recently consecrated archbishop and appointed Apostolic Vicar of Chile. Muzi, who had been entrusted with the task of examining the needs of the Church in Chile and perhaps regularizing relations between Rome and the new government, welcomed Mastai to the delegation. The archbishop asked the Pope to appoint Mastai auditor of the delegation going to America, thus joining himself and Don Giuseppe Sallusti, who was to serve as secretary.

The Countess Caterina, Giovanni's mother, did not second her son's decision to go to Chile, and in May 1823 she wrote to the secretary of state, Cardinal Consalvi, imploring him to prevent Mastai's participation in the venture. She argued that it was unjust to allow her son to travel to that remote region by means of a perilous sea journey: her son, who because of his weak constitution was legally exempt from the military draft. Consalvi, who appreciated the concern of the countess, wrote back that he had spoken to her son, adding that Giovanni was most determined to answer God's call by participating in this mission and he had no way of opposing his decision. "Your son will traverse the sea in the service of the Church," he added, "and will return safe and sound."[27] In June, when Mastai took leave of the Pope prior to his departure for the New World, the aged Pius informed him that his mother had sought to cancel his selection for this mission but he had calmed her by sending a letter assuring that all would be well.

The countess had cause for concern. Her son's health was delicate, the journey was long and perilous, and there were important groups in Spain and the secessionist republics who were hostile to the mission and the delegation. Indeed the apostolic delegation, which left Rome for Genoa on July 3, confronted difficulties from the very outset. The plan to set sail near the end of July was frustrated first by the captain of the ship, who had not yet concluded his business in the port city, then by the news of the ill health and death of Pius VII, and finally even by unfavorable winds. In the interim Cardinal Annibale Sermattei della Genga, who assumed the Tiara of St. Peter under the name of Leo XII, let them know by means of Cardinal Luigi Lambruschini, the Archbishop of Genoa and subsequently secretary of state, that the authorization for their mission remained intact. Finally, after months of waiting, they set sail the morning of October 5.[28]

Six days later their bark, the *Eloisa*, sailed into bad weather and agitated waters. Conditions grew progressively worse and their safety more precarious so that the evening of the twelfth the seasick Mastai placed himself in the hands of the Lord and made his confession. The next day the ship sought safety in the port of Palma on Majorca, one of the Ballearic islands, but since it was under quarantine they could not see the city. While they were anchored not far from Palma, they were summoned on land by the Spanish authorities, who feared that the Pope was sending a mission to their rebellious colonies. Mastai and his fellow passengers who were rowed ashore were placed under virtual arrest and for some days their fate remained unknown—there was even word that they might be sent to Cuerta in Africa to ascertain the will of the Spanish government.[29] Eventually they were released on October 20, in part because the authorities on the island were preparing for the second restoration of Ferdinand VII, who had been freed by the French expedition, and in part because they realized that the mission of the clergymen was religious rather than political.

Early in January 1824 the delegation reached Buenos Aires. It did not take the papal envoys long to recognize that while the population in the port city was sympathetic, the civil authorities were hostile and opposed their efforts. The reception received by the delegation was no warmer in Santiago, which was reached in March after a long and dangerous trek across the continent. "On three occasions during this voyage I was prepared for death," Mastai wrote, first during the tempest at sea; then while crossing the Pampas when it was heard that a dangerous band of Indians were on the prowl, who three days later killed a group of twenty men who were going to Buenos Aires; and finally while crossing the Andes.[30] "He who has great fear of the world will never do great things for God," Mastai quoted St. Ignatius, finding his teaching most applicable during his trip to Chile.[31]

In Santiago Mastai did not always live up to his own expectations, finding himself weak in the face of adversity, irresolute, and plagued by doubts. He was depressed that he had done nothing to advance the cause of the Holy See and religion. At the same time he decried the fact that having spent seven months in Chile he had never seriously considered work among the savages, never examined if God wanted him to dedicate his life to their service. The reason that God had not sought his services, he concluded, stemmed from his many defects and his unfortunate attitude toward God. He promised to do better and asked that if he should ever again set foot on the American continent, and it was God's will, he be allowed to work among the infidels.[32] To add to his consternation, he was dissatisfied with the course of the mission.

In the report or more appropriately the diary the Giovanni kept of his trip to South America, he noted that the apostolic mission was asked for by the independent government of Chile, that of Bernardo O'Higgins, but the government that followed the revolution was not in the least interested in the mission. Consequently the prospect of regularizing relations between the government of Chile and Rome was very bleak, and the same disappointing situation prevailed in Peru. Painfully aware that the expedition had failed to secure the cooperation of the authorities, the delegation boarded the *Eloisa* and returned to Italy, arriving in Genoa in June 1825, where they had to remain fifteen days in quarantine.[33]

Although the trip had done little to improve the condition of ecclesiastic affairs in Chile or the other republics, Mastai's interest in the missions was tremendously aroused. Furthermore, he saw at first hand the important role of the Church outside the Italian and even the European ambience and became more appreciative of its worldwide mission. It thus provided the basis for Mastai's later efforts to make the Church truly universal—at the First Vatican Council there were Vicars Apostolic from Tonkin, China and Japan as well as Bishops from Mexico, Brazil, Peru, Chile, the Philippines and Australia—and inspired him to the efforts which won him the title of "Missionary Pope."

Following his return from Chile Mastai was considered something of an expert on Latin American developments and was regularly consulted by the Holy See on issues pertaining to that part of the world. The Chilean experience was also important in bringing Mastai face to face with political matters to which he had been more or less indifferent during his youth. He had even ignored the tumults of 1820-22 because he was almost totally immersed in his charitable work, but he was unable to avoid the political factor in Latin America. From his writings it does not appear that he ever denied the right of the people of the New World to claim their independence from Spain and Portugal. His hostility was directed against those men who took advantage of the idea of independence to arrive at irreligious ends and launch an attack upon the Church.[34]

After his long absence from Italy Giovanni spent some time with his family in Senigallia where his mother, father, and brothers awaited him, but it is not clear how long he remained there. Perhaps he stayed only for the summer. He still found Senigallia depressing and less than beneficial for his health, and he was most concerned about conditions in the "Tata Giovanni" in Rome. Removed from nepotism, he very much resented the fact that from time to time he was approached by creditors who looked to him to pay the debts of various members of his family.[35] By November, if not earlier, he was back in the capital. Soon after his return Pope Leo XII, whose ideas and tendencies were decidedly conservative, appointed him the director of the Hospital of San Michele, founded some two centuries earlier by Pope Innocent X. It was one of the largest and most important institutions of the time, housing several hundred individuals. The nomination surprised those who considered it a post for a cardinal.

San Michele was a mixed organization and contained an orphanage for boys and one for girls; a reformatory for wayward girls and one for unruly boys; educational accommodations and workshops and instructors for the teaching of trades as well as accommodations for the destitute and elderly. Assigned to San Michele, Mastai saw to it that all sorts of data were collected on the patients, including their ages and the work assigned to them. The same was done for the lay and clerical employees of the various agencies of the apostolic hospital.[36] Mastai remained at San Michele for almost two years[37] and introduced the system whereby the apprentices would share part of the income produced by their work. During his tenure meticulous records were kept and the cost of maintaining instruction for each child was calculated per year.[38] He often preached to the other priests associated with the hospital.[39]

In recognition of his good work at San Michele Pope Leo, in May 1827, following the death of Monsignor Mario Ancaiani, Archbishop of Spoleto, named him archbishop of that diocese in Umbria. To prepare himself to exercise the functions of a bishop Mastai went into religious retreat in Sant' Andrea al Quirinale, under the direction of the Jesuit fathers, at the beginning of June. As on other occasions of anxiety and stress, Mastai visited the sanctuary of the Madonna of Loreto and prayed for divine assistance through the intercession of Mary. He received the episcopal consecration on June 3, 1827, at the hands of Cardinal Francesco Saverio Castiglioni, who would succeed Leo in the papal chair as Pius VIII in 1829.

CHAPTER 2

The Long Apprenticeship: Mastai-Ferretti as Bishop

IN the first pastoral letter addressed to the clergy and faithful of Spoleto, Mastai traced his own history. Recalling his work at San Michele, he noted that it had suited him very well, for it provided ample opportunity for him to grow in Christian charity. He had accepted the new post only at the behest of the Pope.[1] There were good reasons for his hesitation. The appointment was not an easy one in light of the fact that ill health had rendered his predecessor ineffective, so that the administration was in a deplorable condition and the discipline of the clergy less than inspiring. Furthermore the diocese had been divided for some time by bitter factional rivalry.

In light of the deep divisions and party strife existing in Spoleto, it is not surprising that many of the speeches Mastai delivered there cited the need for charity and Christian love.[2] His library reflected the devotional nature of his thought and talks and was not particularly large or diverse.[3] To achieve pacification the new archbishop devoted much of his time and energy to winning the support of the middle classes while combatting revolutionary ideas. His success won him the respect and admiration of many of his parishioners as well as the goodwill of Rome. Mastai's modest standard of living and his numerous works of charity won him the support of many who had been initially cool if not hostile to him.[4] Indeed he often drew upon his income from Senigallia to finance his charitable activities.[5]

In the Cathedral of Senigallia one of the archbishop's frequent themes was that peace flowed not from an attachment to things of the world but from a true love of Jesus Christ.[6] Nonetheless Mastai received the petitions of various suppliants and did his utmost to meet all legitimate requests.[7] He was indefatigable in his traveling, visiting the whole of his diocese and almost always bringing some sort of assistance or advice. He was particularly generous to the seminary,

The Long Apprenticeship

which managed to graduate fifty new priests per year, a considerable number when one recalls that the city of Spoleto then had only 20,000 inhabitants. His open, smiling face, saintly life, and obvious concern for his flock disarmed even some who were hostile to the clerical government.

Mastai's reputation in Umbria was enhanced by the political events of 1831.[8] In the third year of his episcopate political agitation, encouraged by the death of Pope Pius VIII, who had occupied the Chair of Peter for only eight months, disturbed the tranquility of the Papal States as the conclave left the apostolic seat vacant for some two months. An attempt at revolution was made in the capital itself during the excitement of the carnival, but the attempt proved abortive. In the provinces, however, the authorities proved less vigilant, government abuses were more resented, and the spirit of revolution was stronger. In Bologna, in the absence of the legate, Cardinal Tommaso Bernetti, who was in Rome for the conclave, a provisional government was established, and on February 8, 1831, there was published a proclamation declaring the end of the temporal power.

To deal with the insurrection in Bologna and the marches during which all of the principal cities of the Papal States except Rome, Rieti, and Orvieto were occupied, the new Pontiff, Mauro Cappellari della Colomba, Gregory XVI, invoked Austrian assistance. The Austrians moved quickly to honor the Pope's request and to stifle the revolutionary tempest which threatened the stability of the peninsula and the well-being of their multi-national empire. On March 6 they occupied Ferrara; by the twenty-first they were in Bologna and by the twenty-sixth, in Ancona.

The Archbishop of Spoleto found himself very much involved in the entire matter when a number of insurgents, retreating before the Austrians, moved southward into Spoleto and part of the population welcomed them. To spare bloodshed the archbishop, who in the absence of the legate, Monsignor Meli-Lupi di Soragna, was responsible for the temporal power, convinced the Austrians that these rebels were not representative of the law-abiding population. Exacting a promise from the Austrians not to move into the city if he could get the rebels to lay down their arms, he persuaded them to do so by providing them money and safe-conduct passes which allowed them to return to their respective provinces.

Among the rebels were two sons of Louis, the former King of Holland and brother of Napoleon. One of these died of disease at Forli. The other, the twenty-two-year-old Prince Louis Napoleon, who but a year ago had been a student at the Roman University, survived, and, accompanied by his mother, Queen Hortense, fled to Spoleto, where he was provided with the passport required to leave the country. Mastai thus acted to avoid any excessive reaction and to protect the defeated from the fury of the victors.[9] Early in April he wrote to the Pope asking pardon for those of his diocese implicated in the recent disturbance. While Gregory was not inclined toward leniency he appreciated the sincerity and generous heart of his archbishop.

The people of Spoleto praised him for his truce and for sparing them a possible siege of their city and certain bloodshed. Likewise they were impressed by his actions during a series of earthquakes that shook the province of Umbria in 1832, as Mastai went to the assistance of those stricken bringing consolation and distributing food.[10]

Mastai prayed and asked forgiveness for his sins and those of the population of the diocese, for he saw an intimate connection between the sins of humanity and the travails that afflicted man. In Spoleto, the only city which was undamaged by the earthquake, he ordered a service of thanksgiving for having been spared and collected monies for those areas that had been hard hit. His charity and efforts to wring concessions from Rome on behalf of his sheep won him the love and admiration of a good part of the diocese.

In Spoleto it was widely known that the archbishop sought to satisfy all of their legitimate needs. There was therefore considerable consternation in 1832 when it was learned that Gregory XVI decided to move Mastai to the See of Imola. Indeed the citizens of Spoleto sent a delegation to Rome to appeal the decision. The clergy of Spoleto in a joint letter also sought to keep Mastai there, citing his good work and the esteem in which he was held, but all to no avail.[11]

Pope Gregory, who had personally communicated to Mastai in the first half of November 1832 his decision to transfer him from Spoleto to Imola, had done so in such a fashion as to render impossible any protest on the archbishop's part. Mastai, in his response of November 19, stressed his willingness to comply with the Pope's wishes but once again reiterated the shortcomings he found within himself and expressed the fear that the burden would transcend his abilities.[12]

In the eyes of some the move from an archbishopric to a bishopric represented a demotion, but such was not the case. For one thing the population of the See of Imola was at least double that of Spoleto and offered Mastai a wider field for action. Furthermore the situation in the Romagna, and especially the cities of Ferrara, Bologna, Imola, Ravenna, Forli, and Rimini, remained difficult and therefore required exceptional leadership. The lands of the diocese fell within three jurisdictions: the legations of Ravenna, Bologna, and Ferrara. Finally, the Bishop of Imola was usually honored with the rank of cardinal, so that the appointment promised even greater honors in the future. Thus the year 1833 opened with great promise for Mastai, who arrived in Imola in February after having paid a visit to Mary's shrine at Loreto to pray for assistance in his new assignment. It ended on a sad note with the loss of his father, Count Girolamo, who died in December of the same year.

In Imola Mastai showed the same resourcefulness and energy that earned him the admiration of Gregory. In his first speech in the cathedral on the occasion of his solemn entry, Mastai urged his listeners not to be attached to temporal things but to God.[13] Thereafter he preached regularly in the cathedral as well as before his assembled clergy on a broad variety of topics including: the importance of loving Christ; the need for discipline, obedience, and virtue; Christian virtue; the sacrifice of the Mass; and the importance of Holy Scripture.[14]

As Bishop of Imola he ordained that the clergy of the diocese should convene every year for spiritual renewal. Since his youth Mastai had recognized the importance of spiritual exercises and critical self-evaluation for the faithful in general and the clergy in particular. He found special consolation in reading the lives of the saints and poring over holy scripture with his clergy in religious retreat. He proved to be a strict custodian of ecclesiastical discipline, demanding honest habits and a frugal life-style from his clergy.[15] He explicitly prohibited his clergy from wearing secular garb and urged them to shun popular pastimes, especially in public places.

Stories circulated that during a visit to one of his parishes the bishop had declined the excellent meal prepared for him, urging the parish priests to use the money available to them to provide for the poor rather than troubling themselves about the table of the bishop. He kept a close watch on the pious institutions of the various cities of the diocese and provided all the assistance his budget allowed.[16] It was known that on the occasion of the outbreak of cholera in 1835 he launched a drive to help the victims and personally contributed 1,000 *scudi*, going into debt to provide it. He also went into debt with his friend Monsignor Leziroli, Bishop of Rimini and a native of Imola, in order to assist the seminary.[17]

Although not a liberal in the political sense of the word and ultraorthodox in religious matters, Mastai during his fourteen years at Imola associated with a number of moderate liberals including Count Giuseppe Pasolini and his wife, Antonietta Bassi. He encountered Pasolini of Ravenna, who spent part of the summer in his possessions at Monterico near Imola, in the last period of Mastai's episcopate there. The Pasolini villa soon became a refuge for the sociable bishop. He liked to discuss with the count the possibility of conciliation between religion and progress and between the Catholic faith and liberal principles.[18] In his genial company Mastai expressed the hope for a happier future which he felt might be attained by a little leniency on the part of the rulers.

It was at the Pasolini villa that Mastai read such works as Cesare Balbo's *Delle speranze d'Italia* (On the Hope of Italy) and Vincenzo Gioberti's *Del Primato morale e civile degli Italiani* (On the Moral and Civil Primacy of the Italians), according to the son of Count Pasolini. Gioberti's work, in addition to helping the Italians develop a positive self image, assured them that some form of unity was not only desirable but feasible. Renouncing the dream of a unitary state, it stressed the creation of a confederation under the leadership of the papacy and Piedmont.

The fact that Mastai read Gioberti disturbed some, and stories were later hatched that the conservative Gregory claimed that in the Mastai household even the cat was a "carbonaro" and that Mastai was on the top of Cardinal Bernetti's list to the papal legate of people to watch in the Romagna.[19] Despite the stories there is no indication that Gregory questioned either the political or religious orthodoxy of Mastai. His stress on Christian virtue, obedience, charity, devotion to Mary, and the need for love of Christ[20] could not but appeal to Gregory, who found him a good pastor as well as a good administrator.

In his secret consistory of December 23, 1839, Pope Gregory announced his intention of elevating Giovanni Maria to the cardinalate. Once again Mastai was favored by Gregory, and he promised the Pontiff that he would devote all his energy to the cause of faith and expressed his loyalty to the Holy See.[21] In 1840 he received the red hat and ring from the Pope as his mother watched proudly. Two years later she was to die in her home in Senigallia. Mastai was constrained to go into debt with his family in order to pay the requisite fees for the assumption to the cardinalate.[22]

On the occasion of his entry into the College of Cardinals there were the usual festivities including having musicians play under the windows of the new members. Mastai, ever conscious of how money was spent, inquired if it might not be better to have the money spent on serenading the new cardinals given instead in charity to the poor. He was informed that the musicians were poor, and therefore the money granted them could be considered a form of charity.[23]

In part the red hat was given to Mastai for his effective performance in Imola, an area that remained troubled, as did the rest of the Romagna. For one thing much of the area had never reconciled itself to incorporation into the Papal States, was distant from Rome across the high ranges of the Apennines and quite inaccessible, especially in winter. Then, during the revolutionary period it had been wrenched from the Pope and incorporated first in the Cisalpine Republic and later into the Kingdom of Italy, and part of its population had become committed to liberal and national doctrines. The *Carbonari* and other secret organizations found considerable support in the region, and their agitation had recently led to the revolutionary outburst of 1830-31. While the revolutionaries did not get the expected French support and witnessed an Austrian intervention to restore the old order, they belatedly received the moral support of the major powers, who met in conference in Rome at the insistence of France.

As early as March 1831, Metternich had written to Pope Gregory urging him to reform the administration of his provinces, arguing that this was indispensable for the assurance of tranquility in the future. Austria considered the *Motu proprio* issued by Pius VII in 1816 a good basis for the reorganization of the Papal States. It called for the separation of justice from the administration and the participation of the laity both in the administration and the dispensation of justice. The memorandum of the five powers— Austria, France, Great Britain, Prussia, and Russia—issued on May 21, 1831, went further and encouraged the Pope to provide for municipal government, establish provincial councils, and set up a central assembly which would in part be elected, to control finances.

Although Gregory and his secretary of state, Bernetti, were fundamentally opposed to these measures, on July 5 a papal edict indicated that there would be reforms in the administration of the Papal States along the lines suggested by the European powers.[24] Subsequently Gregory outlined his plans for limited reforms including nominated communal and provincial councils which might express the opinions of his subjects. These measures did not satisfy the opponents of the regime, for when the Austrians withdrew there was a renewed rising in the Romagna in January 1832. The Austrians were recalled and occupied Bologna while the French, to counteract the Austrian influence in the peninsula, sent their fleet into the Adriatic and occupied Ancona. Hence the insurrection in the Romagna and Umbria produced no positive results and the memorandum of the powers remained a dead letter.

Camillo di Cavour, writing to an English friend in 1832, observed that the position of Italy, caught between the furious excommunications of the papacy on the one hand and the bayonets of the Austrians on the other, was deplorable. He noted that the intervention of the powers following the revolution in the Romagna had been completely ineffectual. Even the pressure of the French, he complained, had not been sufficient to wring the "most reasonable" concessions from the Pope. Only the voice of England, he concluded, would enable the people of the Romagna to acquire a reasonable government.[25]

At this time anti-Austrian sentiment was fanned in Italy by the publication of Silvio Pellico's *Le mie prigioni* (My Imprisonment), which described his ten-year confinement in the Austrian prison, the Spielberg, north of Vienna. Others resented the fact that the Austrians had been responsible for the dismissal of the papal secretary of state, Cardinal Tommaso Bernetti. He was succeeded in 1836 by Luigi Lambruschini, who maintained a certain independence in his relations with outside powers but imposed upon the acts of the government a rigid intransigence which increased the liberal opposition to the pontifical regime.[26] The situation in the Papal States thus remained volatile.

Although not a revolutionary, or even a liberal, the Bishop of Imola was critical of the slow and ponderous Roman administration. He was disgusted by the constant round of conspiracy, revolt, and repression. "In my opinion the danger stems from a universal bewilderment," he wrote in March 1844. "The troublemakers say they want to provoke a revolution, good citizens remain bamboozled and all stand idly by waiting the day of divine retribution."[27] He argued that it was necessary for the government to assume the moral initiative and inspire those with evil intentions with a fear of wrongdoing. Nonetheless he admitted that the affairs of the world were not well governed and that this was also true of the government of the states of the Church. It was his conviction, for example, that those who paid for the expenses certainly had a right to know how their money was being spent.

Mastai confided to Count Pasolini that he deplored the sad condition of the Papal States and hoped for a better future, which he felt only a bit of common sense, mildness, and Christian justice in the government could bring about. He desired a more temperate government for the states of the Church, one better attuned to the aspirations of its people.[28]

While Mastai on occasion did privately criticize the government, he generally did not discuss political matters, having little experience in secular or political matters aside from his brief experience in South America and his assumption, for a short period of time while at Spoleto, of the functions of the civil governor of Perugia. Open to every generous idea, Mastai, partly because of inclination, partly because of his long illness, did not have the opportunity to undertake systematic study. Still, few doubted that he had the best interests of the Church at heart and was dedicated to the pacification of his strife-torn native land. He explained his plans for the implementation of reform in a work entitled *Thoughts on the Public Administration of the Papal States.* In it he announced the need for some corporate body, a collegiate institution that would advise and coordinate the administration as well as regulate it. Without these minimal concessions he feared that the turbulence in the provinces would continue.[29]

In March 1844, Mastai wrote to Cardinal Luigi Amat that Ravenna was tense with excitement and there was widespread talk of impending revolution. He urged precaution on feast days to prevent the outbreak of any major disturbance.[30] Others shared his concern, and in the second half of 1845 the four cardinal legates of the Romagna held a congress in Forli to consider means to avoid the outbreak of new disorders. On that occasion Mastai, who admitted that he lacked political education and experience, concluded that the cardinals would do a good deal of talking but would accomplish little. At this early date he already placed little faith in governmental provisions and invoked divine intervention, arguing, "If God does not help us, it will certainly not be the Congress of Cardinals that will save us."[31]

Since repression had proved incapable of restoring tranquility to the Papal States, Mastai wondered if limited reformism might not be the answer. "I do not understand the quarrelsome attitude of our government which mortifies with persecution the youth which inspires our generation," he confessed. "It would be so easy to make them [the young] happy and inspire their confidence and love." Nor did the cardinal comprehend the opposition of the papal government to railroads, illumination, suspension bridges, gas installations, and the calling of scientific congresses. "Theology is not opposed to the development of science and industry," he asserted. But he added cautiously, "I know nothing about politics and maybe I am wrong."[32] Notwithstanding this doubt, Mastai continued to hope that Gregory's government would become reconciled to progress and in particular satisfy the call for the building of railroads, observing that the Holy Father could not but concede in his state that which all the others had already granted.[33]

Gregory, who was in disagreement with much of the intellectual ferment of the period and at times considered even the much heralded railroad as an artifice of the devil, was not prepared to make concessions. Nonetheless he perceived the growing opposition and believed that another storm was brewing. Just before his death he feared the outbreak of revolution and called for strong measures to prevent it. Reformers in the Papal States thus placed their hopes on his successor. Pope Gregory died the morning of June 1, 1846, in his eighty-first year and the sixteenth of his pontificate. Metternich was one of the few to regret his departure.[34]

Giovanni Mastai-Ferretti learned of the death of Gregory on the morning of June 4, but, detained by a number of pastoral duties, he was able to leave for Rome only the afternoon of June 8. He arrived at the Porta del Popolo the evening of June 12.[35] During his last illness the Pope had expressed the wish that the next conclave should open immediately after his death in order to forestall the disturbances which might erupt in the provinces during such a vulnerable period. This was not done, and the customary services were followed. However, no sooner was Gregory in his tomb then the College of Cardinals determined to elect his successor, refusing to wait for the foreign cardinals who might be delayed.

The College of Cardinals wished to avoid foreign intervention. The courts of France, Austria, and Spain had traditionally enjoyed the right to veto the selection of a candidate they found unacceptable prior to his securing the two-thirds vote necessary for election. Indeed many of the cardinals considered the rivalry between the Austrian and French factions responsible for the protracted nature of the last three conclaves which respectively had lasted eighteen, thirty-six, and fifty days. They were determined to avoid a repetition, although preparations were made for a long conclave, some 6,000 ballots being printed, enough to last for three months.

The Long Apprenticeship

By the time fifty of the sixty-two cardinals met in the Quirinale Palace the evening of the fourteenth, the names of four or five candidates for the Tiara were mentioned. The prospective candidates were divided by their attitude toward reform in the Papal States and the expediency of making concessions as well as geography. Cardinal Luigi Lambruschini, who had been Gregory's secretary of state, represented both the Genoese party as well as the more conservative cardinals. In the liberal camp the favored figure was the Capuchin Cardinal L. Micara, who was supposedly willing to make the most radical concessions to the party of progress. When he arrived for the opening of the conclave, he was greeted in the streets of the capital as the next pontiff. Less popular, though still considered a leading liberal, was the legate of Forli, Cardinal Pasquale Gizzi, whose reputation rested largely on the praises heaped upon him by Massimo D'Azeglio in his *Degli ultimi casi di Romagna* (On the Recent Events in the Romagna). Mastai-Ferretti was considered to be midway between the conservatives and the liberals and was therefore an ideal compromise candidate.

Prior to the opening of the conclave most Romans did not consider Mastai a serious contender for the papal throne. He had spent little time in the capital during the last two decades and was little known there. Nonetheless the Bishop of Imola, who was loved in his diocese for his spirit of moderation and conciliation, was selected as one of the tellers to count the votes deposited in the golden chalices.

In the first ballot and the *accesso*, a sort of balloting in another form where the cardinals were permitted to vote for another candidate, Cardinals Della Genga and Mattei shared three votes between them, Cardinals Soglia and Falconieri each had four, Mastai had thirteen, and Lambruschini, fifteen. In the second scrutiny of the same day with the *accesso* of the evening Lambruschini lost two votes while Mastai gained four. In the first ballot after Mass on Tuesday morning Lambruschini received eleven votes and Mastai twenty-seven, but this was not sufficient, for election by a two-thirds majority was required.[36] Finally on Tuesday evening and the fourth count the chief of the conservative party received only ten votes and Cardinal Mastai-Ferretti obtained thirty-six at the *accesso*, securing his election. At this point the college rose to confirm his election by acclamation.

Despite the fact that many of the contemporary biographers of Pius IX, and Ernesto Vercesi as late as 1930, presented the election of Mastai as a general surprise and resulting from an agreement made only after the opening of the conclave, new documents show that such was not the case, and the foreign ambassadors at Rome considered him one of the likely choices.[37] Equally untrue were the rumors of foreign interference in the election. It is true that Count Pellegrino Rossi, who in spite of his liberal past and Protestant wife had recently been appointed French ambassador to the Vatican, advised against the election of an Austrian partisan. However, the count used friendly persuasion rather than a veto to influence the outcome. Furthermore while Austria desired a Pope who would be sensitive to the advice of Vienna, it is not true that the Habsburg state called for a reactionary. The claim that Archbishop Karl Gaysruck, who arrived too late to take part in the conclave, carried Metternich's veto of Mastai is unfounded and was perhaps fabricated in order to increase the popularity of the new Pope.[38] Nonetheless the story persisted and it was claimed that the Austrian chancellor had suffered a double setback; for the same month that Mastai was elected Pope in Rome, in London the formation of a new liberal ministry brought Henry John Temple, the Third Viscount Palmerston, to the foreign office.

"There are others more worthy than I am for the important part to which the Sacred College has called me," Mastai replied to the cardinal subdeacon who asked if he would accept the election, "but long accustomed as the servant of Jesus Christ to denials of my will, I obey that of God."[39] Thereupon Monsignor de Ligne, Prefect of Ceremonies, drew up the act of acceptance and the newly elected Pope was ushered into the sacristy of the Pauline Chapel, where he was invested with the pontifical habit.

Mastai assumed the name of Pius IX in memory of Pius VII, who like himself had been Bishop of Imola and had supported and made possible his vocation. The evening of his election the new Pope wrote to his brothers informing them of the event: "The blessed God, who lowers and lifts up according to his divine will and pleasure, has been pleased to raise me, his humble creature, to the most sublime dignity of this world. May his holy will be ever done!" He then humbly added, "I am fully conscious of the high and weighty responsibility attached to my charge, and I feel my great inability to fill it properly. Have prayers said for me, therefore, dear brothers, and pray for me yourselves."[40]

CHAPTER 3

The New Pope

THE evening of June 16, when the Romans did not see the smoke from the burned ballots arise from the Quirinale Palace, it was surmised that the new Pope had been selected. This was confirmed in the morning which was ushered in by the salute from the cannon of the Castel Sant' Angelo which announced to the waiting capital that the conclave had made its choice. This aroused the anticipation of the crowd on the Quirinal Hill anxious to see their new ruler and spiritual sovereign. The diplomatic community was equally excited and a number of its members were admitted to the Quirinale Chapel to meet the Pontiff. Among the well-wishers was the minister of the King of Sardinia, who made a point of being the first to carry the train of Pius's pontifical garb as he prepared to present himself to the people from the great Loggia.[1]

Shortly after nine o'clock the Cardinal Camerlengo, Tommaso Riario Sforza, appeared upon the Loggia and announced that the new pope was Giovanni Maria Mastai-Ferretti. The spectators, surprised by the announcement, were less than enthusiastic in their response, even though Pius was handsome, aristocratic, and distinquished-looking in his ceremonial robes. In fact, after a long pause, it was the cardinals surrounding the Pope who had to give the signal to evoke the usual, popular acclamation.[2]

The new Pope was handsome in face and figure, a little taller than average in height, with a large chest and small, gentle hands. Possessing a strong head with a high forehead, his eyes were black and expressive, his nose aquiline and well proportioned. His voice was high and sonorous, which contributed to make him an outstanding speaker.[3]

The evening of June 17, when the Pope went in procession to the Vatican to receive the obedience of the cardinals, those who lined the streets to catch a glimpse of the Holy Father seemed to be motivated more by curiosity than affection. The Romans were little more enthusiastic on Sunday, June 21, the day of Pius's coronation in the Basilica of St. Peter, observing the sacred ceremony without displaying by their voices or their hands the slightest degree of fervor. On that occasion, when he had the Tiara, or triple crown, placed on his head, Pius had some 6,000 Roman *scudi* distributed to the poor and released those who had been thrown into prison for debt.[4] It was not the amnesty that was desired but it was something.

Slowly the initial indifference to Pius was overcome. The news that he was determined to carry on the government, even temporarily, by a commission of cardinals did not help matters. Included in the special and temporary commission of cardinals were Vincente Macchi, Pasquale Gizzi, Tommaso Bernetti, Luigi Lambruschini, Mario Mattei, and Luigi Amat, with Monsignore Corboli Bussi serving as secretary.[5] Among these, two were acceptable to those who championed reform: Amat and Gizzi. However, the presence of Lambruschini, leader of the conservatives, and Bernetti, deemed the protector of the Jesuits, caused consternation in the liberal camp. The Pope's apparent desire to conciliate both the liberals and the conservatives was a fatal mistake and led to uncertainty regarding the course he would pursue.

Despite this apparent compromise Pius had decided that he would not continue the policies of Gregory's government, for that would lead to an inevitable revolution in the States of the Church with a consequent Austrian intervention that would provoke French and English counter measures. In fact he had brought to the Quirinale all the papers and documents of the diplomatic conference held in Rome in 1831, not hiding the fact that he was determined to develop the reforms suggested in the articles of the memorandum of the Powers of 1831. In his allocution of thanks of July 1846 to the cardinal electors, Pius declared that he accepted his elevation with the resolution of employing all of his forces to procure the glory of God, the honor of the Church and the Holy See, and the well-being of his people.

Pius believed that Gregory had been animated by the best of intentions, but realized that the results had proved disastrous. He assumed authority in an impoverished and disturbed state, on the brink of revolution. Its finances were exhausted, its commerce was in decline, and its industry, moribund. Unemployment was widespread.[6] Railways were forbidden and agriculture remained primitive. The administration of the state was disorganized and disliked and the clerical monopoly of positions long censured. Equality under the law did not exist and justice was slow and costly. Taxation, too, was unequally and unjustly imposed. Many of the branches of revenue were farmed out to individuals and institutions while custom-house officials, poorly and irregularly paid, exacted their fees with a vengeance from travelers. Intrigue and corruption were rife and the services provided by the state were poor. Censorship was strict if not always efficient, and the avenues for the redress of grievances were limited. Small wonder that dissatisfaction was widespread and the fear of anarchy and revolution loomed large.

The papal government had few friends in Europe and even the conservative states declared that it had to be reformed or face possible extinction. Mastai, who remembered the long discussions at the Villa Pasolini, felt that reform was possible. He believed that his states and indeed the entire peninsula could be regenerated gradually and with tranquility, as had been claimed in a number of recent publications. Anxious to make improvements and please his people, from the first Pius did not have a precise picture of the severity of the problems or any precise plans for dealing with them.

The new Pope did succeed in his first task of convincing his people and the European powers that he would pursue the path of reform. His personality helped in this regard, for Pius made himself accessible to all, breaking many of the rules of etiquette and procedure in the process. He invited guests to his table, gave audience after audience, and, always smiling, seemed ready to converse with one and all. In part this reflected his concern for his subjects; in part it reflected his curiosity, one of his chief characteristics, which made him anxious to know as much as possible about those around him.[7] Pius, who spoke French as well as Italian and Latin, was a persuasive speaker, and this also worked to increase his popularity.

"It is said that the new Pope is a man of talent," Massimo D'Azeglio wrote to his friend Luigi Carlo Farini, June 26, 1846. "All expect an amnesty and a revocation of confiscations," D'Azeglio continued; "if this should materialize, by God, even I will go to Mass."[8] Furthermore it was rumored that Cardinal Gizzi, considered a leading liberal in the hierarchy, was to be selected as secretary of state.[9] This materialized in August, with broad popular approval. However, the most important single step in earning Pius a liberal image and the love of his subjects was the decision to grant an amnesty.

At the Pope's request the matter of the amnesty was given priority during the first session of the special commission of cardinals held before him the evening of July 1. One of the Cardinals—most likely Lambruschini, who had signed most of the warrants against political prisoners and exiles—noted that a wide amnesty by the government might be construed as a criticism of the former pontificate and this might be the wedge for other and more far-reaching concessions. Another [Bernetti?] observed that the return of the exiles might prove dangerous for the security of the Holy See. However, most of the others considered a general amnesty necessary to extinguish the hatred of many families against the government. It was their feeling that few were really enemies of the Papal State and few were its ardent champions, with the vast majority indifferent to it. An amnesty would serve to win support for the government.[10]

During the course of the second session of the commission on July 8, the cardinals decided to exclude from the amnesty certain types of criminals: those with an ecclesiastical background, those belonging to the military or administration, and finally those who combined political and common crimes. It was also determined that those who would avail themselves of the amnesty be required to make a solemn declaration that henceforth they would be faithful subjects.[11] The minutes of these and subsequent sessions throw into dispute the story that Pius forced the amnesty upon the cardinals, and when a number of them dropped a black ball in the basket when polled on the issue, Pius covered these negative votes with his white hat, exclaiming, "It's all white, the decree is approved unanimously."[12] The amnesty, signed on July 16, a month after the election, was affixed on the walls of Rome the evening of July 17.

In the amnesty the Pope announced his sympathy for the "inexperienced youth," who were dragged by fallacious promises into the vortex of political disorders, deeming them to be less seducers than seduced. "All our subjects who are in prison for political crimes are to be pardoned," read article I, "provided they make a solemn declaration in writing that on their word of honor they will not in any way or at any time abuse this our act of grace, but faithfully fulfill the duties of a good subject." The same conditions were to be applied to all political refugees. As the commission of cardinals had stipulated, the depositions in the amnesty were not to be applicable to ecclesiastics, military officers, and government employees as well as common criminals.[13]

Moderates such a Luigi Carlo Farini saw the amnesty as a generous act of justice in substance, an act of reparation in form, because it condemned a system and wiped away all the accusations against those condemned. He thus shared the enthusiasm of the masses. The Bishop of Gubbio, Monsignor Giuseppe Pecci, in a pastoral letter of July 24, considered the amnesty the beginning of a new age. The clemency of the Pope, in his opinion, was the sign that he was the man sent by God to give rise to a new era of peace, concord, and universal harmony. The letter was widely circulated and had a tremendous impact. "The events at Rome are such to delight us all," wrote D'Azeglio; "the appearance of a Pope who has entered the realm of moderate liberalism is a fact of new and immense importance."[14] Rome now throbbed with excitement as the Romans abandoned their former indifference and passionately proclaimed Pius the father of his people and savior of the peninsula.

Prince Klemens Von Metternich, the Austrian chancellor, concurred that the Pope's concessions would have a profound consequence, but did not share the optimism of Farini or D'Azeglio. In private he compared the amnesty to an invitation to thieves to enter one's home. Reports already reached him that in Ancona the population celebrated the amnesty with cries of "Long live Italy" and "Down with Austria" while the cries of "Long live Pio Nono" were intermingled with the call, "Death for Metternich." While the Austrian chancellor had seen the need for some papal action, perhaps a limited pardon, he considered the Pope's generosity excessive. God pardons, but does not grant amnesties, Metternich reminded Pius.[15] His analysis proved correct, for the amnesty proved to be the spark that set all of Italy aflame.

Under the terms of the amnesty hundreds of political prisoners were released while scores of exiles were permitted to return home. It thus recalled to Rome the leading and secondary figures of the various sects and revolutionary groups. Among those who decided to return was Pietro Renzi, who had led the insurrection which broke out in Rimini in September 1845. He and others who returned found a state that was being transformed. They were amazed to see Pius accord awards and honors to various known liberals and even to some who a short while ago were persecuted by the papal regime. At Bologna while the excitement and gratitude for the amnesty was at its height the noted composer Gioacchino Rossini set to music some verses celebrating the occasion, and the chorus was joyfully taken up by the entire population.

Pius, determined to improve the position of his people and preserve their goodwill, continued along the path of reform. The price of salt was decreased and extraordinary tribunals were abolished. He appointed commissions of eminent Italian jurists to trace additional reforms. The Pope let the commission of cardinals know of his intention to reform the process of criminal justice and argued that the public should be given some indication that this was coming in order to calm the impatience of the masses.[16] There was the systematization of land for additional cultivation and an agricultural society was planned to improve the agronomy practiced on the land about Rome. Railroad lines were projected and telegraph companies were chartered.[17]

While funds were increased for various public services, the Pope won the heart of his people by cutting his household expenses.[18] He reduced the number of horses in his stable and the monies saved were diverted to the needs of the capital. The funds lavished upon the upkeep of the pontifical gardens were also cut. He was a priest of Jesus and not a Lucullus, he reportedly told those in charge of his table, asking that he be served as a poor priest.

A new press law liberalized censorship and permitted the publication of liberal and national sentiments. As a result the information in the *Diario di Roma*, an official publication and the only newspaper which circulated in Rome, was supplemented by sheets of various political coloration. Pius not only showed himself willing to open the press to the forum of ideas, he also made provision for a box to be placed in the Vatican so the ordinary citizen found a means of voicing complaints and making suggestions. The cardinal secretary of state, meanwhile, brought forward a proposal for the establishment of a council of ministers.[19]

For the first time subjects of the Pope were permitted to attend a scientific congress, traveling to one which met in Genoa in 1846. Among the Romans who went to the port city was Charles Lucien Bonaparte, the Prince of Canino and nephew of the great Napoleon. An ardent champion of Italian nationalism, he delivered the Pope's prayers for a successful completion of the congress. At the same time that Pius seemed to recognize that he was after all the head of an Italian state, he continued to display a deep sensitivity to the economic and social needs of his people. In a circular letter Pius called upon the heads of the various provinces in his state to provide public work projects to minimize unemployment and thus reduce crime.[20] The selection of the young and liberal Monsignor Corboli Bussi as his chief counselor at once reinforced his liberal tendencies and won him increased popularity.

It was the custom of the Romans at the accession of a Pope to wear his colors, and soon they were seen everywhere in gratitude to the new sovereign. Pius's carriage was showered by flowers, and from time to time the young men of the capital sought to unhitch the horses from his coach and pull it themselves. The popular hymn to Pius by Rossini was sung in Italy and abroad. His reforms were greeted by shouts of joy, reunions, marches along the Via del Corso, and popular demonstrations before the Quirinale Palace. These manifestations of public gratitude, often clamorous if not disorderly, increased daily. The Roman public, politically inexperienced, was inebriated by the Pope's spontaneity and affability. A popular ruler, removed from nepotism and genuinely concerned about his subjects, Pius was seen to be making the most profound revolution not for himself, not for his family, but for the public and for Italy. How far would the Pope go? No one knew, but all assumed that any hesitation stemmed from reactionaries in the Curia and Habsburg pressure.[21]

There were those such as Massimo D'Azeglio who feared that some would attempt to push the Pope to move more quickly than he desired and cautioned against such endeavors, urging Italians to trust the promises and character of Pius. "I say that such a man has done more for Italy in two months than have all the Italians together in twenty years,"[27] he wrote. Prince Metternich had even graver fears.

Austria, still sovereign in Lombardy and Venetia and exercising great influence in Naples as well, had her ambassador, Count von Lutzow, who enjoyed seniority among the diplomatic community in Rome, complain about the more obvious anti-Austrian demonstrations.[23] This pleased Giuseppe Mazzini, the founder of Young Italy, who instructed his followers in the peninsula to interject a national note into the demonstrations for Pius to exasperate Austria and prepare the groundwork for the national crusade.

Metternich suspected as much. The chancellor's postion was clear and focused upon two points: first, that the administrative reforms that were necessary should in no way assume the character of concessions that would weaken the government; second, that the moderate party was a sham which provided cover for the radicals and therefore no alliance with them was possible. As early as July the Habsburg minister had noted that every concession represented a renunciation of sovereignty which the Pope did not have a right to make, for he was obliged to transfer his full authority to his successor. A prince who behaved in this fashion, he concluded, was similar to a capitalist who consumed his capital rather than relying upon the profits derived from it.

Metternich's views were in large measure shared by Cardinal Gizzi, the secretary of state. Possessing a broad diplomatic background and accustomed to compromise in order to realize his goals, his amiability had brought him to the attention of Massimo D'Azeglio, who more than anyone else had popularized his liberal image. The image did not reflect the man. Fundamentally Gizzi was a centrist if not a conservative, at once anti-liberal and legitimist. Despite his poor health and frequent attacks of gout which confined him to his bed, he was a man of firm and decisive will. Called to the position of secretary of state by popular opinion which knew the image rather than the man, Gizzi did not share the optimism of the Pope about the prospects of reformism and sought to counterbalance the popular manifestations which seemed to influence Pius.

The secretary of state distinguished between progress and constitutionalism, accepting the first as necessary but rejecting the second as closely tied to nationalism and Italianism, that is to those tendencies that led logically to the destruction of the Papal State. Prepared to support the removal of the restraints on trade, the building of railways, the reform of the penal and civil codes, he shied away from the political concessions demanded by moderates and radicals. Like Metternich he believed that the radicals, under the pretext of laicization of the government, really sought the end of the temporal power.[24]

Pius, on the other hand, believed that God directed humanity and initially believed that the many demonstrations in his favor were motivated by religious fervor and renewed love for the Church. He did not believe that his people were deceived when they abandoned themselves to enthusiastic demonstrations for their prince, who was also head of the Church.[25] Confronted by disorders in Bologna, he had given orders to satisfy the just complaints of its citizens. He hoped that his obvious goodwill on behalf of the population that God had entrusted to him would be reciprocated.[26]

Few in the Curia shared the Pope's optimism, and even some who had earlier supported a moderate reformism reconsidered their positions. Cardinal De Angelis, Archbishop of Fermo, wrote Cardinal Amat that Pius was apparently not appraised of the seriousness of the situation, that a virtual revolution was being waged in his name. Conservatives were even more alarmed by the actions of Pius and saw more therein than weakness and political naiveté. In Ancona

The New Pope

Cardinal Cadolini claimed that a carbonaro had been elected Pope while at Faenza a number of intransigents vandalized the papal coat of arms, arguing they did not want a Jacobin Pope. In the capital itself a number of directors of religious houses urged their members to pray that the Church be spared the harm caused by a liberal Pope.[27]

As early as July 19, 1846, there was issued a note from the secretary of state, which indicated that the Holy Father was moved by the spontaneous demonstrations given for him by the inhabitants of Rome in the last few nights, but added that moderation increased the value of every beautiful gesture. It was not until October 1846 that the Pope finally spoke out against the noisy demonstrations which took his subjects from their work and undermined the tranquility of the state. In his note the Pope expressed the desire that the manifestations of joy at his elevation to the throne and at the various reforms cease, and that the monies used for them be put to some constructive work of public utility. His subjects were urged to await peacefully the further reforms his government planned.[28]

It was assumed that the Gregorians who surrounded the Pope were responsible for this statement and restrained the Pope from forging ahead with all the political changes he hoped to introduce. On November 4, when Pius went to the Church of San Carlo on the Corso, the reception of the public was cold, in part because of dissatisfaction with his statement, in part because of dissatisfaction with the pace of instituting the promised reforms. In response the Pope broadened the commission for the reform of the civic code and instituted other changes. This was apparently appreciated by the Romans, for when Pius visited Saint John the Lateran for the taking of possession on November 8, he was warmly applauded.[29]

During the course of the demonstrations, which continued despite the Pope's statement, cries of "Long live Pius IX," "Long live the Italian Confederation," and "Death to the tyrants and enemies of the Pope" were heard. Rumors were circulated that Pius was being pressured by conservatives to change his course, frightening even the more educated classes. That same month Marco Minghetti had an audience with the Pope and expressed the hope that he would continue along the path of progress. Pius agreed to do so, but added that time and stability were necessary. At any rate he was happy to see the press publish his call for patience and calm.[30] The promise of timely and gradual change satisfied the moderate element, but the radicals remained impatient.

Early in the pontificate of Pius the liberals split into moderate and radical factions. The former wanted to institute reforms without violence and sought a conferation of Italian princes to confront Austria. It was their determination to preserve much of the existing structure in the peninsula and thus assure harmony between princes and people along the lines suggested by Vincenzo Gioberti. The radicals, on the other hand, saw the Pope's reforms as only the prelude to more fundamental change. It was their intention to arouse the people of Italy to a fever pitch and push Austria out by a people's war which would set the stage for the emergence of an Italian republic as envisioned by Mazzini.

From the first the radical plans were unacceptable to the Pope, but even the dream of an Italian confederation called for by the moderates was not supported by the Pontiff, who did not want to do what Mazzini wished and felt he could not do what Gioberti wanted. In fact, as early as August 1846, a short while after his elevation, Pius declared to Pellegrino Rossi that he had no desire to change matters outside his own state and that it was utopian to think of an Italian league presided over by the Pope. A Pope, he told the French ambassador, could not throw himself into utopian dreams.[31]

Neither the liberals nor the radicals were pleased by Pius's first encyclical letter, *Qui pluribus*, addressed to the universal church on November 9, 1846, and understood by some to be an exposition of the fundamental lines he intended to pursue. Following a eulogy of Gregory XVI Pius frontally attacked the incredulous and the enemies of Christian truth. This first encyclical condemned rationalism, indifferentism, and the theory of progressive revelation. Its entire tone was pessimistic, following the initial observation that a war was being planned against all Catholic interests. Referring to the "monstrous errors" of the times, it noted that nothing could be more insane or impious. The letter was especially critical of rationalism, which rejected all truth known by faith and revelation, and indifferentism, which blurred the distinction between virtue and vice.[32]

Qui pluribus urged the hierarchy to watch over their flocks and to combat with fortitude and constancy the enemies of salvation, exorting them to protect the faithful from being led astray by any specious pretext of human progress. Stressing the danger stemming from the activities of secret societies and Bible organizations as well as evil books and mistaken periodicals, Pius repeated much of Gregory XVI's condemnation of liberalism's fundamental principles. Included in the encyclical was a brief but important reminder that power was granted to Catholic sovereigns not only for the governance of their subjects but also for the defense of the Church. Thus at a time when he was in the midst of political reforms, Pius showed himself conservative and traditional in the defense of the rights of religion and his condemnation of the errors of the day.

In substance, if Pius sought to pursue a new path in political matters, in the religious sector he displayed the same attitudes of his predecessor. The *Qui pluribus* was thus the first and best confrontation of the "myth of Pius" and the reality of the man, although one must admit that there was considerable difference between the warm character of the Pope, displayed in his audiences and talks, and the cold, pessimistic tone of the encyclical. In part this was a real reflection of the division in the heart and soul of Pius.[33] This contradiction, as well as the Pope's decision to celebrate a *Te Deum* in the Church of the Gesù on New Year's Eve, at a time when the Jesuits were under increasing criticism from liberal and national elements, led to the reemergence of the rumor that Pius was being pressured by conservative cardinals and led to the cry, "Long live Pius IX, alone."

At the opening of 1847 Pius enjoyed an unprecedented popularity. The new year witnessed an impressive festival in which a good part of the population of Rome marched to the Quirinale Palace, bearing banners and garlands of flowers, to express their love and devotion. Later in the evening the diplomatic community, the cardinals and bishops, as well as the religious, military, and civil authorities came to express their best wishes. In February a deputation from the English colony in Rome, traditionally hostile to the Church, was received by Pius in the Quirinale and thanked him for the help he had offered Ireland, which had been hit by famine. At the end of the same month the Turkish ambassador to Vienna, Chekib Effendi, arrived in Rome to compliment Pius upon his accession to the pontifical throne. Immense crowds assembled in the streets of the capital to witness the novel spectacle of the ambassador and his exotic entourage proceeding to the Pope's residence.

Daniel O'Connell, the Irish emancipator, who was on his way to see the Pope but who died in Genoa en route, left instructions that his body be transported home but that his heart be taken in a silver casket to Rome. Pius was moved to tears by the arrival of this relic. Wanting the greatest possible eulogy of O'Connell, Pius called upon Father Gioacchino Ventura, the renowned orator, to deliver it in the Church of S. Andrea della Valle. Ventura attempted to shun the responsibility, arguing that he could treat the subject only one way and by so doing he would either anger Pius or create too many enemies for him. Pius asked Ventura what he saw in the life of O'Connell that would justify such fears and Ventura announced that he saw an ardent alliance of religion with liberty. "This is also my view," responded Pius, apparently not aware of the commotion that such a eulogy would provoke. "I therefore beseech you to write the funeral oration so you can deliver it on June 28."[34]

In the eulogy, which the Pope permitted to be published, Ventura claimed that by sending his heart to Rome the liberator of the Irish Catholics paid homage to Pius, who would be liberator of Italy. Pius, who did not plan to undertake such a liberation, did wish to be loved by his subjects and was progressively intoxicated by the shouts and praises, the crowds and the processions, and the music and flowers that greeted his every appearance. As he passed by, men, women, and children sang out:

> He is as beautiful as hope,
> Strong as a lion,
> Gentle as a lamb,
> As just as God.

The Pope was transformed into a mystical hero as the enthusiasm of the masses passed into ecstasy. Pius, apparently inebriated by the applause, granted additional concessions which served as the pretext for new demonstrations.[35]

Margaret Fuller, the American author and literary critic who was associated with the Transcendentalists and Ralph Waldo Emerson and who had served as editor of the *Dial*, found herself in Rome as a correspondent for the *New York Tribune*. She noted the childlike joy and trust of the Romans in the first reforms of Pius and wondered if their praise was not premature in light of the insurmountable difficulties he had to confront. In her opinion a cool head and a firm hand were required at the helm, but she found in the Pope's expression more tenderness of heart than intellectual greatness. "He is a man of noble and good aspect, who it is easy to see has set his heart upon doing something solid for the benefit of man," Fuller wrote, adding, "but pensively, too, must one feel how hampered and inadequate are the means at his command to accomplish these ends." Considering his dilemma she concluded, "I often think how grave and sad must the Pope feel, as he sits alone and hears all this noise of expectation."[36]

Pius, in fact, was not unaware of the dangerous situation he found himself in and realized that he had been forced to make concessions in the face of public demonstrations. "We know where they want to lead us," he confided to Father Luigi Taparelli D'Azeglio, the Jesuit brother of Massimo. "We will cede as long as our conscience permits us, but arriving at the limit which we have already preestablished, we will not, with the help of God, go beyond it by one step, even if they tore us to pieces."[37] Despite this assurance the Pope's mentality and subsequent actions, as well as his tendency to confuse the natural, political realm with the super-natural, religious one, did not permit him to adhere to fixed limits, if he had indeed established them other than in the most general manner.

Already there were those who called for the removal of every restriction from the press and an end to all censorship. Pius considered such a move dangerous and argued that the government had to keep newspapers, short tracts, as well as major works under some sort of control. Recent developments confirmed him in this conviction. He was not pleased with the publication and subsequent circulation of Vincenzo Gioberti's *Il gesuita moderno* (The Modern Jesuit), which came out in mid-1847 and claimed that the Order was hostile to liberal institutions.[38] This blistering indictment of the Company's morals, politics, and teaching Pius felt had contributed to the anti Jesuit sentiment in Italy and Europe. Nonetheless he was willing to reform the press law, perhaps in order to avoid more substantive changes.

In the middle of March the edict revising the system of censorship was issued. In the words of Cardinal Gizzi it aimed neither to shackle the just liberty of the press nor to permit it to degenerate into fearful licentiousness. Under its terms:

It is forbidden to treat anything that would bring disrepute to religion, the Church, and the dignity of its Ministers. It is also forbidden to print anything that would offend the honor of the magistrates, the military, the families of citizens, governments and foreign powers, reigning families and their public representatives. Equally forbidden is the printing of any discourse which would directly or indirectly render the acts, forms, or institutions of the pontifical government odious to the subjects of the State or which would feed the factions or excite popular movements against the laws.[39]

Those who considered the press measure restrictive if not repressive expressed their dissatisfaction by substituting the coat of arms of Gregory XVI for that of Pius on all the copies of the edict plastered on the walls of Rome. They also grumbled because Pius had not established a National Guard. The Pope considered the latter institution inadmissable, confiding to Cardinal Amat in March 1847 that it would make people outside the state laugh and would lead those inside to cry.[40] By this time Pius had more serious reservations about the clamorous demonstrations made in his favor which exerted a subtle but persistent pressure for greater and more immediate change. He was beginning to sense what one follower of Mazzini freely admitted, that the demonstrations were the arms by which they stormed the Pope in order to coax and bully him into concessions.[41] Nonetheless, Pius saw no alternative to reform. He warned those who called for Austrian intervention that such a step would arouse the Powers to call for a European Conference, which would impose broader changes than the Pope would have to make if he acted freely and with dignity.[42]

CHAPTER 4

The Failure of Reformism

ALTHOUGH the popular frenzy had hitherto been free of ferocity, Cardinal Gizzi warned Pius not to let the excitable and fanatical imagination of the masses go unrestrained. The cardinal favored strong and decisive government and saw the need to contain the influence of the masses. Disturbed by the policy of concessions in the face of the popular demonstrations, as early as April 4, 1847, he offered his resignation, but the Pope tearfully urged his secretary of state to withdraw it. Pius apparently valued a man of strong principles in a government that was weak and vacillating.

The Pope, determined to provide for the welfare of his people, sought to do so by means of institutions compatible with the peculiar nature of the state he governed. His health remained excellent so he was able to busy himself with temporal as well as religious affairs. He gave innumerable public audiences and consulted all sorts of experts and specialists. In the evening he either presided over a congregation or worked with those cardinals who were entrusted with administrative responsibilities, often remaining at his desk past midnight. Pius's constitution did not seem to suffer from excessive work as much as from the grave thoughts which troubled his mind.[1]

To please his people Pius announced his intention to call from the capital and the provinces a number of persons who would form, if not a council of state proper, at least an advisory council. A number of cardinals opposed the measure, and at their head were Lambruschini and Bernetti. Gizzi accepted the proposal with the understanding that it would remain within a moderate framework and was not a movement toward representative government. In mid-April he published the edict which revealed the Pope's decision to choose from each province a person to venture to Rome to collaborate with him on the public administration. Three respectable individuals were to be proposed to the Pope, from which he would select one to represent each province in the *Consulta di Stato*.[2]

The *Consulta* was to sit at Rome for at least two years and would advise the government on matters of administration, the ordering of municipalities, and other public needs. It was to have a legislative section, a second for finances, another for internal administration that would concern itself with commerce, industry, and agriculture, and a fourth to deal with military matters.[3] The delegates from the provinces were to assemble in Rome at the beginning of November. The reaction to this proposal was quick and favorable. Pius IX, the masses shouted, was the greatest figure of the age. The Romans, ecstatic with joy, rushed into the streets and main squares of the city, proclaiming their devotion to the Pope-Sovereign.

An American who witnessed the spectacle found the reaction excessive.

A week or two ago the Cardinal Secretary published a circular inviting the departments to measures which would give the people a sort of representative council. Nothing could seem more limited than this improvement, but it was a great measure for Rome. At night the Corso in which we live was illuminated, and many thousands passed through it in a torch-bearing procession. I saw them first assembled in the Piazza del Popolo, forming around its fountain a great circle of fire. Then, as a river of fire, they streamed slowly through the Corso on their way to the Quirinale [Palace] to thank the Pope, unbearing a banner on which the edict was printed.[4]

While Pius and his secretary of state considered the *Consulta* the capstone of the reformist program, there were those who saw it merely as a foundation. For some each innovation, each concession, only stimulated the appetite for more. Indeed a memorandum was presented to the Pope calling for administrative and municipal reforms in the capital and provinces, the establishment of a system of municipal councils, and most important of all, the general admission of laymen to all administrative and judicial functions. Others called for some central body to coordinate the government, just as the *Consulta* would coordinate the administration.

By the *Motu proprio* of June 12, 1847, there was instituted a council of ministers which was assigned the task of discussing the most important questions of state before they were placed before the Pontiff for his approval. Previously these matters were submitted separately by the heads of the various departments for the sanction of His Holiness. The council, composed only of prelates, was to be presided over by the secretary of state, except in those instances when the Pope himself chose to chair its meetings. It included the Cardinal

The Failure of Reformism

Camerlengo, responsible for the superintendence of Commerce, Agriculture, Industry, and the Arts; the Cardinal Prefect of Aquaducts and Roads, the Monsignor Treasurer-General, and the Monsignor President of the Department of War. Heads of other departments might from time to time be called to take part in the discussions of the council of ministers, and those who were cardinals would have the same voice and vote enjoyed by the regular members.[5] In this first "cabinet" only Gizzi and Giacomo Antonelli, respectively secretary of state and treasurer, were believed to possess liberal tendencies; the others were perceived as staunch conservatives.

The transformation initiated by Pius in the States of the Church was bound to have repercussions in the other states of the peninsula, and some accused the Pope of sowing the seeds of revolution in the entire peninsula. From Vienna Metternich understood that others were latching on to the Pope's reformism as a lever to expel Austria from the peninsula.[6] The Grandduke of Tuscany was no less concerned about the Pope's cessions to the pretensions of the extremists.[7] Piedmont, according to Carlo Alberto, echoed the agitation of the surrounding states.[8] There were demonstrations in Piedmont, Naples, and Tuscany and in the Grand Duchy an ordinance was issued for establishing the liberty of the press.

The spectacle of an Italian prince exciting the national sympathies of the people of the peninsula filled the Austrians with apprehension if not exasperation. Moderates as well as conservatives were alarmed, and during May and June the most fantastic rumors spread rapidly about the alleged plots of counter-reformists. It was claimed that the "Gregorians" and Jesuits were conspiring against Pius and hatching plots to take possession of his person or end his life. Even those who discounted these stories did believe that certain cardinals, the so-called apostles of the Metternichian system, worked to restrain the Pontiff and prevent him from following his liberal inclinations.

The conviction that Pius was the prisoner of the conservative clique led some to favor more fervent demonstrations on his behalf, revealing that the people were with him and thus providing him the means to stand fast in the face of opposition. On June 17, more than 20,000 flocked from every part of the Papal States to Rome to commemorate the Pope's election of the previous year. The Pope, who on that June day looked out the Vatican Loggia and blessed the mulititude, was already aware that the throngs who were so devoted to the Vicar of Christ remained suspicious of the ecclesiastical government which he headed. There ensued a noisy, at times wild demonstration, which worried the Pope and his secretary of state as well as the resident foreign ministers, who counseled that such gatherings be prohibited in the future. By this time Cardinal Gizzi saw the real possibility of having to call for Austrian intervention if things got out of hand.[9]

On June 22, Cardinal Gizzi played his last card by issuing a proclamation recording the reforms already executed, indicating the willingness of the government to proceed with administrative reforms, but underlining that there were limits to the reforms that could be granted given the special nature of the papal government. The secretary of state stressed that, after a year in office, the Pope was aware of the love and devotion of his subjects and called for an end to the popular reunions and extraordinary manifestations. Gizzi, in his statement, observed that Pius had been pained to learn that some wished to use the current excitement to advocate doctrines and opinions contrary to the fundamental principles of the supreme head of the Church. "The Holy Father cannot forget the sacred duties which constrain him to maintain intact the depositary which has been confided to him," Gizzi explained.[10]

Pius confessed to those close to him that he did not know whom to listen to. On the one hand there were those who feared a revolution every time the public applauded. Others, on the other hand, called for measures he could not concede. In a moment of depression he confided that if God did not have mercy on him and show him what road to pursue, he would have no recourse but to follow the example of Saint Celestin and abdicate.[11]

The Romans, who had seen the Pope issue reforms which others had deemed impossible, realized that Pius was often moved by the very demonstrations his secretary of state wished to see curtailed. Those who wanted to push him further understood that the applause of the masses or the threat of popular discontent carried far greater weight with the Pontiff than any reasoned argument or formal presentation. The people could wring much from a Pope who genuinely sought to please them.[12] For the moment the radicals who orchestrated the demonstrations urged the masses to desist from such actions and receive the Pope with a coldness and silence that contrasted sharply with the boisterous rejoicing and adulation of a few days earlier.

Public hostility was generated to increase pressure upon the Pontiff to grant the civic guard. Both Pius and his secretary of state still opposed this institution as a dangerous innovation. Likewise the

The Failure of Reformism

council of ministers considered it inopportune to place arms in the hands of potential revolutionaries. At the end of June, during the meeting of a number of cardinals and Roman princes before the Pope, the need to grant the civic guard was stressed as the only means of quieting the public agitation. Gizzi preferred another solution and on his own initiative on July 1 asked the Austrian ambassador how his country would react if confronted with a call for intervention. Some days later Metternich gave an evasive reply, while Pius did not seem to appreciate the seriousness of the situation.[13]

Pius was not prepared to contend with the mounting public hostility and feared even graver consequences should he persist in his refusal to grant the guard. Consequently on July 5 there appeared a decree authorizing the controversial institution, whose members were to be recruited from citizens between the ages of twenty-one and sixty.[14] Prince Rospigliosi was nominated commander of the guard and a series of banquets were held by the clubs to congratulate him and win him over to their cause. The guard, which was outfitted in dark blue uniforms with red cording, produced the greatest consternation in Vienna, where Metternich concluded that Pius had virtually sealed his own fate. Cardinal Gizzi shared his pessimism and believed that the guard would lead to chaos. He signed the proclamation authorizing it but resigned days later. He predicted that if he had remained by Pio Nono's side for a year, those who followed would not last for more than six months because it was impossible for a minister of common sense to cooperate with the Pope.[15]

At this juncture Pius wrote his cousin Cardinal Gabriele Ferretti that Gizzi had turned in his resignation for the second time and he had had to accept it. "Do you know who is the new Secretary of State?" he asked, and answered, "His Eminence Ferretti. Come to Rome quickly. Courage! God is with us." Metternich doubted that he could set things straight.[16]

Cardinal Ferretti, who had been Bishop of Rieti, Nuncio at Naples, Bishop of Fermo, and Legate of Pesaro, was no statesman. The absence of statesmanship was to be revealed within the course of the next few days. The government knew that various individuals and groups had plans for a riotous celebration of the anniversary of the amnesty. Fearing the consequences on July 14, the secretary of state issued an official proclamation forbidding the celebration planned for the seventeenth of the month and had the order communicated by telegram to the provinces. Since Pius had not spoken on the matter, it reinforced the rumor that those around him were attempting to prevent the people from displaying their gratitude to their sovereign.

The notion that there was a conservative conspiracy underfoot to take possession of the Pope's person and force him to bring about a total change in his policies in an antireformist sense resurfaced. This and other stories were credulously and irresponsibly circulated. In the excitement the Romans seemed to have abandoned all reason and acted only on the impulse of the moment. Not surprisingly, disturbances erupted on the evening of the fourteenth, which Cardinal Ferretti made no serious attempt to curtail.

The demonstrations also resumed, and there was devised a type of extralegal tribunal which daily examined the course of government and applauded and condemned its actions. The papal authorities had clearly lost control of the situation, according to an English observer, who noted that one individual, Angelo Brunetti, known by his nickname of Ciceruacchio, or big-boy, more than anyone else was responsible for keeping the peace in Rome.[17] Vain, noisy, and credulous, this wine and horse dealer from the Trastevere, who wore an earring in his left ear, coordinated the tumultuous ovations to Pius and all but controlled the civic guard. Capable of fiery speech, Ciceruacchio moved the masses with ease.

The impotence of the papal regime disturbed the Austrians, and Marshall Josef Radetzky in particular. Alarmed by the agitation, on July 17 a force of 860 Austrians crossed the Po and in full war regalia entered Ferrara to reinforce the Habsburg garrison. Partly housed in the citadel, partly in local barracks that had been previously assigned to the imperial occupation troops, some of the officers were assigned to private houses in the vicinity. All of this was undertaken under the terms of article 103 of the Congress of Vienna, which accorded the Emperor of Austria the right to maintain troops there. The timing, however, was unfortunate. Rumors were still rife in Rome of a conservative counter move against the reformers and the public was agitated by the riots of July 14 and 15. The entry of Austrian reinforcements into Ferrara at this time created the impression that the Austrians supported the conservative faction and sought to extend their sway in the peninsula. Patriots demanded their expulsion.

The tense situation deteriorated further when an Austrian official was attacked by a mob in early August as he was entering the fortress from the City. The attack provoked an Austrian occupation of the area surrounding the barracks outside the citadel. This unilateral and

The Failure of Reformism

unauthorized extension of their treaty rights prompted a spirited protest from Cardinal Ciacchi, the Apostolic Legate of the City, as well as the new secretary of state, Cardinal Ferretti. The papal reaction, which included letters to the emperor and empress,[18] eventually induced the Austrians to withdraw to the citadel. The cost was considerable, for the public opposition of the Pope to the Austrian move aroused the patriotic sentiments of Italians and created the impression that Pius was prepared to champion national interests to the point of spearheading the drive to expel the Austrians from the whole of northern Italy. Thus to the myth of Pius the liberal Pope was added the myth of Pius the anti-Austrian Pope who would proclaim a holy war against the ancient enemy of Italy.

In Paris François Guizot, the chief minister of Louis Philippe, was displeased with the Court of Rome's attitude of bringing questions of foreign policy immediately to the attention of public opinion without having first attempted to settle the issue by negotiation with the interested party. There was also concern about the mounting tide of demonstrations and fetes in the Papal States, so that most of the diplomatic community welcomed the strong words of the statement issued on September 11, 1847. It warned that the Pope would not tolerate demonstrations which disturbed public tranquility, such as the clamorous events of the evening of September 7 and 8, and that offenders would be quickly punished.[19]

At the same time Pius wanted the Curia to know that he did not sympathize with those who wanted to revolutionize the papal government or transform the political framework of the Italian peninsula. At the beginning of October the Pope in his allocution to the Sacred College informed them that all his thoughts and actions, rather than being directed by political motives, aimed to spread the influence of the religion of Christ. While he desired that the princes of the earth promote the welfare of their subjects, he was scandalized by the actions of those who abused his name in their demands for change and withheld their legitimate obedience from their sovereign rulers. "Pius IX for one is just what I thought him from the first day," wrote Mazzini, "a good man, who wishes his subjects to be a little better off than they were before. *Voilà tout.*"[20]

Metternich, too, was dissatisfied with Pius, but for quite other reasons. The Austrian chancellor decried the destruction of a government and a regime under the pretence of reform, and warned that the party that daily gained ascendancy in Rome aimed for the union of Italy under one government. Italy, he argued, was a "geographical expression," for the peninsula was composed of sovereign and mutually independent states recognized by international law, and this was the system which the Austrian emperor was determined to preserve. Metternich charged that under the banner of administrative change to which Pius had dedicated himself with benevolence some sought to subvert the legitimate status of the peninsula, establishing in its place a federal republic on the model of the United States or Switzerland. This dangerous course, he wrote Count Dietrichstein, the Austrian ambassador in London, had already commenced, observing that Central Italy was in the midst of a revolutionary movement inspired by the chiefs who had long menaced the peace of Italy.[21]

The Viscount Palmerston, foreign secretary in the Liberal ministry of Lord John Russell, thought otherwise, expressing the conviction that reforms would weaken the position of those few enthusiasts who wanted to unite the peninsula and sought far-reaching changes. "In fact the reforms which have been either made or are in contemplation in Rome and in Tuscany, would naturally tend to counteract any such design," he wrote, "because, in proportion as grievances are removed and nations become contented with their existing conditions, in the same proportion each man among them devotes his mind to the improvement of his own individual condition, and ceases to think of or wish for any great alteration in the political state of the country to which he belongs, be that country great or small."[22]

To assure the reformists further of England's continued support, Palmerston sent Gilbert Elliot, Second Count of Minto, who was Lord Privy Seal since 1846, on an extraordinary mission to Italy. He visited Tuscany, Rome, and Naples, advising their governments to continue their liberal reforms while offering moral assurance to those princes who feared Austrian intervention. In Rome Minto was surprised and pleased by the sincerity and amiability if not the simplicity of Pius, but also noted with concern his lack of political experience and his excessive sensitivity to the applause and silence of the demonstrating Romans. "The Pope's head is less good than his heart," he wrote Palmerston.[23] Pius was in a most difficult position, he observed, not so much because he lacked really capable advisors but because of the difficulty of harmonizing the absolute independence of the Pope as head of the Church with a government of liberal character. Pius asked Minto if he knew that his government could not concede "liberal institutions" such as might be established elsewhere, and Minto indicated that he understood. However, this relative of

The Failure of Reformism

Lord John Russell argued that the Pope as a temporal sovereign could initiate a number of important innovations for the public welfare.[24]

This was precisely the path that Pius was inclined to pursue. Having received the recommendations of the commission charged with the task of devising a new system of municipal organization, Pius acted. His *Motu proprio* of October provided for administrative rather than political reform and extended to Rome and the *Agro Romano*, the territory immediately around it, the municipal system existing in other parts of the Papal States. Under its terms there was established a deliberative council of 100 members and a senate or body of magistrates composed of a "senator" and eight "conservators," all of them chosen from the council by its members. The first was charged with the task of examining all of the decrees applicable to the municipality while the latter was accorded part of the responsibility for their implementation.[25]

At the same time the secretary of state, in the Pope's name, issued a communiqué setting forth the basis for a commercial and customs union which would include the Papal States, the Kingdom of Sardinia, and the Grand Duchy of Tuscany. It was hoped that eventually it would extend to the entire peninsula. Pius, who had cherished the idea of establishing such a league from the beginning of his reign, thought it would lead to material improvement and provide a type of moral unity. Others saw the league as a first step toward political union.

Monsignor Corboli Bussi, who was close to the Pope and shared many of his ideas, wrote that it was impossible to disarm the factions in Italy without taking from their hands the banner of Italian nationalism and independence. He saw two ways to achieve this: the one was to declare war against the Germans and push them out of Italy, but this was dangerous. The other means, slower but more secure, was through the formation of the Italian League and would eventually assure that the entire peninsula from the Alps to Sicily was truly Italian. The League was therefore the best means of consolidating the peace and tranquility of the Italian states.[26] Sent to Piedmont with the mission of acquiring the adherence of Carlo Alberto, Corboli Bussi was able to inform the Pope in October that the Sardinian king agreed to adhere to the tariff League under certain conditions.[27]

In early November a convention was signed in Turin by Corboli Bussi, domestic prelate and intimate advisor to the Pope, Cavalier

Martini, Chamberlain of the Grand Duke of Tuscany, and Count Ermolao Asinari di San Marzano, the Sardinian foreign minister. It sought the well-being of the peninsula by means of cooperation that would fuse the material interests of the populations that constituted the respective states. It was hoped that the King of Naples and the Duke of Modena would adhere to their resolution and that the specifics of the pact could soon be elaborated. Unfortunately these two monarchs gave evasive answers, with the Duke of Modena explaining that, though an independent prince, he was a member of a family that had its head at Vienna and therefore could not give an immediate answer as regards the projected tariff league.[28]

While awaiting the formation of the tariff league Pius continued his program of domestic reforms and in mid-October 1847 there was issued the *Motu proprio* constituting the *Consulta* or High Council promised earlier.[29] Composed of a cardinal who presided over the body as president and a prelate who functioned as its vice-president, it contained twenty-four counselors divided into four sections. The body's functions were consultive; it had no power of initiative and its sessions and discussions were not to be made public. Nonetheless many insisted on interpreting the *Consulta* as an essentially political organ, almost a mini-parliament.

The latter view was not in keeping with the Pope's intention, who from the first had envisioned the *Consulta* as an administrative rather than a political organ. He instituted it to assist him in administration, to provide its opinions on matters of government concerning the general interests of the state and those of the provinces, and to provide technical aid in the preparation of laws as well as the imposition or reduction of taxes. While it is true that the various sections of the *Consulta* were empowered to examine all financial, administrative, and military proposals and report upon them, Pius insisted upon the right, after having heard the *Consulta*, of seeking the opinion of the College of Cardinals.[30]

The Pope confided to Cardinal Amat that the policy of his government was to execute all of the concessions granted while preserving all of its rights. On the issue of the press he did not feel that the head of the Church should call for a repressive policy. However, he was aware of the grave difficulties that were raised by excessive demands and he feared that freedom would degenerate into license. Having confided in God, he felt certain that moderation would overcome the utopian calls of the radicals. Should such not prove to be the case, he would not be able to provide instructions for future

The Failure of Reformism

matters because they would develop in a totally unexpected manner.[31]

Confident that he could remain in the reformist camp without bowing to the call for changes he could not accept, Pius moved ahead. On November 3, his secretary of state wrote to Cardinal Antonelli that the Pope had appointed him the president of the newly formed *Consulta* and would like the group to meet in the apostolic Palace of the Vatican.[32]

The opening of the *Consulta* was fixed for November 15 and it was to follow a rigidly defined, extremely formal ceremony both to underline the importance of the act and to satisfy the public, which enjoyed such spectacles. For the celebration of their installation, the Roman princes had placed at the disposal of each of the deputies a state carriage attended by servants in full livery, in which they proceeded to the Quirinale Palace. When they assembled before Pius in the throne room, he told them that, inspired by God, he sought to do all within his means for his subjects, "without, however, ever lessening even by an iota the sovereignty of the Pontificate, which having received from God and from his predecessors, whole and entire, so he was bound to transmit the sacred deposit to his successors."[33] He added that anyone who saw it as the germ of an institution incompatible with papal sovereignty was sadly mistaken. In effect, Pius implied that the status quo was to be preserved.

Properly warned, the members set off for the Vatican Palace in a splendid pageant that seemed to emphasize the importance of the body, despite the words of the Pope to the contrary. The Duke Marino Torlonia brought the deputies the best wishes of the inhabitants of Rome and the provinces and related that they could make the country prosper by the introduction of timely reforms in the civil administration.[34]

Following the installation of the *Consulta*, Pellegrino Rossi, the French ambassador, called upon the Pope, urging a greater laicization of the temporal power as a means of silencing the radicals. Pius, who once again admitted that he was a novice in political matters, promised to do his best. He reaffirmed this to Marco Minghetti, making it clear that he would not accept all that the *Consulta* proposed, insisting that he retained the right to give or withhold his approval on all issues. As before, Pius spoke of his obligation to transmit intact to his successors all of the rights of the Holy See. On the issue of whether or not the acts of the *Consulta* should be published, Pius made it clear that he preferred secrecy.[35]

While the Pope determined to hold the line on changes he deemed inadmissible, the Romans suspected that the conservative Curia was responsible for his wavering. This presumption disturbed Pius, as did the prospect of civil war in Switzerland between the Catholic and Protestant cantons. To make matters worse, Pius soon learned that the Swiss Diet had declared the *Sonderbund*, or separate league of seven Catholic cantons, illegal and decreed its dissolution, as well as the expulsion of the Jesuits, who were accused of organizing the league. On the issue of the Order in Switzerland, Pius found himself in a most difficult situation. While he did not want the war there to assume a religious nature, he was not prepared to issue orders to the Jesuits to leave Switzerland. In the face of the increasing hostility, Pius assumed a position of neutrality, unable to make a decision either way, and therefore played the part of a passive spectator.[36]

The radicals in Rome, inspired by developments in Switzerland, demanded that the Jesuits be thrust out of the States of the Church as well. Pius, torn between his need to protect the Church and his desire to please his people, found himself in a dilemma. He was scandalized by the cries of "Long live the Diet," "Long live Gioberti," and "Death to the Black Robes," in allusion to the Jesuits. Nationalists and radicals claimed that the issue of the Order was one of a sovereign versus his people and made it an important test of their ability to constrain the sovereign to their bidding.

The Pope's obvious sympathy with the Jesuits angered the radicals, who spread the rumor of his insincerity and urged the Romans to obtain by direct action what their ruler had refused by petition. "The Pope shows visible signs of retrogression," Mazzini wrote his mother in mid-November 1847. "His refusal to receive the Belgian agent because he was an enemy of the Jesuits, the expulsion of Pescantini by the gendarmes because he was the bearer of a petition from the Swiss to the Pope for the recall of the Jesuits, his general speeches, all prove this, and the people note it, and their enthusiasm diminishes."[37]

Pius, in his allocution of December 17, 1847, *Ubi primum* criticized the demonstrations made in Rome before the Swiss Consul following the fall of Freiburg and in anticipation of the defeat of the Catholic cantons. He also protested against the notion that he would consider the slightest diminution of the authority of the Holy See or sanction laws that cherished traditions other than those of the Church. "As to the Pope, it is as difficult here as elsewhere to put new wine into old bottles," Margaret Fuller wrote to Emerson in December 1847, "and there is something false as well as ludicrous in the spectacle of the people first driving their princes to do a little justice, and them *evvivi*-ing them at such a rate."[38]

By the end of 1847 not only the Papal States but much of Italy was in turmoil. In the Kingdom of Sardinia there were disturbances in the port city of Genoa against the Jesuits and in Turin, the capital, some of the leading men of state, including Count Camillo di Cavour, urged Carlo Alberto to grant a constitution. In the Kingdom of the Two Sicilies there were disturbances in Messina and Palermo which sought to persuade the monarch to grant the civic guard. Disaffection was increasing daily in Milan while Sicily was on the verge of insurrection. These developments troubled but did not overwhelm Pius, who remained convinced that God would assist Rome, Italy, and above all the Church.

Pius was advised by the moderates as well as the English that the best way of dealing with the radicals and revolutionaries was by timely reforms. With this thought in mind, on December 29, 1847, just as the year was drawing to a close, Pius issued a decree reorganizing the council of ministers, a sort of Christmas present to his people. Under its terms the government was to be divided into nine ministries: foreign affairs; internal matters; public instruction; grace and justice; finance; commerce, fine arts, industry and agriculture; public works; war; and police. The heads of the above departments were to compose the council of ministers, which was entrusted with the task of supervising every ministry as well as discussing the most important affairs of state. Indeed it was specified that vital issues could not be brought before the sovereign for approval unless they were first discussed by the council of ministers.[39]

Article seven of the *Motu proprio* of December on the council of ministers touched upon the most important problem in the Papal State, the matter of lay participation in the government. By this decree the Pope felt he had conceded all that he legitimately could on this question, for by its terms the only post reserved to a cardinal was that of secretary of state, who was to have a prelate for undersecretary. The other ministries were all to be open to laymen. Unfortunately not one of them was filled by a layman at the time, so the impact of this concession from the Pope was not immediately felt. In fact, rather than proclaim that laicization was integral to the new system, an attempt was made to minimize its impact. Thus the reform that Farini termed one of the most important of the pontificate remained sterile, so that the clerical domination of the reorganized ministry increased agitation in Rome and contributed to the convulsions of 1848.

CHAPTER 5

Toward Revolution

THROUGHOUT the winter of 1847–48 the Eternal City was feverish with excitement, despite the *tramontana*, the icy wind that blew from the north. On January 1, 1848, Pius wrote Carlo Alberto, king of Sardinia, that the difficulty of directing the people increased daily.[1] By this time he was fully aware of the danger of being pressured by popular demonstrations. This awareness as well as his belief that too much was being squandered on celebrations led him to insist that no unusual expenses should be incurred by his people for the public celebration of the New Year. Unfortunately neither the secretary of state nor the minister of police took any precaution to translate the Pope's will into reality. On the contrary the two permitted various groups in the capital to make all sorts of preparations for the day.

A popular procession to the Quirinale Palace was planned for the evening of January 1, both to present its good wishes to the Pope for the new year and to petition him for further change. It was only at this juncture that the authorities acted, and in an arbitrary manner ordered the military to prevent the marchers from reaching the Pope. While the crowd was gathering on the Piazza del Popolo, word spread that the Pontifical Palace was cordoned off to prevent the public from reaching the sovereign. Complaints were immediately made to Senator Tommaso Corsini, and the prince, accompanied by Ciceruacchio, went to see Pius to persuade him that the Romans meant no harm. The two secured from Pius the promise that the following day he would venture forth through the principal streets of the city, placing his complete trust in his people.

The Pope, who was disturbed to hear of the disorders which followed the implementation of an order he had inspired, sought to calm opinion by having his open carriage driven along the great thoroughfares the next day. Perhaps he wished to show that he was not a prisoner of the reactionaries as some claimed and that he did not intend to remain aloof from his people. More likely his decision stemmed from the realization that in Rome the means of control were weaker than the forces which wanted to sway the government.[2] Whatever the cause for his concession, the consequence was to strengthen the belief that a liberal Pope was being adversely pressured by a conservative curia.

Rather than holding Pius responsible for banning the procession, blame was placed upon the shoulders of his secretary of state, Cardinal Ferretti, and the minister of police, Monsignor Savelli. Above all the Jesuits were seen to be at the root of the reaction and this increased the animosity against the Order. This explains why the crowds Pius encountered on January 2 shouted, "Long live Pius IX, alone" and "Down with the Jesuits." Ciceruacchio, whose carriage followed the Pope's, unfurled a banner which read, "Courage, Holy Father, the People are with you."[3]

A number of steps hastily undertaken by the Pope in reaction to the disturbance seemed to corroborate that he was responsible for reforms, and those about him responsible for the reaction. On January 3, Monsignor Savelli was dismissed and Francesco Perfetti, a popular figure, was entrusted with the ministry of police. Equally significant was the appointment of Prince Pompeo Gabrielli, a general and a layman, to the ministry of war. The moderates who had urged gradual but consistent reform as well as the laicization of the ministry were upset by the conduct of their sovereign. They considered it dangerous that such innovations were obtained by the applause of the crowd or the threat of disorder and that reforms resolutely denied to the friends of the regime were precipitously conceded following a popular demonstration.[4]

Interestingly enough, both those who desired to sustain the Pope in a moderate reformism and those who wished to utilize him to undermine the status quo in Italy questioned his political wisdom. Although Pius spoke of the limits of his reformism, his asking the crowd not to make certain demands was more of an exhortation than an authoritative assertion. On January 10, the council of state received a memorandum signed by some of the most influential citizens of the Papal States. It called attention to the increasing tension in the peninsula and warned that their state lacked an adequate army for defense. The *Consulta* seconded the plea for a reorganization of the army, and as a result the pontifical government called upon Carlo Alberto of Piedmont to provide Rome with a military man of distinction who would assume the task of creating a

Toward Revolution

papal army. Subsequently it was learned that this delicate assignment was entrusted to General Giovanni Durando.

While the army reform was being considered in Rome the people of Palermo rose in rebellion against the government of Naples and defeated the Bourbon soldiers in ten days. Ferdinand II, not certain of the loyalty of his capital and frightened by disturbances elsewhere on the mainland, granted a constitution at the end of January. This was the first of a series of revolutionary upheavals in 1848. On January 30, the first night that Rome received word of the Neapolitan constitution, there were illuminations, songs, and other demonstrations of public exaltation. The events in Naples were seen as the logical consequence of the work initiated by Pius. The various clubs in Rome planned further demonstrations and the municipality, unable to restrain the enthusiasm without creating new difficulties, provided them with legal sanction by inviting citizens on February 3 to celebrate the restoration of peace in the Kingdom of the Two Sicilies.

From Turin came word of demonstrations against the Jesuits as well as news that the Genoese had sent a deputation to the capital, petitioning Carlo Alberto for the expulsion of the Order and the formation of a civic guard similar to those in existence in Rome and Tuscany. The journals which had mushroomed in Rome reported that at a conference of journalists in Turin the editor of the reformist journal *Il Risorgimento*, Camillo di Cavour, had called upon the king to grant his people a constitution. Following disturbances in Turin, Genoa, and Novara the reluctant monarch promised early in February to grant such a *Statuto*. Reports from Florence indicated that the grand duke promised to do likewise. Furthermore, the Jesuits were driven from Piedmont and Naples was soon to follow its example. In Austrian-controlled Milan the population commenced the New Year with a boycott of tobacco, which was an Austrian monopoly, provoking a massacre that aroused a good part of Lombardy.

In Rome Cardinal Ferretti was overwhelmed by the turn of events throughout Italy and felt he could no longer direct affairs. At the end of January he left Rome by night, like a fugitive, leaving his post because of his strong disagreement with the Pope, whom he found to be too weak and too prone to make concessions.[5] He was replaced by Cardinal Giuseppe Bofondi, the Governor of Ravenna, on February 7. Lacking broad political experience, Bofondi soon proved himself incapable of coping with the explosive situation. He was the third

Secretary of State in eighteen months. Pius, too, found his position increasingly difficult despite his desire to sanction all the reforms that were needed and were compatible with the character of the papal government.[6] He longed for peace in his state and the peninsula, but subsequent events only increased the agitation and tension in Italy and the whole of Europe.

On February 8 an unruly, threatening crowd gathered in the main thoroughfare in Rome, the Via del Corso, and shouted, "Down with Moderation," "Down with the Ministry," and "Long live Pius IX, alone." These menacing slogans and the increasingly vocal demands for laicization worried the Pope and moved him to increase the number of laymen in his ministry. He announced his intentions in a declaration of February 10, published by the *Gazzetta Ufficiale di Roma* on February 11, which noted that the Pope was neither deaf nor insensitive to his people's desires and needs. On the contrary he thought constantly of developing the political institutions of the state, without, however, violating his obligations as head of the Church.[7]

In the first part of his message Pius confirmed the concessions already granted and proposed others along this line: the reorganization of the militia, secularization of the ministry, and the maintenance of close ties with the other reforming princes in Italy. At the same time, however, he issued a clear warning against impetuous disorders and demands not in conformity with the dignity of the Church and his duties as Pontiff. Above all, he showed himself adverse to a foreign war. Criticizing the attempt to seek public well-being by means of terror, Pius indicated that Italy faced no danger so long as a bond of confidence united the power of the nation with the wisdom of her sovereigns.

In the second half of the message Pius pointed to the unique position of the States of the Church, which he claimed was beneficial to the whole of Italy and preserved it from ruin. Noting that the Romans had 200 million brothers abroad, who would protect their father's house in the center of Catholic unity, Pius argued that Italy would always be preserved so long as it contained the apostolic chair. "Therefore," he continued, "oh great God, bless Italy and always preserve for her this most precious of gifts—her faith."[8] These last words were taken out of context and interpreted in a far broader sense than had been intended. As a result it was assumed that Pius approved the cause of Italian independence as an essentially religious invocation was given a political significance.

Toward Revolution

Meanwhile the promise of increased lay participation in the ministry had satisfied some but not all so that perhaps for the first time Pius realized that concessions did not bring the peace he sought and a show of force might be necessary, as conservatives had argued all along. On February 11 the Pope called the fourteen leaders of the battalions of the civic guard to the Quirinale Palace and asked them if he could rely upon their loyalty and support. They replied affirmatively, but when the Pope inquired if he could also count upon the loyalty of the men they commanded, they lowered their heads rather than respond.

Visibly perturbed, Pius nonetheless altered the ministry as he had promised earlier by including three noted laymen in his cabinet. He appointed his friend Giuseppe Pasolini, minister of commerce, agriculture, industry, and fine arts; the lawyer Francesco Sturbinetti, minister of public works, and Michelangelo Caetani, minister of police. The evening of February 12, when a demonstration was organized before the Quirinale to thank Pius for the changes as well as his "blessing of Italy," Pius issued a stern warning. Before imparting his blessing upon the state, and even all of Italy, Pius pleaded that it was imperative that there not be requests contrary to the sanctity of the States of the Church. Certain shouts and demands, he continued, he could not, must not, and did not wish to permit. This being understood, and under these conditions, he gave his blessing.[9]

In the middle of February Pius created a committee of cardinals and other ecclesiastics and assigned it the task of developing and coordinating the institutions already conceded as well as proposing other institutions compatible with the authority of the Supreme Pontiff. Above all the committee was asked to determine if the concession of a constitution would violate the special nature of papal authority. The committee found no theological hindrances to the introduction of constitutionalism in the temporal realm and noted that politically it had certain advantages—namely the avoidance of two other alternatives: revolution or foreign intervention.[10]

It was only the pressure of circumstances and the demands of the masses that led Pius to consider constitutionalism, a development he had earlier deemed inappropriate for the Papal States. In conference with his new minister and friend Giuseppe Pasolini, he opened up his heart and expressed his feelings. "What ingrates," he told the count. "I have given amnesty and reforms." He was shocked that he had not satisfied his subjects, who always seemed to want more and who had not accorded him the gratitude he believed he deserved. He resented the call for laicization of the state.[11]

The situation was to deteriorate with the outbreak of revolution in Paris on the twenty-fourth and the subsequent flight of Louis Philippe to London. On Sunday, March 5, Rome received the first certain news of the revolution in France and the consequent installation of the Republic there. The first impression in the capital, both in moderate and liberal circles and in the Roman Court, was one of guarded optimism and a sense of relief that reforms had already been granted in Italy. Marco Minghetti was the first to tell the Pope of the revolution and to his surprise Pius was pleased, perhaps because he never did like Louis Philippe and because he felt relieved of the burden of having to take the initiative.[12]

Pius did not have much time to ponder the impact of the revolution upon Italy, for on March 6 Senator Corsini and members of the municipality presented themselves and asked for the establishment of representative government in the Papal States. The Pope was persuaded to follow this course by moderate liberal circles, upon whom he increasingly relied for advice and agreed to meet the request for a constitution. On March 10, he announced the formation of a new, liberal ministry, the prelude to the constitutionalization of the state. Where it would lead, the Pope himself did not know. However, he was haunted by the problem of conciliating constitutionalism with the full independence of the papacy in all questions that even indirectly touched upon its mission.

The Holy Father sought security by selecting ministers who were at once popular and had his confidence. Thus Cardinal Giacomo Antonelli, whose expertise and loyalty were beyond question, was informed that the Pope had nominated him secretary of state and president of the council of ministers.[13] Under him was formed a ministry of six laymen and three clergymen: Gaetano Recchi was selected as minister of the interior; Luigi Carlo Farini, deputy minister of the interior; Marco Minghetti, minister of public works; and Giuseppe Pasolini, minister of commerce. These men were leaders of the moderate faction. In addition Prince Aldobrandini was named minister of war; Giuseppe Galletti, minister of police; Francesco Sturbinetti, minister of grace and justice; Cardinal Mezzofanti, minister of public instruction; and Monsignor Luigi Morichini, minister of finance.

On March 14, the *Statuto Fondamentale*, or Roman Constitution, was published. In accepting it Pius had ceded to necessity but was not certain of the viability or wisdom of the new system and very possibly hoped to be free of it. "He did not affect at all to believe that the Italians were yet capable of conducting the free representative government which they had now everywhere established," Minto wrote Palmerston, "but he seemed to accept his share of it very frankly, and with the desire to contribute as far as is in his power to its success."[14]

Under the terms of the Roman Constitution the Sacred College of Cardinals was invested with the functions of senate inseparable from the Pope. Likewise the council of state, nominated by the Pope, was retained. It was entrusted, under the direction of the government, to draft laws, provide rules for public administration and give its views on governmental matters. In addition there were instituted two deliberate councils for the formation of law: a high council and a council of deputies. By the terms of the constitution the members of the first were to be nominated for life by the Pope; the members of the second were to be elected by procedures to be established.[15]

It was specified that the councils could not propose any law which appertained to ecclesiastical or "mixed matters" or that was contrary to the canons or discipline of the Church. Indeed by article thirty-eight the two councils were prohibited from even discussing the diplomatic-religious relations of the Holy See.[16] When both councils approved a law, this would be presented to the Pope in secret consistory. The sovereign, having heard the vote of the College of Cardinals, would grant or deny sanction to the law. If he failed to accord his approval to a measure passed by both houses, it could not be brought up again during the course of that session. The Pope was to convoke, prorogue, and close the sessions of both councils.

These various safeguards were provided because the Pope could not separate his principality and temporal power from his independence as head of the Church. It was frankly stated in the constitution that the Pope had perforce to reserve for himself and his successors the supreme right to approve all laws which might be sanctioned by the aforementioned councils. It was further specified that, for the security of all Christianity, this new governmental form must in no way limit the rights of the Church or the Holy See. Nor could it in any manner violate the sanctity of the religion which the Pontiff had the obligation and mission to preach to the entire universe.[17]

No sooner was this document made public than it was criticized on two grounds. In the first place, there was dissatisfaction with the provision whereby the College of Cardinals was provided with the powers of a political senate. To make matters worse, its deliberations were to be kept secret, which provided it with immunity despite the fact that it exercised an important influence. Secondly, there was opposition to the prohibition which prevented the assembly from concerning itself with "mixed matters"—political and administrative questions that touched upon the moral mission of the Church. Liberals were upset that political rights were contingent upon one's profession of faith and that the constitution did not provide for complete freedom of religion, including the right of all cults to seek adherents. Hence, though the *Statuto* granted all that Pius felt he could legitimately accord, if not more, it failed to satisfy those who wanted to convert the Papal States into a modern, constitutional state.

The debate on the constitution had just commenced when Italy received word on March 17 of the students' revolution in Vienna and that Metternich, the coachman of Europe since 1815, had been forced to flee shamefully from his capital. "We live in really stupendous times," wrote the Mazzinian Giovanni Ruffini from Paris. "I defy any one to be calm in the midst of a cataclysm of this sort.... Metternich, the great High Priest of Immobility in flight! What lessons!"[18] With old Europe crumbling, with absolutism reeling, the level of expectation had risen remarkably. Farini explained that one could no longer speak in terms of reforms for it was now a struggle between the principles of absolutism and liberalism; it was no longer an Austro-Italian conflict but universal war.

Pius witnessed these events with mixed emotions. He was moved by developments in Vienna and Budapest, the withdrawal of Radetzky from Milan, and what seemed to be the triumph of nationalism over the multi-national empire. All of this the Pope interpreted as the will of God that overturned those who were proud and exalted the humble. At the same time he was disturbed by the new demands made upon him, which he did not wish to sanction.[19] The first of these unpalatable demands was the call for disbanding the Jesuit order in Rome. The second and even more explosive issue was that of papal participation in the national war against Austria that had been precipitated by the heroic resistance of the Milanese against the Austrians on March 18 and broadened by Carlo Alberto's decision to aid the Lombards in their struggle on March 23.

On the issue of the Jesuits, the elimination of the Order in Piedmont and Naples inspired their opponents in Rome to increase the pressure upon the Pontiff to expel them from the Eternal City as well. In the Papal States as in the rest of the peninsula there were demonstrations against the Jesuits, who were forced by popular pressure to withdraw from Faenza, Loreto, Camerino, and Ferrara. The Pope, whose first aim was to safeguard the Church, considered the proposal to expel the Jesuits from Rome an outrage. Stung to the core by what he considered an attack upon the Church, Pius clung desperately to the Jesuits, letting it be known that he had no reason to desire their departure and creating a major impasse. Only at the end of March did the resourceful secretary of state, Giacomo Antonelli, orchestrate a compromise. He arranged for the fathers to leave voluntarily to assure their own safety, thus satisfying the clamor of the radicals while attempting to soothe the scruples of his sovereign. Pius acceded to this solution reluctantly, noting that some, posing behind the mask of self-government for the Papal States, sought to control the affairs of the universal Church.

The issue of papal participation alongside Piedmont in the war against Austria was even more explosive. On March 22, the council of ministers decreed the opening of voluntary enlistment in case of possible conflict and in a few hours thousands had inscribed. Among the first to enroll and offer money for the campaign was Ciceruacchio.[20] On March 23, when the forces of Carlo Alberto crossed the Ticino into Lombardy, a demonstration was held in the coliseum in order to arouse the rest of the Romans. Later the demonstrators marched before the Quirinale and asked the Pope to bless their banners, which called for Italian independence. Pius refused, explaining privately that as a minister of the God of peace he could not bless the torches that might set all of Italy aflame.

While the Pope found it difficult, if not impossible, to attack Catholic Austria openly and perhaps provoke a schism in Germany, his constitutional government, including the president of the council, Antonelli, maintained a patriotic stance. Perhaps this is why Pius did not make his antiwar position clear and allowed money to be collected for the war effort as well as the enlistment of volunteers. This would also explain why he allowed General Durando and the papal army to march northward, followed shortly thereafter by the volunteers under the command of Colonel Andrea Ferrari. However, when the troops who left Rome for the North on March 23 asked for the Pope's benediction, he refused to bless their banners publicly and warned a delegation of this force, which he received, that they were being sent solely to protect the papal frontiers. He explicitly explained that they were not to cross the frontier—although the public was not made aware of the Pope's instructions and misinterpreted the Pope's motives for sending the army north. Publicly Pius did not clarify his position; indeed his statements seemed to support the national effort.[21] "The events which these two months have seen succeeding and pressing on each other with so rapid change, are not the work of man," he wrote at the end of March. "And we, to whom is given the word to interpret the mute eloquence of the works of God, we cannot be silent in the midst of the desires, the fears, the hopes which agitate the minds of our children."[22]

These words, which included a warning to those who did not heed the voice of the Lord in this period of agitation, some interpreted as the opening of an anti-Austrian crusade. However, Pius did not promise his support for an Italian war of liberation. He seemed to be walking on a tightrope in his actions as well as his words; for while the public assumed that sending the army north signaled papal participation in the war, Durando had been carefully instructed to move the troops to the frontier but not to cross it under any circumstances. The papal government did press for the formation of an Italian League which would enable it to participate in the war while freeing the Pope of the responsibility of declaring it.[23] However, Carlo Alberto preferred to act unilaterally and the failure of the Piedmontese to send representatives to Rome to conclude the league increased Pius's suspicions and reservations concerning the war of liberation.[24]

As an Italian Pius seemed to welcome the extraordinary events of 1848, but as head of the universal Church he could not forget that his first responsibility was to defend its independence and preserve intact the powers of the Pontiff.[25] For a number of reasons both religious and political, he hesitated to implicate himself in a war which the Piedmontese had commenced and whose course they largely controlled. In his opinion his position did not allow him to pronounce for the cause of Italian independence as the grand duke had at the beginning of April. Despite his restraint, he was already being criticized in Austria and southern Germany for making war on his fellow Catholics. In the English Parliament he was attacked by the conservative Lord Brougham, who argued that "he, who assumes to be the head of the Religion of Peace, chose to be the first mover of those convulsions which have all over Europe placed that peace in Jeopardy." The pro-Austrian lord charged that "he, who owes his triple crown to the Treaty of Vienna, is the first to draw the sword against it...."[26]

Disturbed by criticism from Protestant England, Pius was profoundly distressed by the impact of his position upon Catholic Austria. He revealed to the Tuscan representative at Rome the pain caused him by the diffusion of demagogic ideas and the threat this posed for Catholic unity in the German world. Consequently he clung tenaciously to the claim that the movement of his forces aimed to protect his frontier rather than to initiate aggression by the head of the Church against part of his flock. When warned that General Durando would lead the papal forces beyond the Po, Antonelli, aware of Pius's position, responded that in such a case the pontifical government would have no other recourse than to protest.[27]

In March and even more so in April Pius was haunted by the fear of a new German schism. Both Monsignor Viale Prelà, nuncio at Vienna, and Monsignor Carlo Sacconi, nuncio at Munich, forwarded urgent messages to Rome indicating that the participation of the Roman government in the war against Austria was turning the South Germans against the papacy and warned that it might even result in a disastrous schism. Viale Prelà's dispatch of April 7, which reached Pius about the sixteenth, proved particularly decisive, for the emotional Pope was stunned by the reported anti-Roman sentiment in Austria and the fact that the Austrians held him responsible for the war which was being waged against them in his name.[28]

For this reason Pius was infuriated by the proclamation secretly written by Massimo D'Azeglio but issued by the commander of the papal forces, Durando, on April 5. It announced that Radetzky and the Austrians were waging war against the cross of Christ. The Italian struggle was therefore depicted as one of civilization against barbarism and was termed not only national but eminently Christian. The soldiers who were fighting for the Pope, the proclamation continued, were to be adorned with the cross of Christ and their war cry was to be, "God wills it." Pius, angered that his troops were passing the Po contrary to orders, was even more upset to learn that his commander was not only making him a participant in the war, but the central figure in the anti-Habsburg crusade. He wished to lash out against the proclamation, which placed him in an impossible position, but his government cautioned restraint. Thus only a brief statement was inserted into the *Gazzetta Ufficiale* (Official Gazette) on April 10, referring to Durando's statement and observing that "when the Pope wishes to express his opinions on an issue, he speaks for himself, never from the mouth of a subordinate."[29]

Cardinal Antonelli hoped that this would suffice to calm the Pope and maintain the precarious harmony between the ministry, which favored entry into the war, and Pius, whose religious mission led him to shun it. Carlo Alberto was also concerned and wrote the Pope a letter indicating that the aim of the war was not only the independence of the Patria but also the triumph of their holy religion, which was oppressed and insulted by the Austrians on their soil.[30]

Pius had not yet spoken publicly about the war. Rumor had it that in a subsequent consistorial address he would speak about the war of independence, and the ministry hoped he would favor the cause. The participation of the Papal States, open and direct, was called for by the times, the ministry declared in a unanimous resolution. Pius, however, thought otherwise and tenaciously refused to declare war. "Italian nationalism is overruning the whole of Italy and it is a natural sentiment," he wrote in a letter of April 25, "but my position is such that I cannot declare war against anyone."[31] On April 27, he wrote his friend and advisor Monsignor Corboli Bussi that two days hence he would speak to the cardinals in consistory and would let it be known that the government could not wage war against anyone.[32]

On April 29 he made his position public in a controversial allocution which revealed that as a prince of peace and common father of all Catholics, he was not prepared to declare war, although he could not prevent his subjects from entering the conflict as volunteers if they chose. "We have at length thought it our duty that ... we clearly and openly declare that this [war] is wholly abhorrent from our counsels," he wrote, "seeing that we, although unworthy, discharge on earth the office of Him who is the author of peace and lover of charity and agreeably to the duty of our supreme Apostleship, regard and embrace with equal paternal earnestness of love, all tribes, peoples, and nations." Pius let it be known that he wished to extinquish the fires of discord, reconcile the hearts of the combatants, and reestablish peace.[33]

The reaction to the allocution in Rome and throughout Italy was immediate and negative. The day after it was issued the Piedmontese and Tuscan representatives met with the Pope, who told them that as an Italian he desired the well being of Italy and considered the independence and federal union of the peninsula to be the foundation of such well-being. He added, however, that as head of the Church and as a man of peace he should not and could not declare war against a power that had given him no cause to do so.[34]

Toward Revolution

The Italians did not understand or did not want to undestand the distinction that Pius made between the Pope, who was both a sovereign and a religious leader, and other temporal princes, who could quite readily declare war. There were those who argued that Pius was the victim of dark, sinister forces while others placed the responsibility for the refusal to declare war upon his shoulders. "He has betrayed us," Ciceruacchio repeated with tears in his eyes, and the cry resounded throughout the peninsula. Since the valor of the Italian troops was motivated principally by religious sentiments, Carlo Alberto feared the consequences of the allocution on the conduct of the war and the future of Italy.[35]

Pius had problems of his own. Following the publication of the allocution the civic guard took up arms and occupied the gates to the city of Rome, arresting the couriers and intercepting all correspondence with the outside world. Meanwhile there were a series of disturbances in the provinces as well.[36] The Antonelli ministry resigned, observing that, given the public mood and agitation produced by the papal allocution, it could no longer maintain the public order of which it was the custodian. Pius, stunned by the reaction his words had produced, urged his ministers to remain at their posts, promising them he would issue a statement which would elaborate upon the allocution and satisfy his people. However, the statement issued in early May confirmed the principles contained in the allocution and above all reaffirmed the Pope's aversion to a declaration of war against Austria.

According to Monsignor Francesco Pentini, who revealed the story only years later, the Pope had asked him to produce a statement in favor of the war or at least one that would quiet the outcry of his subjects. Antonelli, however, allegedly entered the press room and emasculated the message that Pentini had drawn up and Pius approved, thus provoking the rift between the Pope and his people.[37] This story has never been substantiated. Indeed the secretary of state made no substantial changes to the text of Pius's proclamation—and if he had the Pope could have easily set the matter straight. Pius did no such thing. On the contrary, in statement after statement, both public and private, he adhered to his original aversion to a declaration of war, and it was this unwillingness to enter the war that led to the revolution and his exile.[38]

CHAPTER 6

Revolution and Flight

"PIUS IX is the real Vicar of Christ, he is the greatest of all Pontiffs," said his people. "He is a Jacobin, and a Mason," said the princes. Actually Pius was first and foremost a priest who wished his people to share the elation he felt at being elected Pope. However, as their elation took a revolutionary turn and threatened the position of the papacy, he regretted his concessions and recalled that his first responsibility was to protect the interests of the Church.[1] Pius, who would brook no interference with his spiritual authority, found it difficult if not impossible to play the part of a constitutional ruler and submit to a real limitation of his temporal authority. This was the fatal flaw of constitutionalism in the Papal States and the difficulty had arisen as early as March 1848, when the Pope had agreed to the *Statuto*. The war issue served to illustrate dramatically this fundamental weakness and the inability of Pius to separate his spiritual and temporal powers.

Having placed himself in opposition to his ministry and the vocal element of the population that demanded war, Pius sought to quiet their outcry by writing a letter to the Austrian Emperor on May 3, urging a German withdrawal from Italy. The language of the letter, which spoke of "natural boundaries" and made reference to the "Italian nation" as opposed to the "German nation," showed that Pius was not insensitive to Italian nationalism, according to Giacomo Martina of the Università Gregoriana.[2] In point of fact the letter was the work of Giovanni Corboli Bussi, and in his original draft submitted to Pius he warned the Austrian emperor that if he did not withdraw from the peninsula he would be induced to take up arms. This Pius deleted, to the dismay of the monsignor.[3]

The amended letter, sent by the Pope to the emperor on May 3, only antagonized the Habsburgs without satisfying national sentiment in the Papal States or silencing criticism in the rest of Italy. To restore some semblance of order, on May 4 Pius empowered the liberal Terenzio Mamiani to form a new ministry presided over by Cardinal Ciacchi, the least unpopular of the cardinals as a result of his protest against the Austrian occupation of Ferrara. Mamiani, who had taken an active part in the revolution of 1831 in the Papal States and had several works on the Index, accepted, while Cardinal Ciacchi declined, so that the position of secretary of state was given to Cardinal Soglia, a good bishop but a figure lacking both political experience and courage.[4]

Count Mamiani, the real head of the cabinet, assumed the post of minister of the interior while Count Giovanni Marchetti, a childhood friend of Mastai, assumed the ministry of secular foreign affairs and Giuseppe Galetti remained as minister of police. Branding the ministry ultraliberal, Pius wrote Cardinal Amat that the temporal power of the Holy See could not survive if it acceded to its demands.[5] The two pressing issues were the separation of the temporal from the spiritual power and the question of papal participation in the war, which emphasized the need for the first.

Count Mamiani believed that the Papal States should declare war upon Austria, although he understood the Pope's reluctance to do so personally because of his role as spiritual father. The issue could be avoided, he felt, by having the ministry declare the war for him.[6] Pius had reservations about this as well and sought the advice of a number of theologians. Pointing to the agitation born in his states after the allocution and the prospect of anarchy and civil war erupting therein, he asked if it would be legitimate to avoid these possible evils by taking an active part in the war against Austria for the conquest of Italian independence.[7] Only two out of the twelve questioned responded affirmatively. The others indicated that the Pope should avoid such a step, noting the relativity of the principle of nationality and the legitimate rights of Austria.[8]

Pius, whatever his feelings for the Italian cause, let himself be guided by the theologians' decision on the war issue and determined not to alter his neutral stance. At the same time he refused to accept the Mamiani thesis on the separation of the temporal and spiritual power, insisting on his full liberty and authority not only in the religious realm but also in "mixed matters." The Pope did not believe that the *Statuto* could be developed so that the constitutional system he had accorded could be converted into the parliamentary one the liberals desired. Regarding the league, which Mamiani hoped might help resolve the crucial question of participation in the war and therefore the constitutional question, Pius let it be known that he envisioned it as a defensive mechanism rather than an instrument for waging war.[9]

In light of the positions assumed by Pius and Mamiani on the war issue and the question of the separation of the temporal and the spiritual powers, a confrontation between the two was inevitable. It was not long in coming. The discourse that Cardinal Altieri, the delegate of the Pope, was to present on June 5, on the occasion of the opening of the chamber, was edited by Mamiani and rejected by Pius. In turn, the cabinet did not approve the corrections imposed by Pius. The programs of the two differed markedly, above all on the question of waging war against Austria. "Even though the strong desire for Italian greatness grows daily," the Pope responded in July to the continued pressure for a declaration of war from his chamber of deputies, "the entire world must again be told that war cannot be on our part the means of achieving it."[10]

The Pope's reluctance to issue a declaration of war was considered central to the Piedmontese failure to rally the Italian peasantry to their cause and therefore held responsible for the difficult situation in Lombardy. Whatever the reasons, the Piedmontese were decisively defeated by the Austrians in the four-day battle of Custoza, July 22–25. Shortly thereafter Pius wrote Carlo Alberto that he shared the king's affliction as a result of the recent events of the war.[11] The national party wanted action rather than words and, since the Austrians by this time had returned to Ferrara, urged Pius to redeem himself by repelling the invader. The inaction of the Pope led to the resignation of Mamiani.

Mamiani was replaced by another layman, the ex-revolutionary Count Edoardo Fabbri, who was given the task of forming the new cabinet on August 2. The count enjoyed considerable popularity because of his past record and especially his imprisonment and exile during the years of Gregory XVI. Once in power, however, Fabbri found himself trapped between his attempt to follow the directives of the Pope, who had not changed his views, while maintaining the posture of a constitutional ministry sensitive to the chambers and public opinion, that still called for war. He proved unequal to this most difficult task, so that his ministry lasted less than two months. Even before then Pius hoped that the French would send troops to Rome "to restrain the passion of that part of the public that would like to see honest liberty degenerate into license."[12] General Eugene Cavaignac was evasive in his reply.

At this juncture there were few men willing to undertake the thankless task of supporting the Pope's unpopular position on the war against public opinion and the country's new political institutions. Abandoned by most of his friends in the moderate liberal camp and despairing of French assistance, Pius appointed Pellegrino Rossi minister of interior and the effective head of the government in mid-September. Rossi, like the other appointees, had commenced his career as a revolutionary, having been a collaborator of Murat and therefore exiled from the peninsula following his fall. His years in exile had afforded him the opportunity for reconsideration and he became increasingly skeptical of radical and revolutionary rhetoric. Because of his talent, familiarity with the Italian situation, and friendship with Guizot, he was appointed ambassador to Rome in 1845, but was *persona non grata* to the republican regime which followed the constitutional monarchy. No longer ambassador, Rossi remained in Rome both out of patriotism and his belief that he could help the Pontiff.

A brilliant administrator, Rossi was austere in his manner and intolerant of incompetence and demagoguery. He was cold by temperament and distrusted by both radicals and conservatives because he did not espouse the program of the first or the second. As a representative of constitutional monarchy he antagonized the repubicans and because of his opposition to war with Austria he was the *bête noir* of the nationalists. Not swayed by panaceas and simplistic solutions, he warned those who counted on French help against Austria that France was not a corporal in the service of Italy. Loyal to the Pope, he was determined to preserve the temporal power of the papacy, combating both revolution and reaction to do so.[13] With Rossi in control, Pius seemed finally to have found a figure capable of pursuing a moderate program and maintaining stability.

The new minister championed a confederated Italy and believed the time was ripe for pressing on the various Italian courts the necessity for a federal league. Negotiations, in fact, were resumed with Naples, Florence, and Turin. As before, however, the Roman initiative received little encouragement from Turin, where the new government instructed Father Antonio Rosmini to present a project for a simple league for offensive and defensive purposes without any organic, federal bond. Rosmini, who was a priest as well as Piedmont's negotiator for the proposed league, refused to support such a project, knowing that the Pope found it unacceptable. As a result the negotiations came to naught and there were those who claimed that

Pius was responsible for the failure. Rossi, however, refused to let the Pontiff assume the responsibility, and early in November defended him in the *Gazzetta di Roma*, noting that others had placed obstacles in the way of the league. More specifically he pointed out that the failure was due to the fact that the Pope, who had initiated the league, was not willing to follow blindly the limited and quite unacceptable Piedmontese plan.

Rossi's spirited response to the Piedmontese accusations as well as his determination to protect the Pope from the utopian demands of the radicals served to increase the opposition of the clubs in the capital to him. Denouncing him as a despot and an enemy of the Italian cause, demagogues in the Papal States were anxious to eliminate the haughty count, whose shadow seemed to thwart their ambitions.[14] Rumor spread that a revolution would erupt on November 15, the day the chamber was scheduled to reopen. At the very least there would be a confrontation between the Parliament that still favored war and the authoritarian prime minister who seconded the Pope's determination to avoid a clash with Austria.

The prime minister knew that there were those who plotted to take his life but insisted that the parliament should meet on the appointed day and he should personally open it on his sovereign's behalf. Aware though not awed by the threats made against him, Rossi did call for police protection before the Palace of the Chancellory where the parliament met, while a majority of his ministers argued that the civic guard would be sufficient.

The morning of the fifteenth Rossi received a message from the wife of one of his colleagues in the cabinet, urging him not to leave his home, and warning of an attempt to assassinate him. When the count met the Pope later in the morning, Pius urged Rossi to take all possible precautions to avoid having his enemies commit some terrible crime which would cause the Pope immense pain. Rossi, however, remained resolute in his determination to attend the opening of the chamber, arguing, "I defend the cause of the Pope which is the cause of God."[15] It was precisely such talk that aroused nationalists and radicals, who considered his murder a patriotic duty.

When the prime minister's carriage entered the courtyard of the Palace of the Chancellory, it was greeted by a volley of hisses, but then a voice cried out in a commanding fashion, *"Zitto! Zitto!"* and a deadly silence ensued. It was at this point that Rossi realized that his orders had been disobeyed and only the civic guard was present. Not one to turn around or to compromise, Rossi determined to walk into

Revolution and Flight

the hall. As he moved toward the entrance, a hostile crowd gathered around him and Luigi Brunetti, son of Ciceruacchio, commissioned by radicals such as Pietro Sterbini and the Prince of Canino, thrust his dagger into Rossi's throat, cutting his carotid artery. Assisting in the assassination was Sante Costantini, who was later charged with the crime. Rossi, whose throat was cut, did not utter a sound but took out his handkerchief and placed it upon his wound before collasping.[16]

The civic guard did not attempt to assist Rossi or to apprehend his assailants. Within five minutes the prime minister, who was carried to the rooms of Cardinal Gazzoli, had bled to death.[17] Pietro Righetti, the deputy minister of finance, who had been with Rossi when he was attacked, rushed to the Quirinale to inform Pius what had happened. The grief-stricken Pontiff could only say, "Count Rossi has died a martyr. God will receive his soul in peace."

The assassination of the sole figure willing and able to uphold the principles of the Pope against popular pressure was the first of a series of traumatic experiences for Pius. He was shocked by the conduct of the civic guard and the attitude of Sterbini, who had reportedly cried out to the agitated deputies who had learned of the murder, "Calm yourselves, it is nothing!" He considered it barbaric that the assembly, on whose very threshold the prime minister had been murdered, took no formal notice of the terrible crime and sought to carry on as usual. Pius was horrified to hear of the illuminations and celebrations in the city that evening as radicals sang, "Blessed is the hand that stabbed Rossi."[18] He considered these events expressive of the most primitive and bloody instincts of the masses and painfully realized the danger inherent in supporting a moderate program.

The Pope found himself abandoned at this critical juncture by most of his ministers, both lay and ecclesiastic, who thought first and foremost of their own security. While his ministers fled for their lives, the Roman nobles and cardinals remained aloof. The leaders of the two chambers advised Pius that he had no other recourse but to accede to popular pressure and appoint the democratic ministry that the Popular Club demanded. Pius, however, burst out that he had another alternative—he would abandon all and leave.[19]

The morning of the sixteenth there were demonstrations which degenerated into rebellion as a huge crowd, with the deputies of the chamber at its head, marched to the Quirinale Palace demanding the promulgation of Italian nationality, the creation of an Italian federation, and the right of the deputies to decide the issue of war or peace. Pius, surrounded by the ambassadors of France, Spain, Bavaria, Portugal, and Russia, met with a delegation of the "people" headed by Galetti and indicated that he would consider their demands but would not be pressured.[20] Before he would name any new ministry, he wanted the menacing crowd on the Piazza del Quirinale disbanded.[21] This demand aroused the crowd and prompted their firing upon the palace, which resulted in injury to some of the Swiss guards and the death of Monsignor Palma. During this time of trouble only the ambassadors and Cardinals Antonelli and Soglia remained at the Pope's side. Pius, who found his palace under siege, noted that the Quirinale was deserted and almost all had abandoned him.

Evening interrupted the course of events at the Quirinale and the "people," led by Charles Bonaparte, son of Lucien, whom Pius VII had accorded refuge in Rome, put off until the morning the taking of the palace. Meanwhile a provisional government established by Sterbini sent a delegation to inform Pius of the dangerous situation. Unless he met the demands of the people the palace would be stormed and all would be destroyed save the Pope. Presented with this prospect, Pius finally succumbed, informing the diplomats around him that there was no hope in resistance, and he gave in to avoid fruitless bloodshed and more heinous enormities. When Galletti, who was named general of Carabinieri, went to thank the Pope, Pius retorted, "Go thank the clubs where your partisans are to be found, they have selected you, not us."[22]

Meanwhile the Popular Club of Rome, founded and directed by Sterbini, demanded that the Swiss guard be disbanded and once again Pius submitted, on condition that all of their lives would be spared. When, on November 17, the civic guard occupied all of the places formerly protected by the Swiss, Pius was virtually a prisoner of the revolution. He found this distressing not because he feared for his own safety, but because it would now appear in the eyes of the universal Church that his actions were no longer free.[23] Antonelli, governor of the ponitifical palaces, who was responsible for the safety and security of the Pope, considered his position precarious under the new regime.[24] He advised flight.

After the events of November 16, Pius was undecided as to what course to pursue and prayed to God to show him the way. During this state of indecision he received a letter from Monsignor Pierre Chatrousse, Bishop of Valence, consoling him in his difficulties and sending a small, silver vase—the very one in which Pius VII had carried the Eucharist with him into exile. The Pope interpreted this as a heavenly sign of the road he should take, flight from Rome. Beyond this he had no program for the future; his only concern was to trust in providence to secure his escape from the intolerable position in which he found himself in the capital. Since Antonelli had already suggested abandoning the Eternal City, plans were hastily made with the aid of the French, Spanish, and Bavarian ambassadors. The negotiations to arrange a marriage between the Princess of Bavaria, Maria, and the older son of the King of the Two Sicilies afforded the Bavarian ambassador, Count Spaur, and his wife the opportunity to make a hurried journey to Naples, and it was determined that the Pope, in disguise, would accompany them.

On the evening of November 24, the Duke de Harcourt, the French ambassador, arrived in a gala carriage at the Quirinale and was ushered into the Holy Father's quarters. While Harcourt read in a loud voice, Pius assumed the costume of a simple priest sporting large spectacles and was led out a secret entrance by Benedetto Fillippani. This trusted agent of the Pope drove him to the heavier carriage of Count Spaur, which immediately left for Gaeta. Harcourt, having allowed the fugitives sufficient time by pretending to be in consultation with the Pope, finally left the Quirinale Palace and took the road north to Civitavecchia while the Pope headed south for the Neapolitan frontier.

The next morning the Pope arrived at Mola di Gaeta, some six miles from Gaeta proper, and wrote a letter to Ferdinand explaining that the triumph of the enemies of the Holy See constrained him to abandon his states temporarily. Count Spaur personally delivered the message to the King of Naples, who left at dawn of the next day to visit the Pope and offer him hospitality. Ferdinand's ships, which housed his entourage and corp of troops, entered the harbor of Gaeta after noon on November 26 and the Neapolitan king persuaded Pius to remain in Gaeta as his guest.

On November 27, Pius issued a statement explaining his abrupt departure from Rome. The violence used against the Holy See and the manifest intention to employ still more, he noted, had constrained him to separate himself from his subjects and sons, whom he had always loved and still loved. "Among the causes which has moved us to take this most painful step," he added, "was the need to enjoy full liberty in the exercise of the supreme power of the Holy See, which in the existing situation was impossible."[25] The manifesto declared all actions undertaken by the government selected on November 16 to be null void.

Pius, who saw the hand of God everywhere, believed that the ingratitude of his subjects and his bitter exile were punishment for his sins and those of his people. This did not prevent him from leaving instruction to provide financial assistance and subventions for a number of individuals and institutions in his state.[26] Still, he found it necessary to protest against the violation of the rights of the Holy See. At the same time he created a commission of government and early in December issued another decree proroguing both of the Roman chambers. The houses, however, continued to meet; they set aside the governmental commission created by the Pope and in a joint resolution established their own committee to discharge executive functions in the Papal States.

The Pope responded by declaring that the entire world knew the conditions that had driven him into exile and what gross abuse was made of the concessions he had granted to his people. Furthermore, though he had prorogued the chambers, the authors of the recent violence continued along their arrogant way. In order to preserve his sovereignty and transmit it in its entirely to his successors, Pius felt he had to raise his voice before God and the world against the sacrileges attempted. At the same time he declared invalid all the actions and commands issued by the junta established in Rome, arguing that there could be no legitimate authority other than that deriving from the papacy.[27] He lamented to Monsignor Corboli Bussi that at Rome the most deplorable actions were being committed.[28]

While developments in his states troubled the Pope, he found reason to be content with the foreign situation. The Neapolitans were friendly and most generous in their hospitality. They and the Spanish were disposed to act on his behalf. From Vienna, Antonelli, who on December 6 was named head of the pontifical government with the title of prosecretary of state, received word that the Austrian press and public opinion were favorably impressed with the Pope's declaration to his subjects at the end of November. Furthermore the accession to the throne of Franz Josef, who had received a Catholic education and was considered a firm supporter of the faith, was considered advantageous to the Holy See.[29] From France, where there was strong sympathy for the Pope, General Cavaignac offered asylum. Likewise Carlo Alberto expressed sorrow at Pius's difficulties and offered hospitality in his states, suggesting Nice, which was close to France.[30]

Pius, who had been constrained to choose between his role as head of the universal Church and national leader, had acted to safeguard the former to the detriment of the latter. Thus while he was assured increasing support from abroad, national and liberal journals in Italy and particularly Piedmont deplored the decision made by the Pope. The editors of the *Risorgimento* who had decried the attitude of the Pontiff to the war of independence considered it worse still that he had been pushed into a part he would not play. By this pressure, they surmised, the Pope had become an enemy not only to events in Rome but perhaps to the entire Italian movement. The *Opinione* deplored the fact that the Pope, a constitutional prince, had been directed by foreign diplomacy and feared that his flight would serve as a pretext for foreign intervention in Italy. Pius tended to disregard much of this criticism, taking solace in the prayers of the faithful and urging additional prayers to show him the path to pursue.[31]

The news of the Pope's flight created a worldwide sensation and made Rome the focus of the Italian revolution, but the consequences were not immediately felt by the masses of Romans, who remained tranquil. They went about their business oblivious of the anxiety of the Catholic world and the concern of the major Catholic powers. Yet even as the Romans completed their preparations for the Christmas holidays, the Spanish court proposed the calling of a congress attended by the representatives of France, Spain, Portugal, Austria, Bavaria, Sardinia, Naples, and Tuscany to examine the most opportune means to reestablish the authority of the Pope.

The leaders of the revolution sensed the danger and urged Pius to return to his states. Rumors were in fact rife in Rome that the Pope would return the evening of January 5; instead, on January 6 there arrived the Pope's refusal and what amounted to an excommunication of those who had taken part in the events of November 15 and 16. Pius, who had expected some sign of repentance,[32] refused the invitation to return, noting it was sterile and without any guarantees that the recent excesses and flagrant violations of his rights would not reoccur. Instead of the testimonies of remorse he had expected he was shocked by what he termed "a monstrous action" and "an act of real rebellion," the call issued by the decree of December 29 for the convoking of a general assembly of the Papal States to reorder its political life. It was the first to be held in Italy on the basis of secret, universal manhood suffrage for all those over the age of twenty-one.

Pius argued that the authors of this "detestable step" added iniquity to iniquity and sought nothing less than to destroy the temporal authority of the Roman Pontiff. Mazzini termed the Pope's flight an abdication, insisting that the temporal power was dead. Pius considered such talk no less than a sacrilege and worthy of human and divine retribution.[33] Citing the decrees of the Council of Trent, he warned that the major excommunication would descend upon those who threatened the sovereignty of the Pope and undermined the patrimony of the Church. He thus prohibited everyone of whatever class or condition from taking part in the constituent assembly.

The Pope's state of mind in the months following his flight can be ascertained not only from his own pronouncements but from the correspondence he exchanged with a number of sovereigns as well as the testimony of a host of other figures who had access to him. He sincerely believed that his capital had fallen into a state of anarchy but did not despair. Rather he abandoned himself to providence, which had guided him up to this point, and he believed that it would continue to direct him in the future. Pius accepted with resignation the trials and tribulations sent him from on high, certain that in the end the Church would triumph.

By this time Pius had lost whatever faith he had in the political good sense of the masses and believed that they were misled by evil men. Guided by religious sentiments rather than political realities, Pius nonetheless assessed that the revolutions of 1848 were a parenthesis that was about to conclude. He believed that only the appearance of a strong contingent of regular troops would suffice to terminate the anarchy in Rome and reestablish his temporal authority. This, he was determined to regain and defend, not out of territorial ambitions, but because of the temporal power's importance in the spiritual governance of the Church. His conviction that a mere show of force would be sufficient to end the turmoil in Rome helps to explain in part what would otherwise appear a contradiction—that the Pope who was always reluctant to have blood shed now invoked foreign intervention.[34]

A number of the men of the Second French Republic feared that once Pius was restored to Rome he would abrogate the constitution and restore absolutism. Pius retorted that such accusations were without foundation and when informed that no one questioned his goodwill but feared that of those around him, he let it be known that before he had granted the *Statuto* he had consulted the Sacred College on three occasions and it had assented unanimously.[35] Thus at the end of December Pius had not yet decided against resuming his constitutional course once he had been properly restored and law and order prevailed in his states. In January of the new year he wrote Leopold of Belgium that he was in Gaeta not to destroy the

Revolution and Flight

institutions he had accorded, as the suspicious claimed, but to destroy anarchy.

Under no circumstances, however, was Pius disposed to negotiate with the men who he claimed had forced him to abandon his capital. For this reason the emotional Pope was shocked by the conduct of the Piedmontese government, which sought to mediate between the papacy and the men whom he considered rebels and murderers, open enemies of the Pontiff and the Church. Pius charged that under their influence Rome, the principal seat of the Church, had become a "den of wild beasts" overflowing with apostates, heretics, and the leaders of socialism and communism, all sharing a common hatred of Catholic truth and determined to combat it. He did not look kindly upon the fact that when the diplomatic body followed him to Gaeta, Sardinian representatives chose to remain in Rome.[36]

The questionable relations of the Piedmontese with the Roman rebels led the Pope to hesitate recognizing the credentials of Ernico Martini as Sardinia's ambassador to the Papal States. Papal distrust was further aroused when the Turin government announced the appointment of Domenico Pareto as extraordinary minister plenipotentiary of the King of Sardinia to the Holy See. Pius feared that Sardinia wished to maintain relations with the "illegal and sacriligious regime" established at Rome and that is why it desired to send one representative to the Pope as head of the Church and another as head of a sovereign state.[37] He took issue with the assertion of Gioberti, the Piedmontese prime minister, that a benevolent interposition, such as his country's mediation, should be more pleasing to the Vicar of Christ than a violent recourse to arms.

The Pope expressed his dissatisfaction with Piedmont's diplomatic maneuvering directly to Count Martini. He revealed in no uncertain terms that he no longer had any confidence in the Italian governments. The Church as a universal rather than a national institution had perforce to look abroad for effective assistance and therefore could not follow the Piedmontese suggestions that the Roman question be settled by the Italians themselves. Austrian intervention, he let it be known, was not only possible but welcomed, and he was neither prepared nor willing to place obstacles in the path of forces which were being sent to aid him.

The priest and philosopher Antonio Rosmini also urged Pius not to rely upon foreign, especially Austrian, arms and opened negotiations with the Irishman John Sherlock concerning the possibility of organizing a corps of volunteers which could topple the rebel regime and restore the Pope to Rome. The plan came to nought because the pragmatic Antonelli did not consider it feasible despite the best of intentions.[38] Soon after Rosmini left Gaeta for Naples, well aware that the Pope was following counsel other than his own.

Pius and Antonelli were convinced that only the Austrians could restore papal authority. For this reason they welcomed the arrival of the new Austrian representative to the Holy See, Count Mauritius Esterhazy, who appeared in Naples on February 3 and presented himself at Gaeta the following day. The forty-year-old representative did not assume the rank of ambassador but that of minister plenipotentiary. Nonetheless he was empowered to address himself to the crucial question of returning the Pope to Rome and restoring to him all the prerogatives of the temporal realm. Small wonder that Antonelli, at the Pope's behest, informed the Austrian foreign minister that he was delighted with the appointment of Esterhazy and expressed the intention of nominating Monsignor Viale apostolic nuncio to Vienna.[39]

No sooner had Pius and Antonelli expressed satisfaction that the Austrians appreciated their plight in early February than they were forced to endure yet another humiliation and therefore could better sustain their unwillingness to negotiate with the Roman regime. On February 9 the bells of the capital were rung in honor of the proclamation of the Roman Republic.[40] The following day a procession of deputies, with much pomp and ceremony and escorted by the civic guard, mounted the stairs to the city hall of Rome. They bore the flags of the various Italian states, but that of Naples, for obvious reasons, was draped in crepe. In the procession the Prince of Canino, the nephew of Napoleon, marched by the side of Giuseppe Garibaldi, who had recently returned from South America, both having been selected as deputies. The great majority of the representatives, who were lawyers or other professional men, wore the tricolored scarf as their sole badge of distinction. Garibaldi, the hero of Montivideo, was more dramatic in his dress, sporting a red tunic and a black felt hat adorned with an ostrich feather.

Once settled in City Hall the deputies were read the fundamental decree which deposed the temporal power. It argued that the papacy had lost its sovereignty but was promised all the necessary guarantees for complete independence in the exercise of its spiritual powers. The new form of government of the Roman states was to be that of a pure democracy with the name of Roman Republic, and it was stipulated that the Republic would establish close relations with the rest of Italy

Revolution and Flight

on the basis of common nationality. As each of its provisions was read by one of the deputies, the great bell of the capital was rung, a cannon answered, and the crowd roared, "Viva la Repubblica! Viva L'Italia!"

In the interim the assembly was to govern the state by means of an executive committee responsible to it and composed of Carlo Armellini, Aurelio Saliceti, and Mattia Montecchi. Some days later a decree of the Assembly invited Giuseppe Mazzini to Rome and conferred Roman citizenship upon this hunted exile who had provided much of the inspiration for the Republic and the national awakening.[41] In his first address to the Assembly Mazzini prophesied that after the Rome of the emperors, after the Rome of the Popes, would come the Rome of the people. Mazzini quickly assumed direction of the Republic and sought to put into practice the ideals which he had long championed. The Pope considered him a false prophet if not an anti-Christ.

CHAPTER 7

Restoration

THE proclamation of the Republic aroused the righteous indignation of the Pope, who believed that a sort of anarchy reigned in Rome. He cried when he thought of the youth of the capital being dragged along by demagogues. On February 14 he complained that the uninterrupted series of attempts made against the temporal dominion of the Church, proposed by some through blindness and others through viciousness, had reached the culmination of culpability with the decree of the "so-called" constituent Roman Assembly which declared the papacy fallen and the temporal power at an end, creating in its place a pure democracy with the name of Roman Republic. Pius felt it was once again necessary to raise his voice against this latest iniquity, declaring not only that the temporal power was legitimate but absolutely necessary to exercise the Catholic apostolate of the Holy See.[1] Chagrined that his reformism and constitutionalism had endangered the Church and the papacy, the Pope hardened his heart against both movements.

Pius and his secretary of state sought foreign assistance in suppressing the "sacrilegious" regime which prevailed in Rome. On February 18, Antonelli transmitted to the diplomatic corps a note calling for the armed intervention of Austria, France, Spain, and the Kingdom of the Two Sicilies to restore peace in the States of the Church and Christendom and asked for the moral support of the other powers. While the Pope formally invoked the aid of the four powers, he above all addressed himself to the House of Habsburg, and from it expected salvation. Observers noted that while Pius had included Naples in his appeal, Sardinia had been excluded. The Turin cabinet was distressed by this obvious rebuke.

The Piedmontese were also upset by the call for foreign intervention since they had decided to renew the war against Austria on March 20, following the expiration of the Armistice of Salasco of August 1848. They did not have long to ponder the impact of the papal decision, for within three days the forces of Carlo Alberto were routed by General Radetzky at Novara, paving the way for Austrian intervention in central Italy. Novara, therefore, was a defeat for the Romans as well as the Piedmontese. The latter saw their king abdicate the throne in favor of his son Vittorio Emanuele in the hope that he would be able to procure more honorable terms for the country. Shortly thereafter the new monarch wrote Pius that by the will of God, the right of succession, and the fundamental laws of the state, he was called to the throne and promised to show constant zeal for the apostolic, Catholic Church.[2]

The Pope, as before, placed his trust in Austrian arms rather than Piedmontese promises, as was clearly evident in the conference of Catholic powers which opened at Gaeta at the end of March. Austria, France, and Spain concurred upon the need to reassert the authority of the Pope but differed as to the best means to effect it. As the debate continued, the Austrian forces moved slowly but inexorably toward Rome. The prospect of a massive Habsburg intervention in central Italy disturbed the French, and Louis Napoleon, who had been elected President of the Republic, decided to send an expedition of his own to Rome. This ex-revolutionary retained his reservations about the temporal power; he favored intervention to oppose Austria rather than to aid the Pope.[3] The French ambassador informed the English government of the aims of the expedition: namely to assure Italy peace and reestablish regular and constitutional government in Rome.[4]

Upon landing at Civitavecchia, the port of Rome some forty miles northeast of the capital, on April 24, 1849, the French troops under General Nicolas Oudinot shouted, "Vive la Republique!" and "Vive l'Italie!" but within a week were marching toward Rome. The ease with which Civitavecchia was taken confirmed the Pope's optimistic view that his authority could be reestablished without much bloodshed. The situation of the Republic was indeed difficult. In addition to the French forces coming from the Northwest and the Austrians from the Northeast, the troops of Ferdinand of Naples menaced the southern frontier while the Spanish expeditionary force, some 4,000 strong, headed for Gaeta. To counter the enemies, General Giuseppe Avezzana, minister of war in Rome, appointed Colonel Pietro Roselli, a gentleman soldier of the old school, supreme commander of the republican forces. Nonetheless it was the more talented if less orthodox Garibaldi and his famous legion, armed with lances, sabers, old muskets, and whatever else they could find, that were destined to play the major role in defense of the Roman Republic.

The commander of the French expedition, Oudinot, branded the leaders of the Republic outlaws of all nations and charged that they had imposed themselves upon the Pope's subjects against their will. His determination to overturn the Republic was increased by the fall of Bologna to the Austrians in early May and the initial defeat the French suffered at the hands of Garibaldi's volunteers at the end of April. Reinforced during the truce arranged with the Republic by Ferdinand de Lesseps, the French began the siege of Rome in earnest the first week in June. Informed of this development, Pius was moved by two opposing sentiments: on the one hand, horror of the revolution and the reluctance to make any concession to it; on the other, a grudging admiration for the skill and dedication shown by the Republicans in defense of Rome. Deep in his heart the conflict raged between his conscience as Pontiff and his sympathy for Italy.

By the end of June the captial had all but fallen. Garibaldi and his forces departed on July 2, when it became apparent that the French would soon assume possession. When Oudinot, who had been less than sincere in his actions toward the Republic, entered the Corso on July 4, the crowd hooted and cried, "Death to Pius IX and the priests!" and "Down with Oudinot and his French Croatians!" The Pope was hurt but not surprised by such talk, considering it the work of the enemies of God and civilization. When on July 5 he received the symbolic offering of the keys of Rome from Colonel Adolphe Niel, chief of staff of General Oudinot, Pius congratulated the French not for the bloodshed, which pained his heart, but for the triumph of order against anarchy and the restoration of liberty to honest and Christian men.[5]

The Piedmontese, who had in the interim indicated a belated interest in participating in the work of restoration, were told that their offer was too late.[6] Their government, as well as the one in Paris, hoped that Pius would return to Rome a constitutional monarch rather than the head of a party that was steeped in ancient abuses and anxious only to reacquire its privileges. However, word soon spread that the Pope was determined to be restored without conditions. Pius let it be known that his first task upon restoration was to throw the light of eternal truth upon the errors, ruses, and frauds of impiety practiced by the "sacrilegious" Roman regime but said nothing about preserving the constitution he had earlier accorded his subjects.

As early as May 3 the Duke d'Harcourt, the French ambassador to Rome, presented a note to Antonelli pressing the papal government for reforms and reinforced the earlier French entreaties that constitutionalism be preserved in the Papal States. He was seconded and supported by the Count de Rayneval, the French ambassador to Naples who in these months had been virtually transferred to Gaeta. Their suggestions were not well received by Pius, who was burdened by the thought that his reformism had jeopardized the position of the papacy and compromised the sacred deposit of Saint Peter. The Pope, resolved not to falter again, was in no mood to hear of concessions. Antonelli, therefore, responded to the French requests that the Holy Father had decided not to make any concession which would in any fashion compromise the temporal power.[7]

The papal position antagonized Turin as much as Paris and relations between Piedmont and the papacy went from bad to worse. In an attempt to bring about some sort of reconciliation the writer, artist, and statesman Massimo D'Azeglio, who became prime minister of Piedmont in May 1849, decided to send the scrupulously Catholic Count Cesare Balbo to Gaeta as minister extraordinary, to assure the Pope of Vittorio Emanuele's filial respect. Beyond this, Balbo's mission was to combat those dark influences and especially the Austrian and Spanish representatives, who were supposedly pressuring the Pope to withdraw the constitutional liberties he had accorded his people. Pius was to be alerted to the fact that his government would be isolated if it established its power on the basis of priestly despotism. Thus Balbo was to stress that the Pope should resist the advice of reactionaries and recognize the political rights of his people, for this was the best means of securing his authority and forming alliances with the other princes of the peninsula.[8]

Count Balbo was courteously received by the Pope and Antonelli, who held a series of discussions with him at the end of May, and after his visit to Naples, continued their talks with him at the end of June and the beginning of July. However, the count was no more successful than the French in his attempts to sway the Pope in a liberal direction. He, too, found the papal court decidedly cool to his constitutional suggestions, and the prospect of improving relations between the Holy See and Piedmont, slim. Consequently, in early July, tired and disillusioned, Balbo asked to be relieved of the mission, citing poor health and a climate which he did not find agreeable.[9]

Father Rosmini, who returned to Gaeta in June, also found that opinions had hardened and liberalism was now suspect there. Pius explicitly revealed to him that he no longer favored constitutionalism, for he had understood, after long prayer and meditation, that constitutionalism was incompatible with the government of the

Church. "You find me anticonstitutional," he blurted out to Rosmini. The latter concurred that the constitution could not be applied at the moment or for some time to come, but believed it best to have his people hope for some future reestablishment of the *Statuto*. The Pope could not concur, indicating that when something was intrinsically bad, it could not be accepted under any circumstances, come what may.[10] The temporal power, Pius maintained, had emerged to assure the Pope full liberty in his relations with foreign powers. Such liberty, however, would be all but worthless if the Pope did not enjoy an analogous liberty vis-à-vis his own subjects, and it was this internal liberty which he believed constitutional government compromised. It is impossible to determine the precise moment that Pius came to this conclusion, which obviously contradicted the constitutional stance he still assumed in December 1848, and even early January 1849. April 1849 was apparently the turning point.

Pius became even more adamant in his anticonstitutional position following the fall of Rome at the end of June and early July, when he learned that the French army was in Rome and the Tricolor flew over the Castel Sant' Angelo. He did not appreciate the memorandum from France on the reforms he should concede in his states.[11] At the same time the emotional strain in his personality remained as can be seen by the fact that his appreciation for the French capture of Rome quickly turned to criticism for the slow pace of restoring pontifical authority. Indeed while he wrote Franz Josef thanking him for reestablishing order in a large part of his territory,[12] Pius seemed to have nothing but criticism for the French. He was especially disturbed by the tolerance shown many republican leaders in Rome, where Mazzini remained until July 16.

The Pope's dissatisfaction with the French occupation of Rome was one of many factors that postponed his return. The French were most anxious to know when Pius planned to return to the Eternal City, but the Pope himself did not know. He was confused by the flood of events. The Lord had raised his hand and stilled the anarchy of Rome, he proclaimed in a message to his subjects, but at the same time assured them of his desire to provide them with peace and comfort. Nothing was said of political rights or responsibilities. For the reordering of the public administration he nominated a commission of cardinals which included Della Genga, Altieri, and Vannicelli, all of a conservative bent, entrusting them with full power to govern until his return.[13] To assert papal authority and assure that all the rights of the Church were preserved, Antonelli insisted that the commission of cardinals enter the capital immediately.[14] On August 3, the governing commission wrote from Rome that it had assumed its responsibility and found the citizens of the capital tranquil.[15]

The French commander transferred to the commission of cardinals a part of the powers that until then had been exercised by the military and urged the Holy Father to return to Rome.[16] The move was less than popular, for the red triumvirate was considered reactionary and its first steps confirmed this opinion. Housed in the Quirinale Palace, the commission sought to blot out all of the memories of the past seventeen months. Their first decree, that of August 2, 1849, in fact, annulled all that had been undertaken since November 16, 1848. A central council of censure was created, composed of ten individuals residing in Rome and entrusted with the task of judging the fate and future of all government employees who had served the Republic. A similar council of censure was created in every province of the state.[17]

While the triumvirate was revising the administrative machinery of state in Rome, at Gaeta plans were being traced for the new political structure of the state. Whereas the French sought to persuade the Pope to preserve the constitutional structure of his state, the Austrians through Esterhazy assumed a different tack. Faithful to the instructions of Prince Felix zu Schwarzenberg, Esterhazy agreed that reforms were necessary but urged that they be granted from above, preserving intact the sovereign authority of the Pontiff and in no way transforming his government into a liberal one.

With the help of Esterhazy, Cardinal Antonelli outlined a fundamental law which was communicated to the diplomats during the twelfth session of the conference of Gaeta, the evening of August 11. The acting Secretary of State opened the session by informing those in attendance of the principal reforms the Pope intended to actuate including an improvement in the administration of justice, the institution of municipal councils elected on the basis of tax payment and supervised by magistrates elected from above, the formation of provincial councils nominated by the Sovereign, as well as a council of state with an essentially technical character and a *Consulta* to examine the entire financial apparatus of the state. There was no indication that the *Consulta* would be granted a deliberative vote, nor was there any talk of further laicization of the administration.

Antonelli and Pius acted as if the events of 1848 were an extraordinary phenomenon which had ended in 1849 with the failure of both liberalism and nationalism. As regards constitutionalism the two held that the great majority in the Papal States were indifferent to it and desired above all the restoration of order. At any rate the Romans were considered too immature for a constitutional government and such a government could not be conciliated with the liberty required by the Holy Father to govern the Church. The Tuscan Ambassador, Scipione Bargagli, found the Sovereign and his secretary of state adamant on this point and preferred to see the outbreak of war rather than incumber the papacy's supreme authority.

De Rayneval, the French representative, issued a passionate appeal for more liberal concessions but was not supported by the Austrian, Spanish, or Neapolitan delegates. Antonelli responded to the French pressure by observing that when Pius called for the assistance of the four powers, it was proposed only to restore order in his state and to guarantee his independence before the Catholic world. The Pope, as far as he could, wished to avoid creating difficulties similar to those which he had recently experienced. On the issue of laicization Antonelli provided exact figures; the pontifical administration before 1848 contained 104 ecclesiastical officials against 5,023 lay ones. The number of laymen, he continued, had probably grown since then. Critics responded that the cardinal's figures were purely quantitative and failed to take into account the importance of the office held by each group.[18] Antonelli, unperturbed, resisted the demands of de Rayneval.

This papal position angered Prince Louis Napoleon, the President of France, who disliked the commission of cardinals sent by Pius to Rome.[19] He was furious with Antonelli, who seemed to have all the answers but none which he found satisfactory; Pio Nono, whose reformism had apparently turned to reaction; and even General Oudinot, whom he considered far too submissive to the commission of cardinals. The general, subject to his control, was the most easily handled and was replaced by General de Rostolan. The Pope was far more difficult to deal with, but the prince-president found it unpardonable that Pius had not sent him a personal note for his part in restoring the temporal power and found unacceptable the Pope's plans for his states.

Aroused by what he considered ingratitude and preoccupied with the future of the Papal States as well as his own reputation, Napoleon wrote a long letter to Colonel Edouard Ney, son of the famous Marshal of the great Napoleon and a friend of the president. The letter sent to Ney in Rome, dated August 18, 1849, stressed that the French Republic did not send an army to snuff out Italian liberty, but to regulate and preserve it by replacing upon the papal throne a ruler who had assumed the leadership of the movement favoring useful reforms. He called upon Ney to remind the French commander in Rome that when their army toured Europe earlier they left the mark of their passage by destroying abuses and spreading the germ of liberty. It must not be said, he warned, that in 1849 a French army acted in another sense, leading to far different results.

Napoleon let it be known that he was perturbed to find the good intentions of the Holy Father as well as French efforts frustrated by hostile influences and passions which sought to return the Pope to Rome on the basis of tyranny and proscription. Such a course, he continued, not only dishonored the French intervention but undermined stability in the states of the Church. Far better results could be expected if the Pope's government were based upon the principles of a general amnesty, secularization of the administration, the application of the Code Napoleon, and liberal institutions.[20]

Ney, who realized that the president's message was for public consumption, tried to have the letter published in the *Giornale di Roma*, the official journal of the capital. The commission of cardinals, however, refused to have it appear without approval from Gaeta, and this Antonelli refused to grant. The secretary of state insisted that the letter had no official character whatsoever and was simply a private correspondence. By way of a further rejoinder to Napoleon, Antonelli informed the cardinals in the commission that the Holy Father was busy granting his subjects reforms which he believed would be truly useful. Nonetheless the president's letter caused great consternation in the Pope and his entourage in Naples,[21] for while the letter did not appear in the *Journal of Rome*, it appeared in the *Moniteur* of Paris on September 7. The letter served to encourage the opponents of the papal regime.[22] It also led General Rostolan to request his recall from Rome.[23]

Despite all of the pressure from Paris, Pius declared that a general amnesty was impossible, refused to base his laws on the Code Napoleon, and did not encourage a rapid secularization of the administration. The Pope, who as early as April 1849 had concluded that constitutionalism was incompatible with his personal liberty as head of the Church, now broadened his opposition and condemned freedom of the press and constitutional government as intrinsically evil. By September he had further clarified his position and charged that liberalism tended to mislead the masses in those countries in which it held sway. Pius's words now transcended his own state and extended to attack liberalism in general. The seeds of the Syllabus of Errors were sown.

Since Pius was not prepared to move in a constitutional direction, Napoleon had perforce to retreat. This was made easier and more palatable when Nuncio Raffaello Fornari finally transmitted the pontifical letter, dated July 31, which formally expressed the Pope's gratitude to the French army for their work in the restoration.[24] Pius also soothed hurt feelings by honoring and decorating the French, Spanish, and Neapolitan troops who had participated in the expedition against the Roman Republic.[25]

On September 4, Pius was transported from Gaeta to Portici by a Neapolitan ship. A few days later he revealed to the world what Antonelli had earlier indicated to the diplomatic community—the institutions he would grant his people. The *Motu proprio* of September 12, 1849, written by Antonelli, promised administrative and judicial reforms as well as immunities for the various municipalities, but said little about specific political liberties and failed to mention the constitution of 1848. Under its terms the two chief bodies of the reorganized Papal States were to be the council of state and the *Consulta* of state for finances. The *Consulta* was to provide its opinion on the imposition of new taxes and the modification of existing ones as well as to determine the most efficient means to stimulate commerce. Provision was also made for municipal, provincial, and communal councils.[26]

The institutions provided for in the *Motu proprio* of September 1849 were in harmony with the Pope's original, moderate reformism and did not represent a reversion to the system which had prevailed under Gregory XVI. Nonetheless, there was immediate criticism of this governmental structure which the Papal States would retain until their collapse in 1870. Pius was particularly concerned with the French reaction and revealed to the French minister to the Holy See that it was impossible for him to set foot in his capital before he knew the effect made by his *Motu proprio* on the French assembly. If badly received, Pius indicated that his position in Rome would be very difficult.[27]

Five days after the issuance of the *Motu proprio,* the Pope granted an amnesty to those who had taken part in the late revolution. Excluded from its terms were members of the provisional government, delegates to the constituent assembly, the members of the triumvirate, and the government of the Republic as well as the head of the military corps.[28] Refusing to grant a general amnesty on principle, Pius was disposed to interpret the amnesty he had granted in the broadest possible manner. Indeed both the French and the Piedmontese were convinced that his natural tendency to forgive and forget was vigorously fought by those around him. However, it was Pius himself who resisted the English and French pressure on behalf of a number of prisoners and especially resented the English efforts on behalf of an ex-Dominican, considering this an unwarranted interference in the internal affairs of the Papal States and even more so a questioning of his authority as Pope.

Napoleon did not stop demanding that the papal government do more in the way of reform, but the man who was soon to undermine public liberties in France found himself in a weak moral position in dealing with the Pope. Furthermore, Antonelli's sources in Paris informed him that the Roman question had become an important political question there, and public opinion tended to support the Pope on the inadvisability of granting further concessions. The president consequently hesitated to push his opposition to papal policy to the point of creating a breach that would seriously jeopardize conservative Catholic support of his government.[29] He had therefore to move slowly and diplomatically.

In November 1849 General Baraguey D'Hilliers, who replaced General Rostolan as the commander of the French forces in Rome,[30] brought the Pope a letter from President Bonaparte which returned to the question of extending the amnesty and urged his speedy return to Rome. Antonelli replied that the Holy Father was most desirous of returning to his capital, as was his entire entourage, but first he had to be certain that he would enjoy complete freedom of action.[31] Pius continued to have doubts that such was possible at present. He was disturbed by the antipapal demonstrations in the capital and was determined to postpone his return until such time as there existed a more visible respect for the law.[32]

Both the Pope and Antonelli felt that they should return only when the economic situation in the State had stabilized and when funds for the restoration were readily available. Such money could only come from a foreign loan, but this was delayed because of the demands made by Baron James de Rothschild on behalf of the Jews in the Papal States and the determination of Pius to concede nothing which was against his conscience. He was particularly upset by the request that Jews be admitted to the universities, considering this the opening wedge for the admission of Muslims and Protestants as well. Eventually Rothschild showed himself flexible and did not insist that juridical equality be accorded the Jews in the Papal States.[33]

After the acquisition of the loans, other problems served to keep Pius away from Rome. Reports continued to reach him of the public opposition to the Pope, the cardinals, and the temporal power. In January 1850 Della Genga, one of the cardinals of the triumvirate, confided to Pius that the multitude in the capital had not yet returned to those religious and political sentiments that would facilitate the Pope's return. Monsignor Corboli Bussi was equally pessimistic and warned that without the French occupation there would be a new and more menacing insurrection than the last. Pius, who was anxious to return home, placed much of the responsibility for the insubordination in Rome upon the shoulders of the French, arguing that they were too tolerant of antipapal sentiment in Rome. Not surprisingly the French and papal authorities were virtually at sword's point in the capital.

Relations between the Pope and the government of Massimo D'Azeglio remained even more strained. Reports reached Pius that journals such as *Il Censore, La Bandiera*, and *La Strega* of Genoa, as well as a host of newspapers in Turin, were critical of the papacy and the Church itself.[34] Count Cavour's journal, *Il Risorgimento*, which deplored the Pope's move to the reactionary camp and considered it no less than a betrayal, was moderate in its criticism in comparison to a number of others.[35] The nuncio in Turin had protested against a series of articles and Antonelli had seconded him, declaring that where religion and its head were not respected, there could be no tranquility.[36] The nuncio informed the king of the Pope's displeasure, noting that the situation had become deplorable, with the press attacking the most sacred things, the most venerable institutions, and criticized the august head of the Church as well as the temporal government. Vittorio Emanuele responded that the ministry would soon present legislation to curb the excesses of the press, and if the chamber did not enact it, he would personally intervene in the matter.[37]

Pius had no reason to doubt the good intentions of the king, who appeared to be devoted to the Holy See and had promised that he would never permit a wrong to be done to the Church in his states. Nonetheless, Pius knew from bitter experience that under a constitutional regime the monarch could not always direct affairs. He remained suspicious of Turin, and the news that its ministry sought to alter relations between Church and State in a separatist sense did not help matters. The almost continuous tension between Piedmont and the papacy resulted in a series of inconclusive conferences, frequent changes in the Sardinian diplomatic staff, and the exchange of extraordinary missions.

At the end of September 1849 the Sardinian ambassador to the Holy See wrote Antonelli in Portici informing him of the arrival of Count Giuseppe Siccardi, who was entrusted by Vittorio Emanuele with a special mission. The count was told by Pius that the first negotiations were to be conducted by his secretary of state, who also was suspicious of Piedmontese intentions. The Pope very much disliked the measures already passed in Piedmont which restricted ecclesiastical control over education and placed supervision of the curriculum in state hands. He sympathized with the Archbishop of Turin, Luigi Fransoni, and the Bishop of Asti, Filippo Artico, both of whom had acted less than prudently and had been compelled by popular pressure to withdraw from their dioceses.[38] If the Bishop of Asti had offered his resignation Pius might have been disposed to accept it, as the nuncio in Turin advised him to do,[39] but both seemed determined to maintain their positions, and Pius was therefore constrained to support them.

The demand of the Piedmontese envoy for the removal of the unpopular bishops was only one of the stumbling blocks to fruitful negotiation. Beyond that, Pius and Antonelli deplored the fact that the press in Piedmont clamored for an end to the privileged position of the Church and the clergy there. In their perception the call for the appropriation of ecclesiastical benefices, the suppression of religious orders, the sequestration of convents, the introduction of civil matrimony, and the termination of the clergy's ecclesiastical courts was not reformism but a vicious attack upon the Church. Siccardi informed D'Azeglio in October that there was a grave preoccupation in the papal court concerning the Subalpine parliament and the government's stance on ecclesiastical matters. In mid-November, Siccardi ended his talks, irritated by the anti-Piedmontese sentiment in the Curia that went so far as to suggest the abrogation of their constitutional regime. The Holy Father, who lamented the position assumed by the Piedmontese, almost daily asked those around him to pray for Piedmont.[40] In response to the Turin government's action against a number of monasteries, Antonelli warned that the Pope could not remain indifferent to the harm done to the Church by a Catholic power and threatened to launch a formal protest.[41]

The new year witnessed a deterioration in the relations between Piedmont and the papacy. In March 1850 the Subalpine parliament passed the Siccardi Laws, which abrogated the various forms of ecclesiastical jurisdiction enjoyed by the clergy, eliminated the Church's ancient right of asylum, provided for the suppression of mortmain, and limited to Sunday and six major holidays official observance of Catholic worship. At the same time it announced the intention of regularizing marriage as a civil contract. Count Cavour, who supported this legislation in the chamber of deputies and thereby began his drive for leadership in Piedmont, saw his newspaper *Il Risorgimento* banned in the pontifical state some months later.

The summer of 1850 Pier Dionigi Pinelli left Turin entrusted with the mission of winning approval after the fact for the recently passed legislation. Such approval would not easily be obtained, for the Holy See considered Piedmont's action unilateral and arbitrary and a violation of the concordat of 1841. Pius argued that the Holy See lived on the basis of principle and was not disposed to undertake any new agreements with Piedmont in light of its bad faith toward the most solemn accords. Pinelli returned home in the fall of 1850, convinced not only that it was impossible to come to terms with the Pope, but that it was impossible even to open preliminary conversations. Pius, for his part, wrote the Bishop of Vercelli that the Church was ready for conciliation but the Piedmontese government was quick to apply the law that it had promulgated unilaterally. This attitude, he continued, had produced both pain and bitterness in his heart.[42]

In contrast Pius was delighted with the Neapolitans and would never forget the warm hospitality he received in their Kingdom. "I bless you, I bless your family, I bless your people," an emotional Pius repeated to King Ferdinand, called Bomba by his people because of his use of canon against them, as he took leave at the frontier on April 6, 1850. He added, "I do not know how to adequately express my gratitude for the hospitality you have shown me."[43] Six days later, on Friday, April 12, the Pope, whose hair was now visibly gray, and his entourage entered Rome from the Porta San Giovanni after seventeen months in exile.

The Romans, tired of the French occupation and even more so of the triumvirate of cardinals, were by and large happy to see the Pope again. His arrival was announced by 101 cannon shots and the sound of all the Church bells of Rome. Descending from his traveling coach, Pius entered the Lateran Basilica, where were gathered the most important clergymen in the capital, the magistracy, the various religious orders, the diplomatic corps, and the French officers, led by General Baraguey d'Hilliers.[44] Shortly thereafter the Pope, accompanied by the French high command, the guardia nobile, and the various ministers, went in procession to St. Peter's Basilica to give thanks. The crowds which witnessed the spectacle were friendly; the applause was proper and dignified, but neither clamorous nor universal. Very likely as many had come to see the returning Pope out of curiosity as had come out of devotion; the mood of the Romans was restrained compared to the enthusiasm of the earlier period.

Pius, who had very unfortunate memories of the Quirinale Palace where he had been besieged, returned to the Vatican Palace instead. That evening there was a general illumination in Rome, with the Campidoglio particularly well lit, and orchestras played in the various squares of the capital. That Sunday a *Te Deum* was sung in all of the Churches of Rome in appreciation of the Pope's safe return home. Antonelli felt that the festive demonstrations made for Pius in his state and especially the warm reception he received in Rome disproved the lie that the Pope was unpopular or that his subjects were dissatisfied with his government.[45]

With the Pope back in his capital, the French forces there were reduced, the triumvirate of cardinals ceased to exist, and their power was concentrated in the hands of Cardinal Giacomo Antonelli, the first and most important minister of the Pope, who no longer placed any faith in liberal solutions. Pius believed that the "sovereign Providence of God" had willed his return and restoration.[46] It was said that the Pope who returned was shorn of his splendor, a man without political ideals. Others argued that Pius had matured politically and now would govern more realistically. All concurred, however, that a new period had opened in the life of the papacy, the Papal States, and Pio Nono.

CHAPTER 8

The Conservative Pope

FOLLOWING the return to Rome in 1850 Pius had as his main concerns the direction of the affairs of the universal Church and the regularization of his State. In these endeavors he was assisted by the cardinal who had remained by his side during the difficult days of the revolutionary upheaval and who made possible the successful flight to Gaeta, Giacomo Antonelli. The secretary of state, like the man he served, had abandoned his earlier liberal sentiments and likewise considered impossible any conciliation between constitutionalism and the temporal power. Nonetheless, Antonelli did believe in administrative reforms and provided these especially during the first decade of the restoration, revealing the talent and energy which made him indispensable to the Pope.

In the years from 1850 to 1860, the calmest and in many ways the happiest of his long pontificate, Pius returned to his usual good humor and gaiety, going out almost every day and meeting with many of the sovereigns, artists, and illustrious persons who visited his capital. Jovial by temperament, when he did not suffer bouts of depression, he liked to surround himself with prelates who allowed him to forget the pressing problems at hand and thoroughly enjoyed the tours and excursions that were planned for him. His majordomo, Monsignor De Medici, who knew him well, did not lose an opportunity to distract the Pope and related anecdotes and rumors that he knew his sovereign enjoyed in his Neapolitan dialect which amused Pius a good deal.[1] The Pontiff, who maintained a hectic schedule, displayed a paternal affection for his subjects and especially the Romans.

Politically, however, Pius seemed so changed that some referred to him as a new Pope, Pio Nono *secondo*. Certainly his actions seemed cautious and conservative in light of the earlier concessions he had been constrained to make, but they did not depart sharply from the course he had originally intended to pursue. As earlier, he looked upon the papal government, spiritual and temporal, as a trust committed to him. He believed he could be somewhat more or less liberal in the exercise of the authority assigned to him, but stressed that he could not fundamentally alter its nature by sharing this authority. Thus the political institutions designed by Antonelli aimed first and foremost to provide Pius with the complete liberty he deemed essential in the exercise of his sacred trust.

The decree of September 10, 1850, put into operation the *Motu proprio* of September 12, 1849, issued at Portici, and instituted a council of ministers and a council of state. The latter, composed of nine ordinary councilors and six extraordinary ones, was to treat governmental and administrative matters under the presidency of the secretary of state. Divided into two sections, the first examined issues of legislation and finance—that is, the affairs of the departments of finance and justice—and the second examined matters flowing from the remaining ministerial departments. Major matters were reserved for the general meeting of the council, which included projection of new general laws, the interpretation of laws and sovereign dispositions, and questions of competence between various ministries.[2]

The Council of ministers, composed of the ministries of Interior, Grace and Justice, Finance, Commerce, Agriculture, Industry, Fine Arts and Public Works, and Arms, met under the presidency of the secretary of state. The council of ministers was to discuss the most important matters of the five ministries therein, including new laws and general regulations, the interpretation of laws and police measures concerning the security of the state, proposed reforms, and all that concerned the economic life of the state and all matters the Pope presented to it. The cardinal secretary of state would direct its discussion and establish which questions should have priority. The deliberations of the council would have no effect until such time as they were sanctioned by the Pope.[3]

The following month there was issued the decree on the *Consulta di Stato* for finances. The principal object of the *Consulta* under the terms of this decree was an examination and possible revision of the anticipated and actual expenses of the state. The *Consulta* would be asked to express an opinion when the government proposed to create or extinguish debts, impose new duties or eliminate existing ones, and to consider all contracts regarding the public administration. The opinion of the body was to be purely advisory, and its discussions were to be held in closed session, with its voting in secret. The

Consulta was to commence operations in 1851, two months after the nomination of its members.[4] In November there was issued the decree on the government of the provinces and local government which left the locus of power in the hands of the Pope, his secretary of state, and the cardinal legates who headed the various provinces.[5]

The policies of the Pope and Antonelli were to conflict with the aims and ambitions of France and constitutional Piedmont, creating tensions and conflicts that accelerated during the course of the decade. As early as April 1850 the director general of the police in Rome had warned the secretary of state that developments in Paris had encouraged the democrats and socialists throughout the Papal States and the danger was magnified by the demagoguery displayed by the chamber of deputies in Turin.[6] The Piedmontese frequently changed their diplomats in Rome following the restoration so that, from the Marquis Ippolito Spinola, who was the first, to Count Domenico di San Vittorio della Minerva, who was the last, they had no less than five representatives. Their policy remained consistently opposed to developments in the Papal States.

The French and the Piedmontese attributed the increasingly conservative stance of the Pope to the men who advised him and above all to Antonelli, but far more important was the impact of the recent revolutionary experience and the attempt to curb the temporal power, which he considered essential for the exercise of his spiritual authority. The outbreak of revolution led Pius to conclude that constitutionalism was incompatible with his dual sovereignty and would lead to confusion in his state while compromising his position as head of the Church. Later, when he was asked to introduce moderate reforms, he responded that those who were scalded by hot water feared even the cold.[7] Rejecting constitutional government and any moves in that direction, Pius relied upon Antonelli to provide a suitable alternative while he concentrated on the religious issues which most interested him.

Even in exile as Antonelli elaborated the general mechanism for the papal government Pius concerned himself with dogma and discipline in the Church. He condemned those clergymen who had shown themselves receptive to liberal ideas, Vincenzo Gioberti for his book *The Modern Jesuit* and Father Rosmini for his work *The Five Wounds of the Church*. Long devoted to the mother of Jesus, the Pope let it be known that he intended to appeal for her intervention to calm the storms buffeting the Church and favored a formal proclamation indicating that though Mary was naturally conceived,

The Conservative Pope

she was from the moment of her conception free from the stain of Original Sin. He therefore addressed an encyclical to the bishops of the world, *Ubi primum*, concerning his desire to define the doctrine of the Immaculate Conception. At the same time he established a commission of cardinals and eminent theologians to examine the matter and report to him.

Upon returning to Rome Pius preoccupied himself with a series of beatifications, commencing with that of the Jesuit Peter Claver in July 1850. Having established the limits of political reform, he allowed his secretary of state to complete the details while he immersed himself in matters such as the reestablishment of the hierarchy in England, which was accomplished in September 1850, less than six months after his return, and the elevation of the Sees of New York, New Orleans, St. Louis, and Cincinnati to the rank of archbishoprics that same year. The Pope's decision to restore the hierarchy in England raised a storm of protest, and the British prime minister even spoke of "papal aggression." Although Pius took a long time to appoint his bishops, the restoration of the hierarchy contributed to the antipapal sentiment in England as well as an increasing public support for the *Risorgimento*.

Subsequently there was a restoration of the Catholic hierarchy in Holland in 1853, recreating five dioceses headed by Monsignor Jan Zwijssen as Archbishop of Utrecht. This action, too, was less than popular and provoked a popular outcry known as the "April Agitation," which led to the fall of the Dutch cabinet. Unquestionably these manifestations of Pius's spirituality and the Catholic revival were a political mistake, for they cost the Papal States important political support at a time when that government desperately needed friends.

Under the Pope's guidance the Curia, responsible for the governance of the Church, was transformed, as nonpriests and the more worldly clergy were progressively removed. Furthermore after 1850 Pius commenced the de-Italianization of the Sacred College, creating ten foreign cardinals in that year alone. Likewise his entourage was far less Italian than had been the case under his predecessor. Taking great interest in the simple priest, Pius encouraged seminarians from the entire Catholic world to study in Rome. In 1853 a French seminary was founded in Rome and later in the 1850s an American College was opened for the same purpose. Under his impulse missionary work expanded vigorously throughout the world. At the same time that Pius showed himself sensitive to the needs of the Church outside the peninsula, he favored centralization of liturgy and pressed for the adoption of the Roman rite in all dioceses.

Pius favored the conclusion of a series of concordats that would protect the interests of the Church in a number of countries. The Madrid government consented to a concordat in 1850. The ensuing agreement was most favorable to Catholicism, which was pronounced the religion of state to the exclusion of all others, while the clergy was invested with far-reaching rights including that of supervising education and settling all matrimonial disputes without civil intervention. Some years later Vienna signed a concordat that was even more favorable to the Church as Franz Josef proclaimed his loyalty and devotion.[8]

The Pope's preoccupation with religious affairs was bound to strain his relations with Piedmont, which continued to pursue an ecclesiastical policy he found objectionable. True enough their king, Vittorio Emanuele, proclaimed his goodwill toward the Holy See and promised to respond to the complaints of the Church, asking in return that the Pope write a letter to his mother, the widow of Carlo Alberto, who was distraught by the religious conflict of Piedmont with the Church.[9] Unfortunately Pius was told not to expect much from the king, because as a constitutional monarch there were limits to what he could do for the Church. Indeed reports circulated that Vittorio Emanuele had admitted that under the present system he could not pursue his own principles. To make matters worse, according to the nuncio in Turin, Pius could not rely upon the Piedmontese chamber. Although its members were by and large conservative, he reported, they went along with the legislation detrimental to the Church in order to protect their own privileges. Likewise the Senate. As for the aristocratic party, it could do little, having lost its influence at court and having been eliminated from the most influential posts.[10]

Antonelli was sent a series of letters from Catholics in Turin who claimed that there was an increasing oppression of the Church and condemned the antagonistic attitude of the ministry toward Catholic publications. Even *L'Armonia*, according to one informant, was in danger of being forced to quiet its presses.[11] This newspaper, launched as a biweekly in July 1848, was for more than two years virtually directed by Gustavo di Cavour, who attempted to show that society and religion could exist in harmony. Unfortunately, from Rome's point of view, Gustavo's brother, Camillo di Cavour, who in 1850 assumed the ministry of Agriculture and Commerce in Piedmont, did not share his brother's reverence for the traditional religion and inclined toward a separation of Church and State. Camillo di Cavour's views, like those of the rest of the cabinet, were suspect in Rome.

The arrest of Archbishop Fransoni of Turin angered Pius, who demanded his release and his return to his seat.[12] To add insult to injury, the left in the Piedmontese chamber increased its criticism of the Papal government, charging that it was more tyrannical than aristocratic and that the once proud Romans were subjects rather than citizens. Antonelli responded with his edict of January 25, 1851, which reconstituted the municipal body of Rome, composed of forty-eight councilors, eight of whom formed the magistracy under the leadership of a senator appointed by the Pope.[13] By another edict at the end of the year postage stamps were introduced in the Papal States, the first state in the peninsula to do so. Steps were taken to reform the tariff, industry and agriculture were stimulated, and the papal territories shared in the general increase in prosperity after 1850.

Under Antonelli's direction postal and commercial agreements were concluded with France and other states while the system of farming out the indirect revenues was abolished as the government assumed the direct management of the salt and tobacco trade. Improvements were also introduced in the administration of hospitals and prisons, and the government awarded prizes for the improvement of tillage and the raising of livestock. "In spite of considerable burdens which were occasioned by the revolution, and left as a legacy to the present government; in spite of extraordinary expenses caused by the reorganization of the army; in spite of numerous contributions toward the encouragement of public works," wrote the French ambassador in Rome, the Count de Rayneval, "the state budget, which at the commencement exhibited a tolerably large *deficit*, has been gradually tending toward equilibrium."[14]

These reforms failed to satisfy the Piedmontese and the President of France. The latter was much more to be feared by Rome after his coup d'etat of December 2, 1851, which provided him with monarchical, indeed dictatorial, power. In Piedmont Cavour was pleased by this turn of events and immediately understood that Italy could profit from the situation.[15] He was soon proved accurate. The condition of Italy might be changed by propitious circumstances, Napoleon told a group of Lombards who pleaded with him on behalf of Italian nationalism, according to a report submitted by the nuncio at Paris.[16] He had similarly encouraged the Piedmontese, going so far as to tell General Collegno, the Piedmontese minister in the French capital, not to despair of French help in the future when the two would find themselves companions in arms for the Italian cause.[17] Such reports alarmed the Pope and Antonelli and made them ultrasuspicious of developments in Paris and Turin.

The Curia was alerted to the fact that liberal emigrants from all Italy continued to pour into Piedmont, settling in Turin and Genoa. They were granted hospitality and protection by the very attorney general who proposed legislation providing for civil matrimony known to be odious to the religion of state. Reinforced by the complaints of the Catholic press in Piedmont that liberals and democrats wanted to dominate the Church, Pius was scandalized by a number of works published and circulated in Turin which he found detrimental to religion and libelous toward his person.[18] To make matters worse Vittorio Emanuele lamented the attitude of the Court of Rome in its relations with Piedmont.[19] Given such sentiments, the prospect of the Holy See's concluding a concordat with Piedmont was not good.

Troubled by events in Piedmont, Pius was dismayed to learn that Cavour took advantage of the news of the coup d'etat in France to separate himself from his colleagues on the right and join elements of the anti-clerical center-left, claiming that this connection was necessary to combat the possible reaction that might result from the move to the right in Paris. In fact the *connubio* or marriage of the center-right and the center-left, as it was dubbed by Ottavio Thoan di Revel, the leader of the moderate right in Piedmont, was undertaken to provide Cavour the broad parliamentary support he needed to oust Massimo D'Azeglio from power. In return the count promised to support the anticlerical measures desired by Urbano Rattazzi and the center-left.

In less than a year the objectives of Rattazzi and Cavour were realized as D'Azeglio was pressured to implement the Siccardi Laws and support a bill which provided for civil matrimony. Pio Nono, having read the decree by which the attorney general presented the bill, wrote to Vittorio Emanuele that it was neither constitutional nor Catholic, complaining that the proposed legislation legitimized relations which the Church considered concubinage and failed to recognize the validity of others which it regarded as legitimate, and pressed for its withdrawal.[20]

The Conservative Pope

The king's compliance by his apparent unwillingness to approve a law "which might displease the Pope" not only undermined passage of the civil matrimony law but precipitated the resignation of Massimo D'Azeglio.[21] Neither Cesare Balbo nor Count Revel, whom Rome found acceptable, were able to govern without the support of the *connubio* bloc so Vittorio Emanuele was constrained to call upon Cavour to form a ministry in November 1852. The forty-two-year-old count, who assumed direction of the ministry of finance as well as the presidency of the council, took office on the understanding that he would enjoy complete freedom of action on ecclesiastical matters. He did promise, however, not to make a cabinet issue of the civil matrimony bill which he allowed to be defeated by one vote in the senate. For Pius this was to prove a Pyrrhic victory.

Antonelli recognized that the key to Turin was to be found in Paris and sought in France the brake upon the designs and ambitions of Piedmont. Unfortunately developments there created some consternation in Rome. On November 21 and 22 the population of that country was asked to approve the reestablishment of the imperial dignity in the person of Louis Napoleon, whose direct line would inherit the throne. Cavour, who had anticipated this step, argued that the proclamation of the empire would clarify the position of the government and more clearly reveal its sympathy for the Italian cause.[22] The delight of the Turin government was not shared by Rome, even though the nuncio at Paris had reported to Pius and Antonelli that Napoleon wished to rely upon the support of Catholics and it had been subtly suggested that Pius crown the emperor. Later Napoleon wrote Pius inviting him to France to crown him. The Pope refused the request.[23] The past conduct of the French ruler was reason enough, from the papal perspective, to question his motives and to doubt the assurances provided by Rayneval, the French ambassador to Rome, that the empire would follow the same peaceful policies as had the Republic.[24]

There were those who hoped that Napoleon's marriage in January 1853 to the twenty-six-year-old, auburn haired, and profoundly Catholic Eugénia de Montijo would prove useful to Pius, the Papal States, and the Church. Indeed the future empress dreamed of being married by the Pope, but Pius, pleading old age and infirmity, did not venture to Paris. Instead the marriage was performed by the Archbishop of Paris in the Cathedral of Notre Dame. While the Pope appreciated the genuine devotion of the new empress, his nuncio at Paris wrote of the generally unfavorable reaction of Napoleon's friends to the marriage, regarding it as unworthy of his station. The diplomatic world also disapproved, according to the nuncio, viewing it as a stubborn and unreasonable decision and feared that these same qualities would render relations with him difficult.[25] While there were doubts in the Pope's mind concerning Napoleon, he was more certain of the political and religious principles of Emperor Franz Josef to the point of sending him as a relic one of the teeth of Saint Peter.[26]

The Habsburgs quickly earned the displeasure of the French emperor, according to the nuncio at Vienna, who informed Antonelli that a number of members of the diplomatic corps felt that Napoleon had a grievance against the Austrians. According to their accounts this was due to the delay of the various German governments in according recognition to the new empire, and Napoleon believed that the Austrians were to blame for the uniformity of conduct of the various German courts. The visit of Franz Josef to Berlin at the time of the reorganization in France only confirmed in Napoleon's mind the notion that a conspiracy had existed.[27]

Napoleon's hostility toward Austria disturbed Rome because the multi-national empire through its direct control of Lombardy and Venetia, while members of its royal house ruled in Tuscany, Parma, and Modena, championed the status quo in Italy against Piedmontese revisionism. Perhaps it was no coincidence that as France became more openly hostile to Vienna the Piedmontese minister in Vienna left his post in protest, entrusting the first secretary with the responsibility of handling Turin's affairs there. Scratch the emperor and you will find the political refugee, Guizot used to remark, alluding to Napoleon's revolutionary past and perhaps his real sympathies.

Whatever Napoleon's inner thoughts, the papal nuncio in Paris suggested that so long as the current political configuration remained the Pope had little to fear from him. In the interim the nuncio encouraged the secretary of state to improve as far as possible the administration of the Papal States. Antonelli did not have to be encouraged in this respect, nor did Pius, who from the first sought to improve the condition of his people. Indeed the Pope continued to take great interest in their lives, visiting schools, hospitals, workshops, convents, and even the most squalid sections of his capital. The Pope tended to favor all measures which would uplift the population without, however, compromising his principles or the temporal power. Within these parameters Pius created a commission to examine the various departments of government and identify problems therein and propose solutions.[28]

Reforms were introduced in Rome. The price of salt was reduced in the provinces of Bologna, Ferrara, Ravenna, and Forli, and when shortages of common wine and grain were noted, their export was forbidden. In the summer of 1853 a new gold currency was coined in Bologna and Rome, having the value of a *scudo*. At the opening of the following year gas lamps were installed on the major arteries of the capital by an English company to the spontaneous outburst of applause by the Romans. These measures were considered palliatives in Paris, and in London Lord Palmerston concurred. The latter noted the impossibility of introducing "modern" reforms in an ecclesiastical state, and even though he did not explicitly call for the abolition of the temporal power, the logic of his opinions inexorably led to that conclusion.[29]

Napoleon, too, was less than impressed with the conduct of the papal government. In fact his government instructed the ambassador in Rome, the Count de Rayneval, to make a searching inquiry into the whole framework of that government, the reforms accorded by Pius, as well as the condition of papal finances. The ambassador sent an elaborate report back to Paris in May 1856 and tended to be positive in his evaluation. He did not pretend that there was no misery or corruption in the Papal States; Rome had its fair share. However, he did not believe that it merited the condemnations of the Piedmontese and Belgian presses and the widespread belief, most strongly held in England, that the pontifical government had done nothing for its subjects and had limited itself to perpetuating the errors of the past.

"I am perpetually interrogating those who come to me to denounce what they call the abuses of the Papal government. This expression, it must be remembered, is now consecrated, and is above criticism or objection. It is held as gospel," the French ambassador wrote. "Now, in what do these abuses consist? I have never yet been able to discover. At least, the facts which go by that name are such as are elsewhere traceable to the imperfections of human nature, and we need not load the government with the direct responsibility for the irregularities committed by some of its subordinate agents."[30] De Rayneval, for all of his goodwill, was not able to alter Napoleon's view of the Roman situation. In fact his report was kept under wraps until 1857, and even then it was not widely broadcast.

Both England and France were less than sympathetic to the problems of the papal regime and the reopening of the Eastern Question ranged these two powers against Russia, Austria's long time ally, as Europe stumbled into the Crimean War. Antonelli, who understood the implications of the conflict, wrote to the nuncio at Vienna that this was a matter which affected all of Europe,[31] a fact which the Prime Minister of Piedmont, Cavour, appreciated.

In Sardinia both the king and Cavour saw the advantage of having their country allied to the liberal powers against Russia and presumably Austria. When the Habsburg Empire, following a tortuous course, chose to remain neutral, Cavour's ardor cooled, for he had no quarrel with Russia and found it difficult to justify intervention. Vittorio Emanuele, however, refused to lose an opportunity to use his army and threatened to overturn the ministry if he did not have his way on the matter. On the other hand Cavour's ally Rattazzi as well as a majority of the cabinet opposed Piedmont's entry unless something tangible was offered by the allies, which England and France refused to do. Eventually Rattazzi and Cavour concluded an agreement whereby Cavour promised to support Rattazzi's Law of Convents, which called for suppression of over 300 religious houses in return for Rattazzi's support of entry into the Crimean War, without conditions.

While the shadow of the Eastern Question threatened the status quo and alarmed Antonelli, to whom the Pope had increasingly entrusted political and diplomatic matters, Pius continued to concentrate upon the religious life of the Church, a task more in keeping with his deep, spiritual sentiments. He was particularly interested in the response of the bishops and Catholic theologians to his inquiry concerning the definition of the Immaculate Conception and was delighted that out of the 600 that reached him over 540 favored the doctrinal definition. With the assistance of the Jesuit fathers Giovanni Perrone and Carlo Passaglia the doctrine of Mary's special position was explained by Pius in the bull *Ineffabilis Deus*, read on December 8, 1854, in St. Peter's to the sounds of the bells of Rome and the cannon of the Castel Sant' Angelo. The proclamation was not only of theological importance but also significant because Pius had assumed the initiative and in the eyes of some already exercised de facto the privilege of infallibility. Afterwards the Pope went to the Chapel of Sixtus IV and placed a gold crown upon the head of the Virgin. That evening Rome was illuminated and the cupola of St. Peter's was brightened by thousands of lights.[32]

The Pope's jubilation was interrupted by the Law of Convents, which appeared before the Piedmontese Chamber and which he considered an unjust attack upon the Church. In addition to the suppression of the convents it provided for a tax upon episcopal and Church property, thereby assuring the ecclesiastical fund the annual sum of almost 500,000 francs.[33] In January 1855 Pius issued a statement deploring the grave damage done to the Church by the Piedmontese government and specifically attacked the present measure. Asserting that the law was impolitic and illegal, he repeated the canonical censure that would descend upon those responsible for it. Vittorio Emanuele, who lost his mother, wife, and brother in the few days between January 12 and February 10, was most susceptible to pressure from Pius and guilt ridden, wondered if the death of his loved ones was not the sign of divine retribution.[34]

Cavour had defended the Law of Convents on economic grounds, noting that while the Church in Piedmont as a whole was rich many of its parishes were poor and required state assistance. He also observed that the projected law would provide the lower clergy with 1 million lire a year. His arguments were effectively undermined in April when the Bishop of Casale announced to a startled senate that the Church of Piedmont, with the consent of Pius, would provide the million lire which the state had promised the lower clergy. Vittorio Emanuele had urged Pius to give his consent to the project and was obviously relieved that the Pope had done so.[35] Confronted with this maneuver, Cavour resigned.

As before, Pius's victory was more apparent than real because the pro-Catholic Revel ministry that the king had promised never materialized and the stopgap ministry of Giacomo Durando proved unable to govern in the face of the opposition from the Cavour-Rattazzi bloc. Consequently the king was constrained to recall Cavour early in May 1855, and the Law of Convents was pushed through the senate and received royal sanction at the end of the month. Pius responded in July by excommunicating all those who had approved, sanctioned, or executed the controversial measure.

During the course of 1855 Pius had to confront a series of crises. Brought word that the tomb of Pope Alexander and a number of martyrs had been excavated, on the morning of April 12, Pius and a considerable entourage went to inspect the exciting find. On the return they stopped at the Convent of Sant' Agnese, where they took lunch and celebrated the anniversary of the Pope's return to Rome. They then returned to the large reception room of the ancient convent which extended over the stables where a large crowd gathered to pay its respects. There the Prefect of the College of Propaganda implored the Pope to receive the students who had earlier welcomed him. The

Pope amiably complied. As the students crowded into the room, however, there was heard the sound of sagging beams and the multitude, including the Pope, plunged into the lower story as into an abyss. Those on the outside were frightened by the immense fall and feared that all had died.[36] However, all 130 escaped unharmed and to some this appeared no less than miraculous.[37] Others considered the event symbolic of the fall of the papacy.

Some two months later the Pope's chief advisor and minister, who had been at his side at Sant' Agnese, was to have another brush with death. As the secretary of state was descending the great stairway of the Vatican at about 6:30 the evening of June 12, he noticed an odd-looking man at the foot of the stairs, obviously holding something beneath his jacket. Although he pretended to be a petitioner, Antonelli was suspicious and his apprehension proved accurate for the stranger suddenly produced a forklike weapon. As the secretary turned about and soared up the stairs calling for help, the hatmaker Antonio de Felici flung his weapon but missed his mark. De Felici was apprehended by the cardinal's servants, who turned him over to the police. Condemned to death, he was decapitated in July. The other enemies of the papal regime could not be so easily handled.

Of continuing concern to Pius was the conduct of the Piedmontese government and the attitude of Napoleon III. He was therefore most interested to learn that, on November 20, Vittorio Emanuele left Turin for Paris to consolidate relations between the two capitals. By the king's side during the visit were Massimo D'Azeglio and Cavour, who were at once to supervise the king's conduct and encourage Napoleon to challenge the Austrian position in Italy. The latter assignment was not a difficult one, for the emperor showed himself most favorable to the Italian cause and one evening in December after dinner asked Cavour and D'Azeglio to write his foreign minister what he could do for Piedmont and Italy. Cavour wrote Count Alexandre Walewski that Austria should be made to treat Piedmont with justice and govern her territory less oppressively; the King of Naples, induced to show humanity to his people; the papal government, secularized; and the Italian question, brought up at the forthcoming Congress.[38]

These suggestions were anathema to Rome and there were those who felt that Napoleon, who relied upon the Catholic party in France and wanted the Pope as godfather for his unborn child, could not support such a course. Cavour, however, was not discouraged and insisted that Napoleon was committed to the principle of nationality, especially Italian nationality, and though he seemed to court the clergy, deep down he resented their pretensions.[39] His calculations proved correct, for it was the emperor's intervention that induced Count Walewski, who did not share his master's Italian sympathies, to bring up the Italian question once the work of the Congress of Paris had been concluded and peace with Russia was secured. Although Pius had written to Franz Josef asking him to use his influence at the Congress to protect the interests of the Church and the emperor had promised to do all that he could, the Austrians were outnumbered and outmaneuvered at the Congress.[40]

On April 8, 1856, the French Foreign Minister, in a special session of the Congress, asked the representatives of the powers to consider some issues which threatened the peace of Europe and thus brought forward the Italian problem among others. Lord Clarendon therefore took the opportunity to criticize both the papal and Neapolitan governments and pressed for reform. Cavour, when he spoke, pointed to the Austrian occupation of the Papal States and argued that it was the irregular state of affairs there that kept the peninsula in turmoil. In this fashion he struck a blow against the Austrians as well as the temporal power.[41]

Rome hoped that the Russian government might become anti-Piedmontese as a result of the state's declaration of war against her, but such did not prove to be the case. Indeed the Russians told Count Buol of Austria that they did not notice Piedmont's actions against them. A big dog does not pay attention to the barking of a small one, Pius wrote his brother, adding that his government had certainly noticed Piedmont's actions.[42] The Pope also noted that Napoleon more or less suppressed the report of his ambassador which was favorable to the Roman administration while he provided Count Cavour with an international platform to criticize the papal government. All of this did not bode well for the future of the temporal power and troubled the Pope.

CHAPTER 9

Pio Nono and Cardinal Antonelli Confront Italian Unification

THE Pope, who had miraculously escaped death at Sant' Agnese in April 1855, attributed his salvation to a special favor granted him by the Virgin, to whom he decided to show his gratitude by a solemn pilgrimage to the shrine of Loreto, which he had not visited since the spring of 1846.[1] The pilgrimage was postponed by the Crimean War and the Congress of Paris and taken at the beginning of May 1857. Accompanied by a select group of prelates which included Monsignor François-Xavier de Mérode, the Pope also wanted to see firsthand the conditions prevailing in the Marches and the legations as well as show himself in these regions which were known to be disaffected.[2]

Almost everywhere the Pope went there were extraordinary manifestations of veneration and affection shown him.[3] King Vittorio Emanuele sent Carlo Boncompagni to Bologna as an act of deference and of respect for the head of the Church and Italian prince. Almost all who saw the Pope felt it inappropriate to make political demands and many did not discuss political matters at all. In Imola, however, his friend and former minister Giuseppe Pasolini asked for reforms, but Pius expressed the concern that liberal institutions would inevitably resemble that which existed in Piedmont, which was anti-Christian and disturbed a good part of the population. As for the Piedmontese press, Pius continued, it cured one of any notion of granting pardons or making concessions. "Major alterations, I do not want," the Pope confided to Pasolini, implying that these would require an army to preserve order in the state.[4]

When he visited Bologna, Pius told Marco Minghetti, another former minister, substantially the same thing when the latter stressed the need for reform and accommodation with Piedmont. The call for such an accommodation incensed the Pope, who charged that the

Piedmontese were dominated by an antireligious current and wished to dominate the whole of Italy. "Religion is persecuted there," he blurted out, "and the Church is spared no outrage! The King, poor man, would be better off threshing grain!" He had harsh words for Rattazzi, whom he termed an atheist, and though he admitted that Cavour had genius, added, "But I doubt that he is any more religious [than Rattazzi]."[5]

Pius did not accept Minghetti's verdict that unless major reforms were accorded it would not be long before the Romagna were detached from Rome. Acknowledging that he had been asked for local improvements which he was prepared to make, he did not concur with Minghetti's rejoinder that something more was required. "I would not know what else to do," he responded. "The demands are excessive; no one is ever satisfied. The pontifical government is assailed from all sides, constantly denigrated."[6] Minghetti's first meeting with the Pope ended with the latter's assertion that the world was too agitated and reforms were therefore inopportune. During the course of a second meeting with Pasolini, Pius again revealed his reluctance to introduce major reforms and his antipathy for the Piedmontese regime. As Pasolini left, the Pope sadly remarked, "Therefore, you too are leaving me?" To which Pasolini, visibly moved, retorted, "No, Your Holiness, it is not we who are leaving you, it is you who abandon us."[7] The prospect of conciliation between the Pope and the moderate liberal elements no longer existed, as Minghetti noted that the die was cast. Pius, in turn, described his former minister as one of the leading enemies of the pontifical government in Bologna.

On September 5, 1857, the Pope returned from the tour of his northern provinces through the Porta del Popolo. The streets were illuminated and 7,000 *scudi* were distributed in bread for the poor. Pius clearly seemed to enjoy the ovation he received and beamed with health and happiness. A few days later on September 8, there was the uncovering and blessing by the Pope of the monument erected on the Piazza di Spagna in commemoration of the definition of the Immaculate Conception on December 8, 1854. Pius seemed to bask in an interlude of tranquility, as all seemed well for the moment.[8] Even the army passed muster, according to the report of General Charles Goyon.[9]

The apparent quiet after the Crimean War was only the lull before a new storm. The Pope's desire to preserve things as they were was seriously compromised by the attitude of the Turin and Paris governments, which had moved closer together following the war and the Peace of Paris. This had contributed to the breaking of diplomatic relations between Piedmont and Austria in 1857 and the increasing tension between Paris and Vienna. He had seriously studied the situation in Rome, Napoleon told Gioacchino Pepoli, sent to Paris by Cavour, and indicated that the solution rested in cutting the government from the hands of the priests without allowing them to cry out.[10]

Felice Orsini's unsuccessful attempt on Napoleon's life in January 1858, for his failure to act on Italy's behalf, rather than turning the emperor against the Italian cause, made him a more resolute champion of Italian nationalism. Cavour addressed a circular dispatch to all the Sardinian representatives abroad placing responsibility for the attempted crime on the unsettled condition of the peninsula and the papal government's frequent recourse to political expulsion of its undesirables. Napoleon apparently accepted the Cavourian thesis.

In June Dr. Henri Conneau, chief physician to Napoleon III and brother to the notorious slave trader Theophilus, once again acted as an intermediary between Cavour and the emperor. The doctor informed the count that Napoleon wished personally to confer with him and in July 1858 Cavour arrived in Plombières, where he plotted war against the Austrians with the emperor. Napoleon clearly favored the reorganization of northern Italy under Piedmontese direction but insisted that the Pope be treated with circumspection. Thus while Pius would lose the legations and the Romagna to the new kingdom, he was to retain Rome and its environs and be honored with the presidency of the Italian confederation that would unite the various Italian states. Cavour, who inwardly questioned the viability of such a confederation, accepted these conditions so long as the emperor was prepared to wage war against Austria.

Although the meeting at Plombières was conducted in the greatest secrecy, diplomatic Europe soon learned that something was amiss, and from Paris Nuncio Carlo Sacconi noted the increasing anti-Austrian and pro-Italian sentiments of the government-controlled press. Rome's apprehension was heightened by the fact that Napoleon was reportedly referring to Cavour as his only true friend in Europe and was planning to establish a journal in Paris to champion the Italian cause. From Paris the nuncio reported to Antonelli that Napoleon had told the visiting Lord Palmerston that the present state of affairs in Italy could not long continue and he therefore expected a crisis which would probably end with great sacrifices on the part of Austria. In Paris, noted the nuncio, there were few kind words for the papal government, and it was argued that the Pope should have a smaller state so he would be less embarrassed and burdened by the responsibilities of power.[11]

Antonelli recognized that it was essential to dissuade the emperor from some reckless enterprise while mending the diplomatic fences of the Papal States, but this was no small task given the determinatioin of the Pope to pursue his principles, no matter what the consequences. His words and actions were such as to arouse and antagonize the diplomatic community rather than win its goodwill and sympathy. A case in point was the so-called Mortara affair. In June 1858 a seven-year-old boy of Bologna, Edgardo Levi Mortara, who at the age of one had been secretly baptized by a poor servant girl of the household, Anna Morisi, during an illness, was forcibly taken from his parents and placed in a seminary. This incident created a sensation in Western Europe, particularly in England and France, where there was great sympathy for the Mortara family, and attempts were made to convince the Pope to return the child.[12]

Pius, however, would not relent under the pressure of public opinion at home and abroad as critics condemned his "medieval" mentality. In response to the pleadings of the Duke di Gramont, who cited the unfortunate results flowing from the action, Pius pointed to a crucifix, saying, "He will defend me." The Neapolitan ambassador was no more successful than his French colleague. The Pope refused the latter's request, confiding, "I know what my duty is in the matter, and God willing, I will let them cut off my hand rather than be found wanting."[13]

Count Cavour, who had instructed the Piedmontese representative at Rome to associate himself with the attempt of the diplomatic community to intercede on behalf of the boy, took advantage of the failure to discredit the Court of Rome before the tribunal of European public opinion. Whether it was the propaganda of the Turin government or the intransigence of the Curia that proved more important is uncertain, but Sacconi, the nuncio at Paris, wrote home of Napoleon's resentment at not having been able to change the policy of the papal government on the matter.[14]

The Piedmontese minister sought to discredit Rome further by his memorandum to the cabinets of London, Berlin, and St. Petersburg which attributed some of the anti-Austrian agitation in Lombardy-Venetia to the fact that the Habsburgs had signed a concordat with the papacy. This memorandum infuriated Pius, who soon had additional cause for complaint. In January of 1859 Vittorio Emanuele in his speech on the occasion of the opening of parliament indicated that his country was not insensitive to the cry of anguish arising from all over Italy. These words troubled Pius, who announced that they were "calculated to inflame the minds of all the revolutionary men of Italy."[15] There were actions as well as words that disturbed Pius, who was told that the Piedmontese were in communication with the revolutionaries of Tuscany through Giuseppe La Farina, Secretary of the Italian National Society and widely regarded as a lieutenant of Cavour. Pius suspected that the Piedmontese would attempt to arouse and organize the revolutionaries in his state as well.

Rome found the conduct of the Emperor Napoleon no more pleasing than his Piedmontese allies. In February 1859 a pamphlet written by Viscount de la Guéronnière and inspired by Napoleon entitled *Napoléon III et l'Italie* appeared, foreshadowing the war in the peninsula. Its reference to the abnormal situation in the States of the Church and criticism of the clerical character of the government aroused Pius, who was not placated by the author's suggestion that the Pope preside over an Italian federation of states. "We are advised to make reforms and it is not understood that those very reforms which would consist in giving this country a government of laymen would make it cease to exist," he told Odo Russell, the English representative at Rome. "It is called 'States of the Church' (Etâts de l'Eglise) and that is what it must remain."[16]

As tension increased between France and Piedmont on the one hand and Austria on the other, the powers suggested the calling of a congress to propose some solution to the Italian problem. Pius responded negatively both to the proposed congress as well as to the creation of an Italian confederation under the existing circumstances. "The Pope has never asked for the advice of any foreign Government, does not require it, and will never accept it," Antonelli told Russell, "and therefore His Holiness will not send a Representative to appear at the bar of a self-constituted tribunal such as the proposed Congress is."[17]

The talk of a congress was rendered academic by the outbreak of war between Piedmont, assisted by France, and Austria in April 1859. Shortly thereafter Napoleon wrote to Pius, personally assuring him that in the war in Italy he would defend the interests of the Church and the temporal power of the Holy See.[18] Pius questioned both his will and power to do so. He was even more skeptical of the promises made by Vittorio Emanuele. The Sardinian king promised the Pope that if the war went well he would have the means of doing many things he could not do at present.[19]

Antonelli was even more concerned and warned the Pope of the potentially dangerous consequences of this war. Nonetheless for a moment Pius was stirred by a sense of Italian nationalism, even though as Pope he was constrained to condemn the movement which might undermine the temporal power. Supposedly when the secretary of state read him an account of the Piedmontese king's successful campaign against the Austrians at Palestro the Pope suddenly raised his hands upwards and with tears in his eyes cried, "Vittorio, Vittorio, my son!" In response to Antonelli's puzzled look, the story continues, Pius added, "And why not? After all, I am Italian!"[20] The Pope did respond positively to Vittorio Emanuele's request that in light of the danger of death during the war he be absolved from ecclesiastical censure and conferred on the king's confessor the power to absolve him. However, Pius warned the king that he would fall under the same censure in case of new attacks made upon the Church.[21]

Despite the promises and assurances that had been given by the Turin and Paris governments, Rome had reason to be concerned. The Papal States were in the embarrassing position of having troops of both belligerents on their territory, and though Austria and France promised to respect the neutrality of the States of the Church, Piedmont did not. In a curt note the Turin government argued that, being in a state of war with the Austrians, it would seek them where they were, and might find it necessary to enter the Marches and the legations.[22] Antonelli hoped that the guarantees of Napoleon would suffice to keep the Papal States tranquil, but such was not the case.

In June, when the Austrians departed from the legations, this was the spark that set the northern Papal States afire. There were insurrections in Bologna, Ravenna, and Perugia, followed by the establishment of provisional governments and declarations in favor of union with the Kingdom of Vittorio Emanuele. Their example was followed by Imola, Faenza, Rimini, Cesena, Forli, Fossombrone, Fano, Fuligno, and Ancona, all of which, with inspiration from Turin, pressed for union with the emerging northern kingdom. Antonelli protested against this development on behalf of the Pope.[23] He also attempted to stem the tide by police action and military measures. In the encyclical of June 18, 1859, *Qui nuper* addressed to the universal Church, Pius stressed the Church's need for the temporal power.

Despite the vigilance of the papal authorities and a series of arrests, by the first half of June the papal government ceased to exist in the legations. "Why did you revolt against the Papal authorities as soon as the Austrians had left the Legations?" Napoleon inquired of the deputation which arrived at his headquarters. "Revolted against whom? Against the Pope? But the French did not come over to Italy to deprive the Pope of his possessions!"[24] Nonetheless this was clearly the consequence of the French intervention. Troubled by the course of events, Pius confided that his position became more difficult every day, but continued to look to God for assistance, who alone knew how to draw good out of evil.[25]

In a consistorial allocution of June 20, 1859, Pius condemned the "nefarious" attempt to destroy the temporal power and called attention to the excommunication and other ecclesiastical censures sanctioned by the sacred canons, by the apostolic constitutions, and by the decrees of the general councils, especially the Council of Trent, which were operative without the need for specific declarations, against those who in whatever way attacked the temporal power of the Roman Pontiff. Antonelli in a note to the diplomatic corps the following month protested against the Piedmontese attempt to usurp part of the Pope's temporal dominion.[26]

Pius prayed for deliverance and for a moment his prayers seemed to have been answered. On July 14, the emperor wrote him of the terms of peace he had concluded with the Austrians.[27] The Pope was delighted by the armistice of Villafranca, which so distressed Cavour, but doubted it would endure because its enemies were, in his words, insane and evil. In fact the terms of Villafranca, which provided for the restoration of legitimate authority in Central Italy, including that of the Pope, were not easy to implement.

Only the use of force by the papal troops brought Ancona, Fano, Urbino, Fossombrone, and finally Perugia back into the papal fold, momentarily and with much adverse publicity, in the summer of 1859. When word spread that the Pope's Swiss troops had behaved brutally during the siege of Perugia under Colonel Anton Schmidt, who was soon after promoted to the rank of brigadier general, Antonelli responded that the stories had been "grossly exaggerated by the Piedmontese party who were at the bottom of the whole insurrectionary movement in the Papal States."[28] Piedmont, he later observed, did not deny having provoked the rebellion in the Romagna, having favored and fostered it, supplying it with arms.[29]

Both Pius and his secretary of state were outraged that the King of Sardinia had sent a commissioner, several officers, and a body of Piedmontese troops to Bologna without any explanation of this extraordinary breach of the neutrality of the Pope's dominion. The cardinal secretary concluded that in the minds of all good Catholics Vittorio Emanuele was already excommunicated and foresaw the total rupture of diplomatic relations with Sardinia. Perhaps to prevent this the king entrusted the *abbé* Vittorio Emanuele Stellardi with the secret mission of informing the Pope that he found it necessary to place the Romagna under his authority to save it from greater danger and to convince Pius to be content with a nominal sovereignty over the area in return for the payment of an annual tribute.[30] The Pope proved unwilling to accept such excuses.

At the end of September 1859 Pius, citing his solemn responsibility to uphold the cause of the Catholic faith and transmit the property and civil principality of the Church *in toto* to his successor, again raised his voice in a consistorial allocution to condemn the spoliation. He warned that those who by their advice or aid take part or approve of this spoliation were included in the ecclesiastical censure. At the same time he wrote his brother Count Gabriele about the disorders in the legations and the Romagna, which he indicated might be termed Italian buffoonery, if it did not result in such unfortunate consequences. Pius made it clear that he confided in the Lord, who alone could put an end to the difficulties, when he willed to do so.[31]

Early in October Antonelli sent a dispatch to the Minister of Sardinia, Count della Minerva, referring to the action of the Piedmontese in the legations and transmitting his passport, observing that the dignity of the Holy Father would not permit a representative of the King of Sardinia to reside in Rome. Shortly thereafter the count was almost clandestinely hurried out of the Eternal City in order not to make his departure an occasion for manifestations and demonstrations.[32]

Despite the loss of control of the legations and the very obvious Piedmontese presence there, a number of events encouraged Pius in 1859. First the logic of the terms of Villafranca favored a return of the Pope's government in the legations. Furthermore Cavour, enraged at receiving Lombardy without Venetia and frustrated in his determination to create a kingdom stretching from the Alps to the Adriatic, resigned in protest. Finally Napoleon seemed determined to keep Piedmont out of Central Italy. "If annexation should cross the Apennines, unity would be accomplished, and I will not have unity," he responded to the requests of the Marquis Gioacchino Pepoli, adding, "Unity would make trouble for me in France on account of the Roman Question."[33]

The Pope hoped that Napoleon would do more, taking an even firmer line against Piedmont's ambitions and perhaps participating in the restoration of order in Central Italy. The emperor, however, was neither prepared to intervene against the provisional governments in Central Italy nor was he willing to let Austria do so. Fearing the development of republicanism and anarchy there, and perhaps stricken by a guilty conscience for his failure to live up to the Plombières agreement with Cavour, by the end of 1859 Napoleon, too, sought to persuade Pius to renounce the Romagna.[34] He wrote the Pope suggesting that he resign himself to the loss of that province, thus providing a great service to the people of the peninsula and the peace of Europe. At about this time there appeared a pamphlet entitled *Le Pape et le Congrès* (The Pope and the Congress), which argued that while the Pope should retain the temporal power, this should be reduced to a minimum. The pamphlet, which suggested that Pius should be satisfied with the city of Rome, or at most the surrounding area known as the Patrimony of Saint Peter, was widely believed to be the work of Napoleon.

Pius denounced the propositions put forward by the pamphlet, which he dubbed a remarkable monument of hypocrisy and a vile tissue of contradictions, and refused to accede to the suggestions of Napoleon. He explained to the emperor that the Roman Pontiffs did not receive their possessions as personal heirlooms which they were at liberty to dispose of, or renounce. Rather each Pope received the pontifical States, the patrimony of the Church, as a sacred trust which he was bound to preserve and transmit to his successor. For this reason he could not compromise his right to rule the Romagna or any other part of the Papal States and rejected the notion that he assume the honorary presidency of an Italian confederation as compensation.

At the beginning of the new year, Edouard Thouvenel, who had replaced Walewski as French foreign minister, also urged the Pope to abandon his temporal interests, claiming that he could thus more fully occupy himself with spiritual matters. Antonelli refused on the Pope's behalf while Pius in his encyclical repeated what he had told Napoleon at the end of 1859, that he could not cede the rebellious provinces. He would not cede them, even if he could, to a government and its agents he considered eminently evil.[35]

The Pope's attitude led Napoleon to shift his position on Central Italy and concoct another scheme with Count Cavour, who returned to power in January 1860. Central Italy was to be permitted to unite with Piedmont, and France would receive Nice and Savoy, all to be sanctioned by plebiscites. Pius soon had indications that Napoleon was again plotting with Cavour. From the Romagna papal agents reported that copies of a speech the emperor supposedly delivered to his troops on the occasion of the new year were being widely distributed. In it Napoleon boasted that the Peace of Villafranca did not prohibit the completion of Italian independence, that three powers were against this development: Austria, Naples, and the Pope, and finally that he would frustrate their opposition to complete unification.[36]

Pius, who had taken his name in memory of Pius VII, whom the great Napoleon had mistreated to the point of imprisonment, now saw himself persecuted by his nephew, Napoleon III. He was so incensed with the emperor that he wished openly to excommunicate him according to Russell, the English representative at Rome. Only the intervention of the more practical Antonelli, who feared the political consequences of such a step, dissuaded the Pontiff.[37] Although expert theologians admitted that the temporal power was not based on dogma, Pius was determined not to surrender an inch of the territory he considered necessary to safeguard the spiritual power. Strengthened by the moral support of the entire Catholic world, he was indisposed to make the least concession. What he found most distressing, he confided to the American seminarians he visited at the end of January, was not the loss of the temporal power but the perversion of ideas.[38]

Although Pius let it be known that he would never negotiate while his rights were being violated and the Church persecuted, as he felt it was, both the French and the Piedmontese persisted in their efforts to convince him to acknowledge the loss of the legations. Vittorio Emanuele, in his letter of February 7, 1860, noted that the impulse in the new political trend in the peninsula, which led to the revolution in the legations, was sparked by Pius at the beginning of his reign. He urged the Pope to renounce the Romagna, Umbria, and the Marches, observing that the Holy See was powerful and venerated for many years before it possessed the legations. At any rate, the Pope could no longer maintain order there. The Piedmontese presence in the Romagna was therefore necessary to save that region from anarchy. Vittorio Emanuele proposed to control it as vicar of Pius, whose supremacy he would recognize and to whom he would pay an annual tribute.[39]

The Pope, confused and upset, turned to the king's envoy, Stellardi, and exclaimed, "Oh, first they spoke only of the legations, now they also want the Marches and Umbria. How can I concede such things?" He also inquired about the nature of the high dominion the king spoke about and asked, "What guarantees do they want to give me and in whom can I place my trust?"[40] Not receiving satisfactory answers, Pius responded that the ideas the king expressed were not worthy of a Catholic monarch of the house of Savoy. He was sad not for himself but for the unfortunate soul of the king, which was already under censure and which would fall under even greater censure as a result of the sacrileges that he and his followers seemed determined to commit.[41] Not to mar his conscience he found himself constrained to refuse every project that would sanction or even indirectly accept the disorders and the violent spoliation.

Meanwhile the French foreign minister circulated a dispatch which maintained that the revolt in the legations was provoked by the discontent of the people rather than by the work of outside agitators, as the Pope argued. He suggested that Pius accept the verdict of his people. Antonelli in his response again sought to explain why the Pope could not accept the loss of these territories. He could not because he had sworn before God to transmit them in their entirety to his successor, a promise which weighed heavily upon the conscience of the Pope. Furthermore, to cede the Romagna would create a precedent which could be applied to the rest of the state, a prospect which distressed the practical secretary of state.[42] For this reason Antonelli asserted that any minister who succeeded to his position would be unable to change this basic policy, which was dictated by the needs and traditions of the Church.

Antonelli did not exercise total control of policy in the Papal States. Although he had always nourished reservations about creating an army of volunteers, in the spring of 1860 the Pope commissioned a prelate and former officer of the Belgian and French armies, François-Xavier de Merode, to create such a force. The legitimist French general, Christophore Juchault de La Moricière, who had distinguished himself in the Algerian war, was made its commander despite the serious reservations of the secretary of state. Antonelli, who relied upon diplomacy rather than arms, realized that the appointment of La Moricière, whom Napoleon distrusted, was bound to alienate France and jeopardize the support he considered crucial. Pius, however, heeded de Merode, whom he made his minister of war, and who now challenged the secretary of state for the ear of the Pope.

Unable to make any progress with Rome, on March 1, 1860, Napoleon addressed the *Corps Legislatif*, affirming that he had advised Vittorio Emanuele to respond favorably to the wishes of the people of Central Italy as regards union with Piedmont, respecting in principle the rights of the Holy See. Shortly thereafter, on March 11 and 12, the Piedmontese conducted plebiscites. In Bologna, where there was some public intimidation, the papal authorities themselves admitted that there was a genuine enthusiasm for union, as in almost all the windows Piedmontese flags were displayed.[43] Nonetheless Antonelli argued that the acceptance of the vote by Vittorio Emanuele was a usurpation detrimental to the Church and therefore illegitimate and void.[44] Pius in his letter to the Sardinian king refused to accept the justification for his actions in the Romagna.[45]

At the end of March the major excommunication was launched against the authors, counselors, and adherents of the rebellion, invasion, and usurpation of his provinces in the Apostolic Letter *Cum Catholica Ecclesia.* The Pope's position was curious, for Napoleon was included in the excommunication, even though the Pope and Antonelli relied upon the French to protect the remaining papal territory. In this as in so many other cases the religious sentiments of Pius prevailed over the diplomatic maneuvering of his secretary of state. It was an unfortunate time to antagonize the French emperor, for the papacy had precious few friends in Europe, and of these almost none was willing and able to do much to protect the temporal power.

Events now moved forward at a frenzied pace for Pius, Napoleon III, and Cavour. In April 1860 an insurrection erupted in Sicily and in May Garibaldi and his volunteers landed there. Pius considered the expedition of desperate men to Sicily on Sardinian ships no less than incredible and predicted that it would appear so to future generations. By the end of June the main Neapolitan force had left the island with Garibaldi in control, already maturing a plan for crossing the straits to reach Naples and from there, Rome. As far as Pius was concerned there was no doubt upon whom the responsibility for the Garibaldi enterprise must fall; he saw Turin pulling all the strings. He was even more disturbed by the incursion of Callimico Zambianchi and his more than 200 followers into the Papal States. They were unleashed by Garibaldi when he landed at Talamone in Tuscany before sailing to Sicily. Although the expedition was short and inglorious and repulsed by papal troops without the aid of the French stationed in Rome, Pius was alarmed. His deepest fears of the Italian revolution all seemed to be materializing, arousing the bitter recollection of 1848.

The Pope knew that Garibaldi considered the papacy a cancer which had to be eradicated, had named his ugliest donkeys on Caprera "Pio Nono" and "Antonelli," and preserved the Mazzinian notion that Rome had to be the capital of a united Italy. Sensing greater trials ahead, Pius accepted them with resignation. "We pray in vain, He does not hear us and our enemies are allowed to triumph over us," Pius told Russell. But he quickly added, "The Papacy has had severer trials than the present one and the Pope knows how to suffer, to wait, and to hope."[46]

Rome did not have to wait long. On August 19, Garibaldi crossed the straits to Calabria and by the end of the month the Neapolitan army of the South had collapsed and Naples was vulnerable. It was only a matter of time before the guerrilla chieftain occupied the capital, and from there threatened to march to Rome, which was still protected by French forces. In the face of the impending doom the Pope was despondent but calm, according to the American consul, William Stillman, who had occasion to see him at the time of the Garibaldi expedition. He seemed convinced, reported the American, that the great day of tribulation prophesied for the Church had arrived and it would have to experience fifty years of oppression before it would rise again, more glorious than ever.[47]

The propsect of Garibaldi's invading the Papal States disturbed Paris as well as Turin, and Cavour sent representatives to Napoleon explaining the need to prevent the volunteers from invading Rome and clashing with the French. They proposed sending the Piedmontese army into the Marches and Umbria, avoiding Rome, and stopping Garibaldi at the Neapolitan frontier. Sensing the need for some action the emperor gave a qualified assent: "If Piedmont thinks this move absolutely necessary to save herself from the abyss, be it so; but it must be taken at her own risk and peril."[48] He advised the Piedmontese to move quickly.

This was precisely Cavour's intention. In anticipation of the invasion he sent the army to maneuver close to the papal frontier under the leadership of the minister of war, Manfredo Fanti.[49] On September 7 he sent an ultimatum to Antonelli demanding the dissolution of the mercenary troops of the government, arguing that the conscience of Vittorio Emanuele would not permit these foreign forces repressing in bloodshed every manifestation of national conscience.[50] To the Pope these "mercenaries" of whom Cavour complained were devout sons of the Church who had come from France, Austria, Belgium, and Ireland to defend the temporal power which had existed for more than a millennium. Hastily recruited in less than a year the papal army was as much a volunteer force as that of Garibaldi. Threatened with invasion, Rome could only rely upon this small force and the promises Napoleon had given. Neither was sufficient to restrain the Piedmontese.

Even before Antonelli had refused Cavour's ultimatum, more than 30,000 Piedmontese troops crossed the papal frontier. The French, to avoid all responsibility, withdrew their ambassador from Turin and sent an additional four regiments to Rome. This was not enough to stop the Piedmontese from marching south, leaving Pius with only a small portion of his state protected by French bayonets. The French, as per their agreement, stayed in Rome and its environs, leaving the Piedmontese free movement elsewhere.

At the time of the restoration the Papal States had consisted of two major regions, the Mediterranean with ten provinces and more than a million inhabitants and the Adriatic with another ten provinces and almost 2 million people. Now the Pope was deprived of all of his Adriatic provinces and was left with only five of the Mediterranean and some 700,000 inhabitants. There were those who hoped to incite insurrection in the capital and bring it, too, under Piedmontese control but this was prevented by the French troops and the increased vigilance of the papal police, who kept a strict watch for demonstrations of national sympathy and support.[51] Nonetheless Cavour in a parliamentary speech of October 11, 1860, declared that Rome must eventually serve as the capital of Italy. The attempt to acquire Rome dominated Italian-papal relations for the next decade, poisoned relations between Napoleon III and Pio Nono, and served to entangle the French Emperor in Italian affairs to the detriment of his schemes elsewhere.[52]

CHAPTER 10

The Syllabus of Errors

THE loss of the greater part of his State disturbed the Pope, who felt betrayed and abandoned. Pius was most upset by the conduct of the French and the failure of the emperor to contain the Piedmontese as the Duke de Gramont, the French ambassador, had promised. Never able to hide his feelings, Pius did not attempt to restrain himself before General Goyon and openly criticized the policy of Napoleon. Antonelli, who realized that what remained of the Papal States could only be guaranteed by the French, made a sort of apology, explaining that when Pius was about to experience an epileptic seizure it was best to avoid certain subjects, for under such conditions the Pope could not be held responsible for all that he said.

The secretary of state had to make a number of apologies, for the Pope's anger and bitterness toward the French seemed boundless. He told Goyon in a fit of anger that the emperor was a "traitor and a knave" and the general was a "fool" to serve him. He lashed out at the Duke de Gramont, whom he described as a legitimist who had sold out to Napoleon and in the process had himself become a "merchant of lies." While the Pope seemed to be in harmony with de Merode and La Moriciere in attacking Napoleon, Antonelli was much more sympathetic, recognizing that while the other Catholic powers of Europe had all but abandoned the interests of the Church and allowed the Papal States to fall prey to Piedmontese aggression, the emperor had guaranteed Pius the possession of Rome and had kept that promise. For this reason the secretary of state did not support the call of the ultramontane party that Pius abandon Rome a second time.[1]

Count Cavour appreciated Antonelli's skill in diplomacy and understood that the Pope's main preoccupation was that the loss of the temporal power would adversely affect his spiritual authority. He therefore sought to reassure him on this matter.[2] For this reason he welcomed the memorandum of the liberal Catholic physician

Diomede Pantaleoni and the ex-Jesuit Father Passaglia, which provided a solution to the Roman question on the basis of "a Free Church in a Free State." Their proposal asked the Pope to renounce his temporal power, including the exclusive right to Rome, and in return promised complete freedom from state interference in Church matters. In the capital the Pope would enjoy nominal sovereignty as well as inviolability; his nuncios and spiritual ministers would likewise share in his inviolability and the complete freedom of all future conclaves would be assured. In addition the Pope would be guaranteed a fixed income and free communication with the entire world.

Cardinal Vincenzo Santucci, who was most desirous of seeing some accommodation between the emerging Kingdom of Italy and Rome, showed the draft proposal to Pius, who was sufficiently interested to consult Antonelli. The secretary of state, who had serious reservations, went along to the extent of not raising objections to Father Passaglia's venture to Turin to sound out Cavour in February 1861. However, the Pope was alarmed and angered when he heard that the Turin government intended to send an envoy to Rome to negotiate on this basis. The Holy Father, scandalized by the Piedmontese occupation of the bulk of his territory and the introduction there of legislation he considered blatantly anti-clerical, could not control his temper. He let it be known that a Piedmontese envoy could come to Rome, but he would not be allowed to leave. This warning the Piedmontese heeded. Meanwhile Pantaleoni was given his passport and told to leave Rome, so that the unofficial negotiations came to an abrupt end.[3]

The rift between Rome and Turin was soon to widen. On March 18, the day after Vittorio Emanuele was proclaimed King of Italy, Pius issued a consistorial allocution *Iamdudum cernimus* in which he argued that the campaign against the Roman Pontiff aimed not only to deprive the Holy See of its civil power but to weaken Catholicism and, if possible, to destroy it. The Holy See therefore could never consent to the "vandalous spoliation" and its consequences, without violating its principles and moral beliefs. There could not be any conciliation, Pius protested, between the principles of truth and error, between virtue and vice, between the forces of light and darkness.[4]

Cavour's response was issued in the Italian Parliament at the end of March. Under his leadership Rome was proclaimed the capital of Italy. This audacious maneuver only increased the nervous agitation of the Pope, who reportedly was unable to sit still even for a few moments. In April the Pope, distressed by the recent course of events, suffered from a sharp attack of fever which led to his collapse in the Sistine Chapel. He was removed from the chapel unconscious and remained in a faint for some ten minutes.[5] In light of his recurring epilepsy and his deteriorating health—it was feared he had dropsy— there were those who considered the death of Pius imminent. However, in 1861 the angel of death bypassed the aged and ailing Pontiff, who would remain at the helm for more than another decade and a half, and took the much younger Cavour, who had just fashioned the Kingdom of Italy. Upon hearing the news the bedridden Pius raised his hands to heaven and said, "Let us pray for him, the mercy of God is infinite!"

Despite Cavour's death, the position of the papacy did not improve after 1861; indeed on the international plane things could not have been much worse. Antonelli feared new tempests. With Austria only the form of international relations remained, the empire having shown itself incapable of intervening in the peninsula to assist its relatives in the Duchies much less the papacy. Pius, who was less than pleased by the changes that the Austrian government introduced in the Concordat of 1855, let the emperor know precisely how he felt. Franz Josef, in turn, was disturbed to see the Holy Father misinterpret the actions of his government which he claimed were rendered necessary by the times and the need to satisfy the religious interests of his non-Catholic population.[6]

Rome maintained only superficial exchange with Spain and there was an absence of official contact with the new Kingdom of Italy. In France the transformation of the empire in a liberal direction did not augur well for Rome. In reaction to a renewed French call for reform and reconciliation of the Papal States with the Kingdom of Italy, Pius responded by a cold refusal, barely tempered by the formal courtesy of Antonelli. The English, even more than the French, were disturbed by the "illiberal" nature of the papal regime which closely censored the press, but Pio Nono refused to allow the press to be free in the States of the Church, arguing that morality forbade it.[7]

Some in good faith, others not so well intentioned, sought to save the Pope by making Cardinal Antonelli responsible for Rome's isolation and the catastrophic failure of papal policy. The inclination to hold Antonelli responsible stemmed from his political preeminence and special relationship to Pius since 1849, the unwillingness of some to criticize the Pope, and the fact that the cardinal secretary of state continued to rely upon the French and diplomacy to salvage what was left of the temporal power rather than rely upon the papal army, as de Merode and others suggested. The opponents of the cardinal argued that the protection of the French was treacherous, deceiving and humiliating the Pope and trapping him in a labyrinth with no visible exit. They called for self-action to remove the Pope from the clutches of the emperor and saw an independent military establishment as the mechanism of deliverance.

Antonelli had never approved of the military tastes and policy of Pius. The romantic Pope had been thrilled by the idea of a Catholic army of volunteers flocking to defend the faith and his frontiers, while the realistic minister looked askance at the proposal. "Such a plan, which in the abstract appears excellent," he had earlier explained, "when put to the test, evokes many problems and obstacles that render its execution difficult if not impossible."[8] For these reasons he opposed the formation of a large, new force and wished to limit enlistment to those who had lost almost everything by the dissolution of the earlier force, suggesting a force of 2,000 men, which would be sufficient for police purposes. The French seconded the cardinal, holding that a division was all that was needed to resist the incursions of the Garibaldini and that the formation of a bigger army would serve only the interests of its officers.

Although Pius appreciated Antonelli's experience and skill in managing affairs, and his profound knowledge of men and matters in diplomatic relations, on the army issue he was prepared to heed the ultramontane suggestions of the foreign prelates around his throne rather than the more moderate counsels of his secretary of state. He did not accept Antonelli's total dependence upon Napoleon and the French and resented their attempt to force him to reach an agreement with the Italian Kingdom. "My goodness," he exclaimed to Napoleon's expressed wish that he come to terms with Turin, "I can do that whenever I wish, and without the help of foreigners. When all is said and done, we are Italian."[9]

Prospects for a negotiated settlement with the Italians, or the Piedmontese, as Pius insisted on calling them, were not good because the Pope had not altered his position since the allocution of March 1861. Indeed it had hardened into an intransigent stand. Conciliation, he wrote Maria Pia of Savoy, could be commenced when her father returned the territory unjustly seized from the Holy See. Nonetheless he sent his regards to the king, instructing the princess to tell her father that despite all that was happening the Pope loved him and prayed for him every day.[10] "I am bound by my engagements and I cannot act in two different ways," he later told Odo Russell. "As to Italy, I am an Italian at heart and love my country, but I cannot countenance the atrocities that have been committed in the name of unity."[11]

Enjoying improved health and dependent on neither a cane nor crutches, as some of the newspapers had reported, Pius actively and energetically fought the new regime.[12] In March 1862, he delivered an address to the clergy in the Minerva and expressed the opinion that while the temporal power was not an article of faith, it was essential for the independence of the Sacred College. Consequently in June when the fathers of the Church assembled in Rome they overwhelmingly agreed with the Pope that the temporal sovereignty was necessary for the independence of the head of the universal Church. The address of submission of June 8, 1862, citing the need for the temporal dominion of the Pope, was signed by twenty-one cardinals, four patriarchs, fifty-three archbishops, and 187 bishops.

Despite the loyal support of the clergy, Pius was upset by a series of other developments in 1862 including the courtesy visit of the French navy to Naples, the visit paid by Prince Napoleon to Turin, and most important of all, the continuing agitation of Garibaldi and his radical volunteers, who seemed bent on seizing Rome for the new Kingdom. Garibaldi, inspired by the cry "O Roma O Morte!" (Either Rome or Death!) decided in the summer of 1862 to march upon Rome. Encouraged more than hindered by the Italian authorities, the general raised a force of some 3,000 men whose avowed purpose was to seize the Eternal City for the Italian Kingdom. At this juncture Prime Minister Urbano Rattazzi, who together with the king had apparently encouraged Garibaldi, now sought to convince Napoleon that he could be stopped only if the Italians occupied Rome. The emperor was not convinced. Consequently after Garibaldi had been incited by the king and Rattazzi, they found it necessary to intercept his volunteers, wounding Garibaldi at Aspromonte.

Aspromonte revealed to the Pope that it was Antonelli's diplomacy and the Frence presence in Rome that saved what was left of the temporal power rather than de Merode's military force. When the Pope received the French officers on New Year's Day 1863, he gave them the warmest expressions of gratitude for their protection, and the best of relations seemed to prevail between Rome and Paris. De Merode, frustrated in his attempt to win first place in the Pontiff's favor, devised another means to eliminate his rival. Early in 1863 the monsignor's envy of the secretary of state inspired an unwarranted prosecution of Antonelli's servant Domenico Fausti, who, on the basis of questionable witnesses and flimsy evidence, was arrested and charged with taking part in a series of liberal conspiracies. The power struggle between de Merode and Antonelli was not only personal but also hinged upon the future policy that the truncated Papal State should pursue.

Antonelli, who favored close relations with Paris, was in a difficult position. If he did not intervene on Fausti's behalf, it would convince many that the accusations hurled against him were true and most would assume that His Eminence was implicated. If, on the other hand, Antonelli acted, de Merode was prepared to charge that the secretary of state was abusing his power. Antonelli did complain to Pius, who retorted that the minister of the interior could arrest whomever he pleased and did not have to answer to the secretary of state. Exasperated, Antonelli resigned in protest, but the Pontiff ordered him to remain at his post.[13] Pius was troubled by the stories circulating that the government of Marco Minghetti in Turin sought to move the capital and feared that a renewed effort would be made to acquire Rome. In such a situation the diplomatic expertise of Antonelli was crucial for the survival of the temporal power.

On September 17, 1864, Rome received word that Minghetti had negotiated a convention with Napoleon by which France promised to withdraw its army from Rome within two years and in return the Italian government engaged not to attack the territory held by the Pope and prevent any attacks upon the patrimony of St. Peter from Italian territory. As if to assure Pius that this settlement would guarantee his possession of Rome, Napoleon included the provision that within six months the Italian capital would be moved from Turin to Florence. At the same time the Italians withdrew their opposition to the formation of a papal army of volunteers from all parts of the world, so long as the force did not threaten their security. Finally the Italians agreed to pay part of the debt of the former papal territory they had incorporated into their kingdom.

The terms of the convention were less than pleasing to Pius, who responded in December 1864 to the Convention as well as to the liberal Catholic movement by his encyclical *Quanta cura*, to which was appended a catalog of erroneous propositions already condemned by Pius or one of his predecessors. For each of these censured propositions there was a reference to the encyclical or allocution in which the particular error had been previously condemned, together with the date of the earlier condemnation. This had been in Pius's mind for some time. As early as February 1862 he had ordered Cardinal Prospero Caterini to place before the Cardinal Inquisitors of the Supreme Sacred Congregation of the Holy Office a list of seventy principal errors for their scrutiny and condemnation.[14] It was the Supreme Sacred Congregation of the Holy Office which proposed that the condemnation be in the form of an allocution to the bishops rather than one emanating from the Holy Office.[15]

The Holy Office, fully aware of the furor that the condemnation of the propositions would provoke in Europe, thought it best that the responsibility not fall upon its shoulders.[16] Unfortunately the form its members suggested, the papal allocution, would place the onus upon the Pope, whose reputation in political circles was at an all-time low. Antonelli especially feared the reaction of Napoleon III. He questioned the wisdom of offending the emperor by publishing a catalog of censured propositions, many of which were dear to his heart, at a time when his forces protected the remnant of the Papal State and Rome from the grasping hands of the Italians. The arguments of the secretary of state apparently convinced Pius, for publication of the documents was delayed. However, when the September Convention was concluded between the imperial and Italian governments without the approval or even the knowledge of the Pope, the latter complained that the French treated him like a minor, and refused to hold the encyclical and Syllabus back any longer.[17]

The secretary of state, whose policy was based upon the support of the European chancelleries and above all that of France, recognized the political damage done the cause of the Papal State by the Syllabus. It seemed to be directed not only against the Italians, who had legitimized their actions by means of the condemned propositions, but also against their accomplice, the Second Empire. To mitigate its impact, Antonelli argued that the Syllabus was a declaration of abstract principles that did not require that one call into question the concrete liberal institutions upon which the greater part of the European constitutions were founded. He also explained that the encyclical had been in the making for the last two years, since the Bishops had assembled in Rome in 1862 for the canonization of the Japanese martyrs and asked for a document condemning the main errors which had grown around them in their respective dioceses. In consequence, Antonelli explained, Pius had the Syllabus drawn up, which was a mere memorandum to facilitate references to earlier condemnations of the propositions in question.[18]

The Syllabus of Errors

The analysis of the secretary of state was accurate, for technically the Syllabus, like the encyclical to which it was appended, was addressed to the bishops and had been issued for their guidance. Furthermore, it was a condemnation of religious liberalism and the growing secularism and materialism of the age. In it such things as pantheism, naturalism, indifferentism, absolute rationalism and latitudinarianism were condemned. However, it departed from the religious sphere to plunge into the most controversial problems of politics and thought of the day, especially in the sections which catalogued "Errors About Civil Society, Considered Both in Itself and in Its Relation to the Church" and "Errors Having Reference to Modern Liberalism."[19] It was the errors listed herein that more than anything else brought the Syllabus to public attention.

There was resentment of the condemnation of the notion that public schools should be freed of all ecclesiastical authority. There was even more opposition to the condemnation of the belief that the temporal power was expendable, including an outcry over the condemnation of the principle of the separation of Church and State, with the greatest agitation produced by the condemnation of liberalism, nationalism, and democracy. Italians could understand that the roots of the Syllabus lay in Pius's personal experience with liberalism and nationalism in the peninsula that led to the assassination of his minister Pellegrino Rossi and the revolution that forced him into exile. However, the language of the document was broad and the condemnations seemed directed against the principles worldwide and for all time. Small wonder that the Syllabus provoked the indignation of non-Catholics, who resented the condemnation of the principle that man was free to embrace and profess the religion he chose, and created confusion in the Catholic world.

Odo Russell in Rome described the encyclical letter and the Syllabus as "the most unbounded pretensions to absolute control over the souls and bodies of mankind" and 'the strongest claim ever put forward by Rome since the Reformation!"[20] "There is no salvation out of the Roman Church," Pius told the English representative, who had inquired about the Syllabus, "yet I, the Pope, do think that some Protestants may by the special grace of God be saved. I mean those Protestants who by peculiar circumstances have never been in a position to know Truth," Pius quickly added. "For those who, like yourself, have lived in Rome at the very fountain of Truth and have not recognized and accepted it, there can be no salvation."[21]

The refusal of the papacy to reconcile itself with "progress, liberalism and civilization as lately introduced" according to some critics revealed the absurdity of its position and spelled the doom of the papacy as well as the temporal power. The government of Napoleon III, sensing that much of the Syllabus was directed against the emperor's policies in Italy, declared the encyclical and its catalog of errors "contrary to the Principles on which the Constitution of the Empire rests."

Later the French protested against the bull *Apostolicae Sedis*, especially its provision which considered as excommunicated all magistrates and lawmakers who obliged clerics to appear before secular tribunals. Although this was the work of Pius, who was outraged by developments in Piedmont and the Italian Kingdom, Antonelli was confronted by the French, who demanded an explanation. Initally the secretary of state responded that he was not sufficiently acquainted with the document to make any observation. However, when pressed by the French ambassador during the course of a second interview on the matter, Antonelli calmed him by announcing that the particular provision did not concern those states that had a concordat with the Holy See.[22]

The storm aroused by the encyclical *Quanta cura* and the Syllabus was somewhat quieted by the pamphlet of Antoine Felix Dupanloup, Bishop of Orleans, entitled *La Convention du 15 Septembre et l'Encyclique du 8 Decembre* (The September Convention and the Encyclical of December 8). In it the bishop argued that it was necessary to differentiate the thesis, the ideal which could exist only in a truly Christian society, and the hypothesis, that which was possible in the existing state of society, adding that the encyclical provided the ideal of a completely Christian society but allowed the faithful to act in conformity with the present political reality. Thus while the separation of Church and State could not be considered the ideal, under certain circumstances in the real world it might be the best that could be attained in a particular area.

Pius did not publicly disavow Dupanloup's explanation of the Syllabus nor frustrate Antonelli's attempts to pacify the French. He seemed to realize that Napoleon represented the last barrier between Rome and the revolution. Thus at the end of the summer of 1865 he removed de Merode, never popular at the Quay D'Orsay, from his position as minister of arms without putting anyone in his place. The papal army, after 1865 commanded by General Hermann Kanzler, was retained, but the Pope increasingly relied upon the diplomatic negotiations of Antonelli to keep the Italians from his door.

Pius found it difficult even to listen to those who suggested reconciliation with the Italian State. Nonetheless he was distressed to see so many vacant sees in Italy and in March 1865 he proposed to Vittorio Emanuele that some trustworthy individual be sent to Rome to deal with the problem.[23] The king responded that he was disposed to some solution and proposed sending Saverio Vegezzi to Rome with appropriate instructions.[24] Unfortunately the matter of royal approval of new bishops and the requirement that they swear allegiance to the government brought the negotiations to an end.

Papal resentment of the Italian government reached a new high at the beginning of 1866 when its parliament, seated in Florence since 1865, passed a civil marriage law under whose terms the State no longer recognized a marriage in the Church and required that couples be wed by its representatives as well. True enough, this legislation did not attempt to forbid the sacrament, it merely deemed it insufficient in the eyes of the State. Thus Pius considered it another blow against the Church. He also resented the law of July 1866, which adopted extreme measures against the Church, suppressing and refusing to recognize all the religious orders and congregations.[25] The mission of Michelangelo Tonello, professor of the University of Turin, to Rome[26] at the end of 1866 resulted in the nomination and transfer of a number of bishops but did not lead to a general improvement of relations between Rome and Turin.

While the Pope was troubled by the ecclesiastical legistation of the Italian Kingdom and the injuries sustained by the Church, Antonelli was concerned by the talk of an impending war between Austria and Prussia for hegemony in Germany. The cardinal feared that the Italians would take advantage of the troubled situation to move either against Venice or Rome. Happily for Pius, they decided to secure Venice and on April 8, 1866, the Florence government signed a secret treaty with Berlin whereby Prussia was to initiate war with Austria within three months and Italy would then enter the conflict alongside Prussia. In June of 1866 she kept her promise and entered the war.

Although the Italians suffered defeats both on land, Custoza, and on sea, Lissa, the Prussians decisively defeated the forces of Franz Josef at Sadowa. Antonelli, upon hearing the news of the defeat, cried out, "Casca il mondo"—the world is collapsing.[27] Striking his forehead with the palm of his hand he later lamented, "Good God, what is to become of us?" The Pope responded with resignation if not fatalism. "When the Almighty allows such trials to afflict the Church," he noted, "the Vicar of Christ on earth can only pray and wait in all humility."[28]

The Vatican found small solace in the fact that the war had not been fought well by the Italians, for they had secured recognition from Austria as well as the Veneto. As before, a plebiscite was held in the region to be acquired, and when a deputation from Venice officially announced the results to Vittorio Emanuele he reportedly said, "Italy is made," and then referring to Rome, "but it is not complete." Rome now remained the major area outside the kingdom and in its isolation became the center of attention.

Pius had other problems, for Carlotta, wife of the Mexican Emperor Maximilian, who sought aid for her husband, who was abandoned by the French, found her way to Rome. Her madness soon became the center of conversation at the Vatican, where she implored the Pope to grant her accommodations and engaged in such antics as seizing his goblet and taking it to the fountain of Trevi to drink water. In response to her frequent queries as to whether he used antidotes against poison, Pius responded, "Yes, the rosary and prayer."[29] Annoyed by her actions as well as the entire political situation, Pius lamented that everything happened to him including having a madwoman as a guest. Fortunately she soon left the Eternal City.

The Pope's difficulties with the Italians remained. Indeed no sooner had the Florence government concluded peace with Austria in October 1866 than the Prime Minister Baron Bettino Ricasoli brought forward the Roman question, which was on the minds of patriotic Italians. Following in the footsteps of Cavour, the baron proposed the complete separation of Church and State. Once the Church renounced the temporal power, Ricasoli promised the State would no longer interfere with the freedom of the Church and allow it complete liberty within its own orbit. He dispatched his agent Michelangelo Tonello to Rome to negotiate on this basis.

The Ricasoli proposal materialized at a time when both the Pope and Antonelli suspected the intentions of the Italians, who were to protect the patrimony of St. Peter under the terms of the September Convention, once the French left. In the mind of Pius this was tantamount to placing the wolves to guard the sheep. He was not alone in this opinion. "The withdrawal of the French troops from Rome will of necessity lead to a reopening of what is known as the

Roman question," Lord Stanley, the British foreign secretary, wrote, "and probably to material changes in the relations now existing between the Pope and the Government of Italy."[30]

While the British could calmly contemplate far-reaching changes in the temporal power, secure in the knowledge that their interests would not be hurt, in fact might be furthered by such a development, Pius sought peace through resignation to God's will and a strict adherence to principle, no matter what the consequence. Despite the obvious danger, he retained his sense of humor. Assured by a member of the French ministry of foreign affairs that he should not worry because the emperor was there, Pius responded, "And I am here . . . and everyone knows that Paris is quite far from Rome."[31]

In December, when the last of the French officers paid their respect to Pius prior to their departure, he predicted that the revolution would very likely reach Rome. "The Revolution thunders at my gate," he informed them, "but like St. Augustin [sic] at Hippo, I pray God that I may die, sooner than assist in my own ruin."[32] His words, echoed by Antonelli, did not augur well for a negotiated settlement. The fact that the Italian parliament, under the pressure of war with Austria, had passed a bill under whose terms over 2,000 monasteries and convents were suppressed and their properties confiscated, did not reassure Rome of the good intentions of the Florence government.

Pius and Antonelli were not the only obstacles to a negotiated settlement of the Roman question of the basis of a Free Church in a Free State. The prime minister's bill entitled "Freedom of the Church" was fought by some liberals, who felt it left far too much power in the hands of the Vatican, and during the election of 1867 Garibaldi popularized the notion that Rome had to be won by arms rather than talk. Ricasoli, realizing that the mood of the chamber and the country did not support his measure, resigned in April 1867. His failure to achieve a peaceful solution to the Roman question brought back to the fore the alternative program of direct action.

In 1867 as in 1862 Vittorio Emanuele turned to his confidant Urbano Rattazzi to form a government, and this in turn encouraged Garibaldi again to promote an insurrection in Rome to be accompanied by an incursion of his volunteers into the Eternal City. Napoleon, upset by the actions of Garibaldi and the inactivity of the Florence government, reassured the Pope that, should Garibaldi invade the Papal State, French forces would reoccupy Rome.[33] Garibaldi was not intimidated. Upon his return from the congress of the International League of Peace and Liberty in Geneva in September, he openly recruited men under the slogan "Redeem Italy or die."

At the end of September 1867 Garibaldi's sons appeared on the outskirts of Rome with numerous volunteers. Rome protested and the general was arrested by the Italian government on September 24 and returned to Caprera. However, the royal ships that were to patrol the waters of his island home failed to do so and in mid-October Garibaldi appeared on the mainland. On October 23 he crossed into papal territory to assume command of the volunteers who had earlier crossed the border. Antonelli complained that, if the Italian authorities did not openly aid the revolutionaries who threatened the Papal State, they certainly encouraged them.[34]

The projected insurrection in Rome, which might have justified outside intervention, failed to materialize and Paris demanded that the Italians honor the September Convention and move against the volunteers. When the Italians failed to do so, Napoleon, who deemed their entry into the States of the Church an infringement of international law, decided to send his troops back to Rome. Once again Rattazzi was in a difficult position. He had apparently encouraged Garibaldi and had permitted the volunteers to be armed with weapons from the national guard. Compromised by his earlier support of Garibaldi and his inaction when confronted with the crisis, he resigned. At this point Vittorio Emanuele belatedly issued a proclamation condemning the invasion of papal territory. By this time, however, the initiative had fallen out of his hands as a Franco-papal force defeated Garibaldi and his volunteers near the village of Mentana and forced them to withdraw across the border into Italy.

During the conflict a number of Garibaldini were taken prisoner, and among these was one Mario Panizza, who was brought to the infirmary in Rome. This radical was surprised to see the Pope visit his adversaries and even more surprised when Pius told him, "Look at me, young man; this way you can say that you have seen the tyrant well," and placed his hand on Panizza's head.[35] The Pope even had kind words for Garibaldi, who had termed him the "vampire of the Vatican," and let it be known that he celebrated Mass on the general's behalf.

Garibaldi found it easier to overturn the throne of Naples than to defeat the army of the Pope, in which not a single case of desertion had taken place.[36] For a change Pius had cause for celebration. The pontifical troops returned to the capital on November 7 amidst cries of "Long live the Pope-King" and "Hurrah for France." The nobles devoted to the papacy met the victors, crying, "Evviva" and waving handkerchiefs. When General Kanzler proceeded to the Vatican, he was immediately received by Pius, who dramatically recited the first octave of *Gerusalemma Liberata.* Later the Pope received the French officers and thanked and blessed them and the emperor. Pius praised the heroic valor of the pontifical army but realized that the enemy, supported in a thousand ways by the government of Florence and its "miserable and pathetic King," might have triumphed, if not for the assistance of the French.[37]

Pius felt secure for the moment. His capital had shown itself completely loyal and had failed to rise in revolution as had his other cities after 1859, disproving the claim of the National party that the temporal power was only preserved by bayonets. Furthermore he was gratified by the fact that the French foreign minister, Eugene Rouher, had announced in the French chamber that Italy would not be permitted to go to Rome, for France would never permit such violence to its honor and its Catholicism. For this among other reasons, when the Italian Parliament passed a bill granting rights of citizenship to all Italians living in provinces not yet united with the kingdom, a provision clearly aimed at what remained of the Papal State, Vittorio Emanuele vetoed it. Antonelli's diplomacy and French forces guaranteed that Rome would remain papal for the present.

CHAPTER 11

The Vatican Council

FOLLOWING Mentana the Menabrea ministry in Florence proposed a modus vivendi to the Holy See, and Napoleon suggested a conference of European powers to secure a solution to the Roman question. Pius accepted the invitation of the emperor to take part in such a congress, but only if the principles of legitimate right and justice prevailed. Since the Holy Father insisted that the only solution to the Roman question he could accept was the unconditional restitution of the provinces and property of the Holy See, the congress never met.[1] Realistically a settlement could not be negotiated on such terms, and Pius seemed to realize this, devoting his attention not to a solution of the Roman question but to the prospect of calling an Ecumenical Council to deal with a number of issues troubling the Church.

It is difficult to determine with precision when Pius decided to convoke a Council, although some such as Cardinal Lambruschini had advised him to do so from the beginning of his reign and the Pope had seriously entertained the idea since his exile at Gaeta. The last universal Council, that of Trent, had been held some three centuries before, the longest period between two general councils. Therefore in 1862 when Pius invited the bishops of the Church to attend the canonization of twenty-six Japanese martyrs it was rumored that he might call for a Council. However, some two years passed before the Pope revealed his intention to do so. On December 6, 1864, two days before the issuance of *Quanta cura* and the Syllabus of Errors, during a meeting of the Congregation of Rites, Pius asked the officials to withdraw and spoke to the cardinals of his conviction that it would be beneficial for the Church to hold an Ecumenical Council. He asked the cardinals in the Curia, those resident in Rome, to study the proposal and then submit their reactions in writing. While two cardinals were clearly negative and half a dozen more expressed grave doubts, the majority favored the proposal.[2]

In March 1865, following a consultation with the cardinals, a commission of five cardinals was appointed to discuss a number of preliminary points. Then in April thirty-six bishops of the Latin rite were questioned in the Pope's name by Cardinal Caterini, prefect of the Congregation on the Council, concerning doctrinal and disciplinary matters they believed should be examined in the forthcoming Council.[3] The following year Pius again invited all the bishops to Rome for the eighteen-hundredth anniversary of the martyrdom of Saints Peter and Paul. As a result between June 15 and June 30 there ventured to Rome forty-six cardinals, six patriarchs, ninety-six archbishops, and 347 bishops who were to assist in the canonization of twenty blessed on June 26. Originally the Pope hoped to have the Council open on this day, but because of political developments in Italy and the pace of preparation for the Council, this was not possible.[4]

On June 26, the anniversary of the martyrdom of the two saints, Pius first publicly spoke of his desire to convoke the Council and revealed that much of the preliminary work had already been done. The date of the opening was not yet fixed, and for a time the Pope hoped that it could be December 8, 1868, but this too proved impossible. Finally, on June 29, 1868, with the bull *Aeterni patris*, Pius fixed the opening of the Council for December 8, 1869, the feast of the Immaculate Conception, in the Basilica of St. Peter's.

It was expected that the Council would continue for at least two years and presumably conclude with the festivities of 1871 to celebrate the twenty-fifth anniversary of Pio Nono's election as Pope. "The Pope believes his Oecumenical Council to be the result of divine inspiration," Odo Russell wrote from Rome, "and that he is chosen to become the Shepherd of one single united Christian flock of the future."[5] News of the impending Council aroused fear and suspicion in Protestant states, disturbed some liberal Catholics, and was the cause for considerable consternation in the Italian camp. Antonelli, who had reservations about calling the Council, for he feared the opposition on the part of the powers, received word of the agitation of the Garibaldian party in Florence.[6]

In April 1869, prior to the opening of the Council, three important events were celebrated in Rome: the Pope's golden jubilee of his priesthood, the fiftieth anniversary of his first Mass; the fifteenth anniversary of the "miracle of Sant' Agnese"; and the nineteenth anniversary of his return to Rome. The three festivities were fused into one and were celebrated by the illumination of a number of churches and streets in Rome and a series of processions. In the face of the praise that reached adulation, Pius retained both his humility and his sense of humor. Thus when a certain lady told him she had obtained one of his socks and placed it on one of her sick legs and was miraculously cured, the Pope responded, "Beautiful, by using only one of my socks you are cured while I who use two am unable to rid myself of my leg problems." When visiting the Villa Borghese an old gendarme threw himself at the Pope's feet, saying, "Holy Father, I have twenty-five years of service and they do not want to give me a pension." "The opposite is happening to me," Pius quickly responded, "I have not yet twenty-five years of service and still they want at all costs to pension me off."[7]

On the occasion of the Pope's fiftieth anniversary as a priest, deputations, addresses, and gifts were sent from every land, arriving daily at the Vatican. From America there arrived six huge chests with instructions that they not be opened until April 11. One was opened and found to contain chocolates among which was hidden gold from California. In all Pius received gifts valued at several million lire. "Say what we may," wrote Gregorovius, who was a resident of Rome at the time, "the papacy is still a moral idea; combat the statement as strongly as we may, it can reckon on the love of many classes of mankind. Facts speak for themselves."[8]

The Pope's joy at the many expressions of love and loyalty was tempered by the death of his brother Gabriele in the summer of 1869. Rome, however, remained festive as religious and lay visitors crowded into the capital in anticipation of the Council, impressing them with her sense of eternal destiny and imperishable grandeur. There was much speculation in the Eternal City and elsewhere as to what the Council would mean for the Church, Italy, and constitutional Europe. There was also considerable interest in how the work of the Council would proceed.

The judgment of an older historiography was that Pius did not play a crucial role in the Vatican Council, leaving a free path to the Jesuits and the cardinal presidents of the various committees. All of the facts are not yet out, but quite clearly the Pope, who had long looked upon the Holy See as the center of unity and the symbol of order in the Church,[9] played a far more important role than was earlier believed. While it is true that he did not initially have a precise program for the Council, he was convinced that earlier councils had played an important role in the Church during difficult periods, such as he assessed the present. He therefore hoped that the new Council would strengthen the Church so it could better cope with the numerous attacks being made upon it.[10]

The Papal bull convoking the Council indicated that its main purpose was to save the Church and society from threatening calamities, correct if not extirpate a number of modern errors, and effect a timely revision of the legislation of the Church. "It is at this time evident and manifest to all men in how horrible a tempest the Church is now tossed, and with what vast evils civil society is afflicted," the bull of indiction read. "In this oecumenical Council must be examined with the greatest accuracy, and decreed, all things which in these difficult times relate to the greater glory of God, the integrity of the faith, the gravity of divine worship, the eternal salvation of men, the discipline of the secular and regular clergy and its wholesome and solid culture, the observance of ecclesiastical laws, the amendment of manners and the instruction of Christian youth," it continued.[11]

In harmony with Pius's belief that there should be a reestablishment of relations with the Church of the East, he sent out invitations on September 8, 1869, to the Eastern bishops not united with the Church. The responses were all negative. A similar refusal was accorded the Pope's letter to all Protestants and other non-Catholics which exhorted them to reconsider their position and return to the Catholic unity from which their fathers had strayed. The Evangelical bishop of Berlin, apparently offended by the Pope's words, spoke in turn of an illicit hierarchy in the Church in his rejection of the invitation.[12]

A sign of the times was the lack of invitations to the Catholic princes who in the past had been invited to the Councils. Émile Ollivier, head of the French ministry, commenting on the failure to mention the emperor or the representatives of the civil power, concluded that the Pope, by this action, had definitely separated the Church from the State. His comment was answered by the Jesuit periodical *Civiltà Cattolica*, which indicated that the rulers had not received invitations because only some of the governments recognized Catholicism as the religion of state. Noting that the Holy Father could not invite representatives from the Italian government, Antonelli informed the Bavarian ambassador that this prevented him from inviting the representatives from the other Catholic countries. Certainly this was not the only reason, but it provided a convenient and obvious explanation. The Court of Rome was determined to exclude diplomats.[13]

It was the *Civiltà Cattolica* in an article of February 6, 1869, which published correspondence from France, and cited the prospect of the Council's unanimously proclaiming the infallibility of the Pope, a dogmatic assertion on the part of the bishops that when he spoke from his chair he was infallible. The notion of infallibility was neither new nor illogical but it provoked a bitter controversy in Catholic countries and aroused the fears of Protestants throughout Europe. It was thought unlikely that the semiofficial *Civiltà Cattolica* would have supported infallibility without the sanction of the Pope, who reportedly said, "In former times before I was Pope, I believed in Infallibility; now, however, I feel it."[14]

Unfortunately the article in the *Civiltà Cattolica* transcended the question of infallibility and seemed to indicate that the Council would approve by acclamation the papal teaching in the Syllabus of Errors as well. This linking of the controversial Syllabus with the question of infallibility made it appear as if the latter were part of a general crusade against the "errors" of the times and part of the Pope's vendetta against Italy.

In Italy there was considerable concern about the consequences of the Council and a declaration of papal infallibility. Menabrea, who was president of the council of ministers until November 1869, was constantly preoccupied with the thought of what the Council might do and feared that this would prove detrimental to Italian interests.[15] The Masons proposed calling a counter-Council at Naples, receiving the support of such notables as Giuseppe Garibaldi and Victor Hugo, and organized popular demonstrations in various provinces under the theme "War to the End against the Papacy." The Italian government, which permitted Count Giuseppe Ricciardi and his freethinkers to open their counter-Council in Naples, closed it shortly thereafter on December 9, under the pretext that it disturbed international relations, there having been used at the counter-Council language offensive to Napoleon III.[16]

In Germany, which had witnessed the rise of a scientific party in the Catholic Church under the leadership of Johann Josef Ignatius von Döllinger of the University of Munich, there was a tendency to disdain the alleged lack of learning among their Italian colleagues and their fanatical devotion to the papacy. At the beginning of September the German Bishops, meeting at Fulda, sent a collective letter to the Pope, expressing their grave reservations about a possible definition of infallibility. The German Bishops also asserted that the Council could not establish new dogmas, could not proclaim a new doctrine not contained in Holy Scripture or Apostolic Tradition, and would only set the old and original truth in clearer light.[17] In France there were liberal Catholics such as Count Charles de Montalembert and Bishop Dupanloup of Orleans who were opposed to the proclamation of infallibility. The possibility of a proclamation was a bitter blow to the champions of Gallicanism, who accepted the papacy as a divine institution but sought to minimize its claims. While this tendency had manifested itself in a number of countries, it found its clearest expression in France.

No sooner had the Jesuits proposed infallibility than a series of articles for and against it appeared. Arguing against the definition was the dominant intellect of the Munich school of Theology, Döllinger, who, under the pseudonymn of Janus, sought to show that no such thing as an infallible Pope ever existed. He and others spelled out the dire consequences of proclaiming infallibility. Some of the royal houses even feared that Pius would claim the right to depose sovereigns, and this rumor was encouraged by a number of writers, politicians, and diplomats.

The chancellories of the various countries were alarmed by the possible political pronouncements of the Council and in April 1869 the Minister President of Bavaria, Prince Chlodwig Hohenlohe-Schillingsfürst, despatched a letter to the Bavarian Ministers at the various courts. "It is unlikely that the Council will occupy itself solely with doctrines of pure theology," his note, drafted by Döllinger, read. "The only dogmatic thesis that Rome would wish to be proclaimed at the Council is the papal infallibility."[18] Arguing that such a definition would become an eminently political question, the prince called upon the cabinets of Europe to undertake joint action in view of the repercussions to be expected from the issues considered by the Council. His call for a conference and a collective protest to Rome was considered premature and therefore went unanswered.

The Menabrea ministry in Italy was one of the few that shared the Bavarian government's fears and concurred that some joint action might be opportune, sending a circular to the powers late in April. The Italian circular proved no more successful than the Bavarian initiative. Harry von Arnim, the Prussian representative at the Holy See, favored some form of intervention, but was overruled by Bismarck.[19] The governments decided on a policy of nonintervention so long as the issues considered were confined to the spiritual order.

In November 1869, on the eve of the Council, the Bishop of Orleans, Dupanloup, wrote an article entitled "Observations on the

Controversy Regarding the Definition of Papal Infallibility at the Future Council." In it the chief Catholic champion in all public controversies and the most prominent supporter of the temporal power in France declared that a definition of papal infallibility was inopportune. Pius was disturbed by this publication from one whom he esteemed for his service to the Church, and Antonelli expressed his alarm. "In the Council he could have said what he pleased," observed the cardinal secretary of state, "but not publicly."[20]

By the end of November some 400 bishops, archbishops, patriarchs, and cardinals had arrived in Rome and others were pouring into the Eternal City at the rate of fifty or sixty a day. Forty-eight bishops and one abbot constituted the representation from the United States. According to the Reverend Thomas Mozley, who covered the opening of the Council for the London *Times*, soon after his arrival Cardinal Bonnechose went to pay his respects to Pius. The Pope supposedly inquired of Bonnechose what public opinion in France thought of the Council in general and his infallibility in particular. When the cardinal replied that it was hoped that infallibility would not be declared a dogma, Pius was perturbed, according to Mozley, who was less than sympathetic to the papacy. "Your Eminence has always been in opposition," the Pope allegedly replied to a startled Bonnechose. "I remember that on a former occasion you were opposed to raising the doctrine of the Immaculate Conception to a dogma, but thank God, we willed that it should be so, and it was so; and we will that the infallibility of the Pope shall be made a dogma, and it shall become one through the influence of the Council of 1869."[21]

On December 2, Pius addressed the bishops in the Sistine Chapel prior to the opening of the Council and noted that it had been called to find suitable remedies for the numerous evils and errors that afflicted the Church and modern society. The Pope spoke of the harmony necessary among the fathers and expressed the concern that the Council would be torn by strife and conflict. Pius was later to note that every Council consisted of three periods: the first was that of the devil, who tried to embroil; the second, that of men, who tried to confound; and only the third that of the Holy Spirit, who enlightened, purified, and coordinated.

Early in December the bull *Multiplices Inter* was given to the fathers, laying down the order of procedure at the Council, its rules and its official machinery. Pius nominated the five cardinals, who, in his name, were to preside over the five congregations or committees of the Council, as well as the secretary of the Council.[22] Referring to the tribulations he had endured, Pius let it be known that he felt strengthened by the presence of so many brethren who were bound to him.

Some days later on December 6, the Pope gave an audience to the Italian hierarchy. The importance of this gathering, which has been overlooked and neglected in the historiography of the Council, is made clear by the diary of Monsignor Giulio Arrigoni, the Archbishop of Lucca. Pius decided to speak to the Italian bishops as a group, thus indirectly providing recognition of the political unity of the peninsula, to express his displeasure at the actions and attitude of the French fathers who were meeting that very day in assembly, even though Pius had made it clear to them that nationality had to cede to ecumenism. The Holy Spirit was to be found in the Council rather than the national assemblies, the Pope told the Italians, adding, "The bishops here are Catholic, not Frenchmen or Germans."[23]

The following day the Pope saw the English hierarchy. "In our audience with the Pope on the 7th, we found him looking very well," wrote William Bernard Ullathorne, Bishop of Birmingham. "He stood, and gave us, the English bishops, a little address on the spirit of the Synod, and then solemnly blessed all our clergy, nuns, and people, and specially our special friends."[24] That afternoon when the noon hour was sounded, all of the 360 churches in the capital rang their bells while the cannon of the Castel Sant' Angleo sounded incessantly to remind all of the impending opening of the Council. In Florence the demonstration against the Council ended in failure.[25]

The morning of December 8, the Pope's favorite day, fifteen years after the proclamation of the dogma of the Immaculate Conception and only five years after the issuance of the Syllabus, the bells of the rain-soaked city alerted residents and visitors to the opening of the Council. At nine amidst the ringing of all the bells of the churches and salvos of artillery from the Castel Sant' Angelo the Pope and a procession of some 700 ecclesiastics entered St. Peter's and assumed their places in the right-hand transept of the Basilica. Of these some 200 were Italian; over 100 were English-speaking; while the rest came mainly from France, Spain, Austria-Hungary, and the other Catholic countries of Europe.

Following Mass the Pope gave his benediction and received the homage of the members of the Council: cardinals kissing his hand, bishops his knee, and religious superiors his foot. After the Pope invoked the aid of the Holy Spirit and a hymn was intoned for its assistance, the prelates by a voice vote approved the decree opening the Council. A second decree announced that the next public session would be held on January 6. The *Te Deum* was then sung and the meeting adjourned at approximately 4:00 P.M. In all, the service had lasted some seven hours.

The first order of business was the selection of the Congregations or Committees of the Council charged with the preparation of reports and responsible respectively for handling matters of faith, discipline, the regular clergy, and rites. Four in number, each one was composed of twenty-four men brought forward by the Pope and his advisors, and approved by the Council. Although some immediately protested that these congregations were merely deputations to receive and organize the papal will, they had to submit all matters to yet another committee, also appointed by the Pope, and finally to the general congregation, that is, the Council as a whole.

Some were distressed that the Pope was playing so active a role in the affairs of the body. He had provided the secretaries and undersecretaries both for the Council and its several committees. It was observed that in comparison to the Council of Trent the initiative had shifted from the fathers to the Pope. At Trent there was no previously prepared agenda and regulations were not prescribed beforehand. Although Pius indicated that the Council would have to determine its own agenda, there were those who saw Pius's hand there as well, especially regarding the question of infallibility.

As Christmas approached, Pius, on December 19, received some 600 visitors in the Vatican Library, his first public reception since the opening of the Council. After a series of presentations and some kind words for all those who paid him homage, he addressed his visitors in French on the subject of pride. "God, in teaching humility, declared pride to be the enemy of man and the author of revolution," he told the assembly, which he blessed amid loud applause.[26] There were those who thought that Pius was infected with pride in favoring infallibility, while the Pope thought that those who opposed it, to the point of going against the wishes of the majority of the fathers, were guilty of the sin of pride.

It was assumed that the Italian episcopate would almost to a man stand with Pius, who desired infallibility. Indeed the Pope virtually assumed the leadership of the infallibilist party, which clearly enjoyed a majority in the Council. The bishops of France, Germany, Austria-Hungary, and the United States, who opposed the definition, about a fifth of all who were present, were a very vocal minority who irritated Pius, who reacted to their protests with petulance. "The Council appears to have been convoked for the special purpose of defining the Papal Infallibility and enacting the propositions of the Syllabus as general laws of the Church," wrote Peter Richard Kenrick, Archbishop of St. Louis. "Both objects are deemed by a minority, of which I am one, inexpedient and dangerous, and are sure to meet with serious resistance."[27]

While the question of infallibility was on the minds of those inside and outside the Council, Pius maintained a hectic schedule and continued to receive clerical and lay vistors. During these audiences the Pope remained amiable and jovial. "Are you statues?" he jokingly asked a group that was so intent upon gazing at him that those in it failed to kneel. "I've the best sculpture gallery in the world and I'm in no want of another." On another occasion, when his vistors rushed at him and showed an unrestrained enthusiasm to the point of making it difficult for him to move freely, Pius said, "I should like to make the rounds of you all and exchange a few words; but you really are too much for me." He then added, "But you've come to see the Pope, and 'Voilà'."[28]

On January 29 Pius visited the American College, presiding at the Mass afterwards in which all the American bishops assisted. Although the Pope delivered a short sermon in Italian on the virtues proper to the episcopate and sought to impress the American bishops, there is no evidence to suggest that an overt attempt was made to win votes for the definition.[29] The Bishop of Birmingham reported that though the Pope was now almost eighty, he managed to fulfill his responsibilities remarkably well and was as active as much younger men. At one of the receptions a number of Frenchmen nearly pulled him to pieces and Pius was only saved from his friends by the papal guards who surrounded him. Like the American lady who shouted to Pius to speak up, the Pope's French admirers were moved by affection rather than rudeness.

The devoted and the curious, as well as the political representatives to the Holy See who were admitted to the Pope's presence, were aware that work was proceeding on the draft of the definition of infallibility. The French foreign minister, Count Napoleon Daru, disturbed by the possible impact of the definition, sent a note to Antonelli, observing that the policy of the Holy See was making the situation difficult for the French government, which would have to justify in the chamber the retention of troops in Rome. Likewise the

Vienna government informed Antonelli of its reservations regarding a definition of infallibility.[30] The secretary of state, supposedly concerned about the consequences which might ensue from the declaration under the present circumstances, led a group of cardinals to discuss the matter with the Pope. Pius, however, refused to compromise. "I have the Blessed Virgin on my side"; he reportedly retorted. "I will go ahead."[31]

Pius was disturbed that Charles de Montalembert, a devoted son of the Church and a strong champion of French support for the temporal power, opposed the proclamation on infallibility. In a letter he had protested that he had never thought or written anything "favorable to the personal and separate infallibility of the Pope, such as is sought to impose upon us; nor to the theocracy, the dictatorship of the Church."[32] Pius responded to the liberal minority in a letter to the Benedictine Abbot of Solesmes, observing that they did not believe, as did other Catholics, that the Council was governed by the Holy Spirit, and criticized their imprudence.

Shortly thereafter the long-ailing Montalembert died. As a Roman patrician he was entitled to a Requiem Mass in the Ara Caeli attended by the senate and the patricians. However, Pius, fearing a demonstration at the funeral of the figure who had joined the party opposing infallibility, prohibited it. The secretary of state, the governor of Rome, and the chief of police, all of whom feared the consequences of the papal prohibition, urged Pius to relent, but he stood firm. He did permit a Mass to be said at another Church and assisted in it.

On March 6 a draft of the *schema De Ecclesia*, which contained three chapters on the Pope's primacy and one on his infallibility, was circulated. By this time Pius was actively involved in the infallibility controversy. "The Pope takes every opportunity of expressing his views on infallibility, both in audiences and in letters that at once get into the papers," wrote the Bishop of Birmingham, who was sympathetic to the majority position in favor of the proclamation. "He has quite changed his old policy on our arrival, when he professed neutrality before the Council."[33]

The other fathers also knew that Pius wished the proclamation issued. "I have just heard that the Holy Father sent for one of the strongest Infallibilists and told him that he must use his best influence to bring on the question at once, as the state of Europe was such that if not settled now it never would be," wrote Bernard J. McQuaid, Bishop of Rochester, on April 17. "Of course if he has said so to one, he has said the same to several. We may therefore expect the all-important question to be placed before us for discussion immediately."[34] Not suprisingly on April 29 Pius agreed to give precedence to the *schema* on the powers of the Pope, taking it out of its proper order despite the opposition of the minority and the reservations of many in the majority. Interestingly enough, this coincided with the news of Daru's resignation. The Infallibilists rejoiced.[35]

The Bishop of Orleans, Dupanloup, wrote to Pius urging him to postpone the discussion on infallibility, but to no avail. "It is right for the Fathers at the Council to put forward clearly difficulties they think stand in the way of any definition," Pius responded to Dupanloup's plea ten days later, "but it is not right to strive by all means to bring all over to one's way of thinking: especially as we know the Council is under the guidance of the Holy Ghost, and that nothing can be defined that is not true and revealed, or that is not for the good of the Church."[36]

On May 13, after many revisions made by the bishops upon the circulated draft, the chapters on the papacy of the *schema De Ecclesia Christi* were placed before the Council as a whole for consideration and the public discussion upon infallibility commenced. The principal speaker for those in favor was the Archbishop of Westminster, Henry Edward Manning, who fought long and hard to secure enactment of the dogma. Both he and the Bishop of Regensburg, Ignaz von Senestréy, while assisting at the papal throne on the feast of Saints Peter and Paul in 1868, had taken vows to do all within their power to secure a definition of papal infallibility.

Pius was perturbed by the clamor of the anti-Infallibilists and became increasingly less tolerant of those who were less than totally committed to a definition. He was clearly disturbed by the speech of Cardinal Filippo Maria Guidi, Archbishop of Bologna and a distinguished scholar who had been professor of theology in the universities of Rome and Vienna. The cardinal, whose words were awaited with great expectation, argued that the assent of the episcopate was necessary for the definitions of the Pope to be recognized as infallible. That evening the Pope called the cardinal into audience and reportedly charged that he made an unworthy and heretical speech and insisted that Guidi subscribe to a new profession of faith. Almost immediately the story circulated that when the cardinal attempted to explain to Pius that what he propounded was in accordance with Scripture, the teaching of the Church, and tradition, the Pope interrupted him angrily with the comment, "I am tradition!"[37]

Although this story, which put into the mouth of Pius the words of Louis XIV, "I am the State!" received wide acceptance, especially among the anti-Infallibilist members of the Council, no one indicated the source of the statement. Certainly no one attributed this to Guidi, who was in the best position to know precisely what the Pope had told him. It is true that Pius wished the cardinal to make a public declaration to the effect that his speech had been misinterpreted, but Guidi convinced the Pope that any further statement would only increase the polemic and would be detrimental to the decorum of the Holy See.[38]

Undeniably Pius was upset by the obstacles placed in the path of the definition as well as the pace of progress of the work of the Council. Alluding to the expenses incurred in supporting the bishops who enjoyed the hospitality of the Pope, some 300 in all, half of whom relied upon his generosity for lodging, the other half for almost everything, he declared that by the time he was pronounced infallible he would have failed financially.[39] He reacted to the opposition to the definition in a personal fashion so that the bishops who favored the definition but had reservations concerning the form were afraid that they might be branded opponents of the Holy See. The Bishop of Birmingham took the precaution of seeking an audience with the Pope on July 6 to explain his position. "I informed His Holiness that from the time of my theological studies I had always been an infallibilist," wrote Ullathorne, "and that all I desired was to see that the definition should be as clear as it could be made." Pius, pleased by his position, patted him on the back and exclaimed, "Bravo! Bravo!"[40]

At the end of June the debate on infallibility was closed and Wednesday, July 13, was the crucial day when the chapter on infallibility, as amended by the congregations, was put to a preliminary vote in the general congregation. The vote taken among the 601 fathers at this sitting produced 451 *placet,* or yea; eighty-eight *non placet,* or nay; and sixty-two *placet juxta modum,* yea subject to certain modifications; while some seventy-six fathers actually in Rome absented themselves from the session.[41] The opponents of infallibility offered to relent if some of their objections to the wording of the dogma were met. On July 15, a delegation of the minority, composed of five bishops, in an audience with the Pope promised unanimous approval for the proclamation if the text were modified to indicate that the Pope had to consult the episcopacy. Pius, however, refused to compromise and rejected the proposed modification.[42]

The Vatican Council

The Bishop of Orleans addressed another appeal to the Pope, pointing to the impending conflict between Prussia and France, and asked that Pius suspend confirming the will of the majority on the issue of infallibility until a more propitious time. Pius did not accept the suggestion and for a moment it appeared that the minority against infallibility would refuse submission and vote against the dogma in public session. To avoid the scandal, Dupanloup convinced those more than fifty bishops who could not bring themselves to vote in favor to leave Rome rather than publicly repeat the *non placet*. Thus on July 18, 1870, when 535 of the fathers voted in favor of infallibility, only two publicly voted against it. On that final vote, twenty-five bishops from the United States voted with the majority, twenty-two either absented themselves or already had left for home with only the Bishop of Little Rock, Edward Fitzgerald, joining the Bishop of Caizzo, Luigi Riccio, in voting against infallibility.

The final vote drew a huge crowd into St. Peter's despite the lightning, thunder, and rain which shattered one of the windows in the Basilica almost above the papal throne. When the spectators in the Basilica and those outside realized that infallibility had been proclaimed, they clapped their hands and waved their handkerchiefs, shouting, "Long live the infallible Pope!" and "Long live the triumph of the Catholics!" The shouting and celebration were only stopped by a solemn recital of the *Te Deum*. Before Pius left St. Peter's the two bishops who had voted against infallibility made their submission. "Now I believe, Holy Father," said Fitzgerald, and Riccio, kneeling before the Pope, said, "Credo."[43] John Henry Newman, who accepted infallibility, noted in his correspondence that the promoters had behaved "cruelly, tyrannically, and deceitfully...."[44]

The dogma, defined and declared to be divinely revealed, read:

Therefore faithfully adhering to the tradition received from the beginning of the Christian faith, for the glory of God our Savior, the exaltation of the Catholic Religion, and the salvation of Christian peoples, the Sacred Council approving, We teach and define that it is a dogma divinely revealed: that the Roman Pontiff, when he speaks *ex cathedra*, that is, when in discharge of the office of Pastor and Doctor of all Christians, by virtue of his supreme Apostolic authority he defines a doctrine regarding faith or morals to be held by the Universal Church, by the divine assistance promised to him in blessed Peter, is possessed of that infallibility with which the divine Redeemer willed that His Church should be endowed for defining doctrine regarding faith or morals: and that therefore such definitions of the Roman Pontiff are irreformable of themselves, and not from the consent of the Church.

But if any one—which may God avert—presume to contradict this Our definition; let him be anathema.[45]

The dogma defined, the fourth session of the Council was closed in the expectation that it would meet again on November 11. However, the next day the Franco-Prussian War erupted, with far-reaching consequences for France, Germany, Italy, the Papal States, and the papacy. Pius's efforts on behalf of peace proved fruitless.[46] At the end of July the French foreign minister told the French ambassador at Rome to prepare Pius for the departure of their troops and found him surprisingly resigned. "Now is the time for prayer," he said, adding, "but everything will end well."[47]

CHAPTER 12

The Collapse of the Temporal Power and the Roman Question

AS the last French troops left Civitavecchia in August 1870, there was little hope that some other power would step into the vacuum left at Rome. The Austrians had denounced their concordat with the Church and since the loss of Venice had shown a distressing disinterest in Italian affairs. Bavaria was sympathetic to the opposition of Döllinger to papal infallibility and had neither the inclination nor the means to act on behalf of the Holy See, while Spain was in the throes of internal conflict. Only the last flicker of uncertainty about the outcome of the war, the attitude of the powers and especially Prussia, and the need for a pretext delayed an immediate Italian move toward Rome.

In preparation for some eventual action against the Eternal City the Florentine government created an army of observation for Central Italy and entrusted command to General Raffaele Cadorna. Its instructions were to protect the frontier and to prevent insurrectionary movements from penetrating the papal border. In the interim Napoleon III sent Prince Napoleon to ask the Italians for an army of 70,000 and hinted that in return the Italians might have a free hand in the peninsula. The Italians were not very interested in intervention in the war but very interested in Rome. The Prussian representative in Rome was inclined to play an active role in the crisis, but Bismark's instructions called for a policy of non-intervention.[1]

Despite the impending invasion Pius adhered punctually to the papal calendar, presenting himself in the churches of Rome, participating in the solemn functions of St. Peter's and in other public ceremonies. Within the Vatican and especially among the Jesuits there were voices that urged Pius to leave Italy, but Pius did not favor a second flight. Twenty years had elasped since his return from Portici and at the age of seventy-eight he did not desire to leave home again. Besides, unlike in 1848 he would now be constrained to leave Italy because he could not seek asylum in Naples.

Nonetheless the Empresse Eugénie, acting as regent, sent the man-of-war *Orénoque* to Civitavecchia to evacuate Pius, if he wished, to France. Antonelli opposed such a step, seconding the Pope's inclination to remain in Rome and face the consequences that became inevitable following the spectacular German victory at Sedan in early September and the establishment of a provisional Republic in France. On September 8 Vittorio Emanuele despatched his envoy Count Gustavo Ponza di San Martino to Rome with a letter. The king, who claimed to write with the affection of a son, the faith of a Catholic, the loyalty of a king, and the sentiment of an Italian, argued that it was necessary for the security of Italy and the Holy See that his troops occupy the rest of the Papal State.[2]

Nice words but ugly deeds, the Pope muttered, as he read the king's letter, adding that it would have been more loyal and sincere simply to admit that he wanted to take possession of all of the pontifical State. "I am not a prophet or the son of a prophet," he shouted to Ponza di San Martino, whom he received on September 10, "but I can assure you that you shall not enter Rome!"[3] The Pope replied to Vittorio Emanuele's letter with a firm refusal.

Count Ponza di San Martino has delivered to me a letter which Your Majesty was pleased to send me; but it is unworthy of an affectionate son who boasts of professing the Catholic faith and glorifies in his Kingly loyalty. I will not enter into the particulars of the letter to avoid renewing the pain which its first reading produced. I bless God, who has permitted that Your Majesty should fill the last years of my life with bitterness. For the rest, I cannot admit the requests contained in your letter nor support the principles contained therein. I once more turn to God and place my cause, which is His, in His Hands. I pray to Him to grant to Your Majesty abundant grace to preserve you from danger and accord you the foregiveness which you so obviously need.[4]

On September 10 the Pope appeared in public to inaugurate formally the opening of a new fountain in the capital, and an immense crowd gathered round him shouting, "Long life, Pio Nono, King, King, King." Quite clearly the Pope was still immensely popular in Rome, and the prospect of another revolution against him was remote. The liberation of Rome, if it were to be achieved, would have to come from the outside. The Italians understood this. On September 11, the Pope's domain, which was defended by a papal force of less than 14,000 men under the command of General Kanzler, was invaded by the more than 60,000 troops of General Cadorna. Pius ordered a three-day intercession before the image of the Madonna della Colonna in the Basilica of St. Peter and continued to hope that the Italians would not dare to attack Rome itself. He refused to accede to the Italian request to enter the Eternal City. "If we are unable to prevent the thief from entering," he replied, "let it at least be known that he enters only by means of violence."[5]

On September 19, when the Italians were poised outside his capital, prepared to enter it the next day, Pius knew that further resistance was useless. He determined that his troops would only offer token resistance, and, once the walls were breached, capitulation would ensue. Fighting within the city he would not permit. Noting that the whole of Europe deplored the numerous victims of the war between Prussia and France, Pius insisted that it must never be said that the Vicar of Jesus Christ, even though unjustly assailed, consented to a bloodbath.[6] In response to Kanzler's request that he and his men be permitted to fight and die, Pius asked them to surrender, realizing that for them this was a greater sacrifice.

The afternoon of the nineteenth Pio Nono went out of the Vatican for the last time, proceeding to the Santa Scala and climbing it upon his knees. At the top he prayed in a loud voice broken by emotion for the Church and the people of Rome. As he left, he blessed the troops on the Piazza di San Giovanni and then had his coachman drive slowly to the Vatican.[7] Very likely he knew that this would be his last drive through the streets of his capital. As he drove through the city on his way home, groups of Romans who feared that he might depart on the *Orénoque* pleaded for him to remain in the capital and Pius reassured them that he would.

Early on the morning of September 20, 1870, the Italians began the bombardment of three of the city gates. As arranged, the diplomatic corps presented itself at the Vatican to be with the Holy Father during this time of trouble. Following Mass the Pope received the ambassadors and ministers of the powers in his private library. Before them he protested to the entire world against the violence of which he was the victim and condemned the "sacrilegious" action. "Sirs, I am giving the order to capitulate: a further defense would serve no purpose," he informed the diplomats. "Abandoned by all, I must sooner or later surrender, and I do not wish to shed blood uselessly."[8] By ten o'clock the fire had ceased all along the line and shortly thereafter the diplomatic corps left the Vatican. When Father

Daniel, chaplain of the papal troops, entered the Pope's presence, Pius said, smiling, "My dear Daniel, here we are really in the lion's den."[9]

At three in the afternoon the capitulation was signed in the central hall of the Villa Albani. Drawn up by General Cadorna, Kanzler brought forward his own points which had been prepared in concert with the Pope and Cardinal Antonelli. Perhaps the most important stipulation, from Pio Nono's point of view, was the one which assured that not only would the Sacred College and the clergy be respected but all religious congregations of either sex be maintained in the capital. The Holy See could not exact very much from the Italians in light of the total indifference of the powers to its plight. Only the Republic of Ecuador raised its voice to protest the invasion.[10]

The Italians now controlled the Eternal City and effectively ended the life of the oldest European state. The inrush of democrats and Mazzinians into the capital disturbed the Pope and Antonelli, and on the evening of September 20 the secretary of state decided to call upon Italian arms to occupy the Leonine City without prejudice to papal interests therein. However, the evening passed without incident and the note written by Antonelli to Cadorna was not sent. The next day the announcement of a popular demonstration against the Vatican promoted the writing of a second note to Cadorna, which was signed not by the secretary of state but by General Kanzler. "His Holiness entrusts me to inform you that he desires you to take efficient and energetic steps to safeguard the Vatican," it read; "since his troops have been dissolved, he does not have the means to stop the disturbances and disorders under his sovereign residence."[11] Shortly thereafter Pius told the cardinals that he felt incapable of freely exercising his spiritual powers as a result of the loss of the temporal power.[12]

On October 1, the Italians forcibly entered and took possession of the Quirinale after futile attempts to obtain the keys and possession from Cardinal Antonelli. The next day the junta formed at Rome under the protection of the Italian army called upon the citizens of what was left of the Papal State to vote yes or no on the question "Do you wish union with the Kingdom of Italy under the constitutional monarchy of Vittorio Emanuele and his successors?" With the help of some violence and electoral engineering the citizens of Rome who had hitherto remained apathetic to the call for union with Italy voted overwhelmingly for inclusion in the unitary state. On October 9 the expected results were hand delivered to the Italian king in the Pitti Palace in Florence by a delegation from Rome led by the blind Duke of Semoneta, Michelangelo Caetani.

Soon thereafter the Italian authorities introduced changes in Rome. The senator was replaced by the *Sindaco* or mayor and later there were elections to municipal and provincial councils as well as for the national parliament. Terracina elected Gregorio Antonelli to the provincial council, but the cardinal's brother promptly resigned, refusing to sit by the side of the king's supporters. Pius set the example to be followed by arguing that he had yielded to illegitimate force and repeatedly claimed that he was King Vittorio Emanuele's prisoner and refused to venture out of the Vatican. He received a series of offers of asylum.[13]

On October 20 Pius issued a bull which suspended the meeting of the Ecumenical Council until a more propitious time.[14] Shortly thereafter, on November 1, the Pope argued in an encyclical that to do violence to the sovereignty of the Holy See, to separate its temporal from its spiritual power, was simply to impair and ruin the work of God and therefore exposed religion to the most serious danger. For this reason he invoked the major excommunication for all those who had perpetrated the invasion, the usurpation, and the occupation of the papal domain as well as those who had aided or counseled the action.

In order to calm the Pope and reassure Catholics as well as the great powers, the government of Giovanni Lanza brought forward the Law of Papal Guarantees. This legislation recognized the inviolability of the person of the Pope and invested him with the full attributes of a sovereign. As compensation for the loss of his territories he was to receive annually the sum of 3,225,000 lire, not subject to taxation, in perpetuity, even during periods when the Holy See was vacant. As regards relations between Church and State the *exequatur* and *placet* were abolished as well as other government mechanisms for controling the publication and execution of acts emanating from ecclesiastical authorities. In fine, the principle adopted though not fully implemented was the Cavourian notion of a free Church in a free State.[15]

The Pope and his secretary of state refused to compromise their position of opposition and therefore did not accept the Law of Papal Guarantees, which was termed a monument of civil wisdom by the Liberals but branded a monument of barbarous ignorance by the Pope.[16] Approved by a vote of 185 to 106 in the Italian Chamber of

Deputies in March 1871, Pius repudiated it in his encyclical *Ubi Nos arcano* of May 15 and again in his consistorial allocution to the Sacred College of Cardinals on October 27, 1871.[17] He insisted that recent events had shown that for the papacy there was no other guarantee than its own civil power, free from the control of any state; any other security was simply an illusion.

When the Italian government attempted to deliver to the Pope the first installment of the annuity assigned him under the Law of Papal Guarantees, he firmly refused it.

Yes, I need money badly. My children throughout the world have adopted various expedients to fulfill my needs and those of so many others. But you, what would you bring me with that delivery. A part of what you have stolen from me? I will never accept it from you by way of reimbursement and will provide no signature of acceptance that might seem to imply an acquiescence or a resignation to the spoliation.[18]

Despite the Pope's opposition to the legislation, once this had become the law of the land in Italy, the capital was moved to Rome in July 1871: the chamber would sit in the Palazzo Montecitorio; the senate, in the Palazzo Madama; and the king moved into the Quirinale. Pius, however, did not accept the *fait accompli*, locking himself in the Vatican and refusing to prejudice in any manner or form the rights of the papacy. If John the Baptist was a voice shouting in the desert, he told a deputation from various Roman parishes, his was a voice ringing from the Vatican. He pledged to use his voice and pen to protest against the usurpation, violence, injustice, lies, corruption, and incredulity he found rampant in the capital.[19] He remained true to his word.

Pius remained adamant because he regarded the total loss of the temporal power a serious threat to his spiritual sovereignty and part of a broader war against the Church and religion. He was convinced that the war was not only against himself but against God and his Christ.[20] This conviction made it impossible for the Pope to compromise himself by dealing with those who had deprived the papacy of its inheritance. In a letter he wrote but did not send to Vittorio Emanuele he explained that he found it necessary to protest the loss of the temporal power now and so long as God gave him life in order to satisfy the dictates of his conscience.[21] In both his public and private correspondence Pius made it clear that he could never cede that which belonged to the Holy See.[22]

The Pope also found it necessary to renew his protests against the seizure because he believed that without his own territory, he would be subject to the Italian government, despite the words of the Law of Papal Guarantees. He explained to his vicar-general in Rome, Cardinal Patrizi, that any concession, by its very nature, implies power over the person to whom it is granted, and this he could not tolerate. "It is not enough that he [the Pope] is for the moment materially free," he told his secretary of state, Antonelli. "He must be and must appear free and independent in the exercise of his supreme authority."[23]

Pius remained shut up in the Vatican as a protest against the occupation of Rome and as a clear sign of his noncompliance. "You have come to see the one they call *the prisoner of the Vatican*, and truly that is what I am," he told a delegation of foreign women who came to visit him. "I have no doubt that physically I could go out, but I could not do so morally, without seeing a spectacle of misery, scandal, and of profound affliction, for the city has deteriorated from what it was."[24] His protests were echoed by the faithful abroad.

The states of Europe, however, one by one recognized the Italian acquisition of Rome and, even though they maintained representatives at the Vatican, sent their diplomats to the Quirinale, the official residence of the king. In France the monarchists who were sympathetic to the papal cause were unable to effect a restoration and the Republic more or less came in through the back door. Furthermore in France there was a sharp division in the Catholic camp. In 1872 Pius called for union, peace, and harmony among the factions in France, noting that the party opposed to papal influence lacked humility while those who opposed them showed little charity, forgetting that without charity one could not be truly Catholic. He recommended humility to the one, charity to the other, and to all union and harmony.[25]

By 1874 the Republic, anxious to maintain good relations with Italy, found it necessary to take some action on the *Orénoque*, the ship the French had earlier placed at the disposition of the Pope and anchored at Civitavecchia since August 1870. Marshal Patrice Macmahon, elected President of France by a predominantly royalist assembly which hoped for a restoration, explained to Antonelli that the presence of the ship at Civitavecchia strained relations with Italy and asked the Pope's permission for its withdrawal. Pius complied with an air of resignation. "I did not ask for the *Orénoque*," he reportedly said in private; "let them take it away if they wish.

Civitavecchia is far away; the *Orénoque* was twenty-four hours from the Vatican; its aid would have been of little avail."[26]

Pius, who celebrated the jubilee of his coronation in June 1871, and was presented with a petitition of loyalty containing some 27,000 signatures, found conditions in the capital deplorable. He prayed constantly that the political and social cataclysm would soon end.[27] Despite his prayers, the protests of Cardinal Patrizi, who spoke on his behalf, and those of the bishops outside of Rome, the Italian government assumed control of the charitable institutions of the capital known as the *Opere Pie*. Ironically the former Emperor Napoleon III who had befriended the Piedmontese and had played a crucial role in the unification of Italy and the subsequent loss of Rome, wrote from his exile that he took courage from the attitude and example of the Pope and was better able to endure his own misfortune.[28]

The Pope's anger with the Italians increased with every new measure he deemed aimed against the Church and religion. In 1872 the Rome government passed legislation which provided for the suppression of monasteries and the sale of ecclesiastical property in Rome as had already occurred in the rest of the kingdom. Subsequently the houses of the religious orders were seized and converted into government buildings with the Minerva being converted into the Ministry of Worship and the library of the Collegium Romanum appropriated. The Convent of San Silvestro was taken for the ministry of the interior and later served as the central post office in Rome.

Pius complained that this legislation and the action undertaken under its provisions represented the logical continuation of Italian government's desire to undermine religion, justice, and morality. In an angry letter to Vittorio Emanuele, Pius charged that the work of the revolution had made Rome not so much the capital of Italy but of disorder, confusion, and impiety, citing the abuses and actions taken against the religious houses and their members. He claimed that the harassment of the religious in Rome rendered it difficult to direct the affairs of the universal Church and worked to undermine his spiritual authority. "Is it possible that after having usurped this last strip of temporal dominion there remains the desire to attack the Pope in the exercise of his spiritual dominion?" he asked the king.[29]

The Pope continued to differentiate between Italy and the revolution, explaining to an Italian delegation—to whom he confessed that, as an Italian himself, he was particularly delighted to receive their proofs of affection—that when he had blessed Italy from the loggia of the Quirinale Palace, his words were misrepresented to seem that he had blessed the revolution.[30] In fact his love for Catholic Italy constrained him to raise his voice against the current iniquities.

The unfortunate position of the Church in Rome motivated Pius to write to Vittorio Emanuele again in July 1872, protesting against the threat made to prevent priests, brothers, monks, and all those lay people that were dubbed clericals, from teaching. Clearly upset, Pius argued that if the Italian government wanted to destroy the Roman Pontiff, it should say so clearly, for then he would inform the Catholic world of the actions he felt constrained to take in response. The manner in which the affairs of religion were treated in Rome increasingly convinced Pius that the Church faced a real persecution.[31]

The Pope admitted to a group of pilgrims that he was weary of so much injustice, disorder, and outrage in a city which had been a model of practical faith and morality. He decried the fact that Catholic processions in which the Eucharist was carried were virtually prohibited while the flag of the International could be unfurled as well as the banners of the freethinkers and Masons. Indeed, he believed that the latter were actually encouraged in their devilish designs.[32] Disheartened by conditions in the Eternal City, Pius was all the more indisposed to treat with those he regarded as the perpetrators of the injustice, remaining firm in his determination to resist all compromises.

In the midst of his conflict with the Italian government and what he interpreted as persecution of the Church in the peninsula and elsewhere, Pius never lost his sense of humor or his confidence that ultimately the Church would emerge victorious. Thus when a foreigner asked him when the battle with the Italians would end, Pius, in contrast to the bitter pronouncements of his official discourses, responded, "I am the Vicar of Christ, not his secretary."[33] To those who asserted boastfully that the bark of Peter would always remain afloat, Pius acknowledged such to be true, but added that this would not prevent those who traveled in the bark from getting a good drink of water.

Pius was convinced that Christ would eventually come to the rescue of his persecuted Church if it remained true to its mission and did not compromise with its persecutors. "It is useless to talk of conciliation," he told a group of Romans and foreigners at the end of November 1871, "for the Church can never conciliate itself with error and the Pope cannot separate himself from the Church. No, no sort of conciliation is ever possible between Christ and Belial, between light and darkness, between truth and lies, between justice and usurpation."[34]

While the Pope awaited the day of retribution, he lived simply in the Vatican, his room all but bare except for an ugly bed and a kneeling stand.[35] He appreciated those things which money could not buy: music, the open air, and the simple piety and friendliness of the poor, who had a special place in his heart. "Let me not be attached to the things of this world" was his constant prayer, which the Italians seemed determined to answer. He, Garibaldi, and Mazzini, Pius observed on one occasion, seemed to be the only three who got nothing out of the *Risorgimento*. Such was not completely true, for the seizure of the Pope's state aroused part of the faithful, who determined to provide for the needs of the Holy Father.

The cardinal secretary of state, Cardinal Giacomo Antonelli, informed the Catholic world that the Holy Father, who did not wish to accept money offers from any particular government, was inclined to see the faithful come to its aid by means of Peter's Pence. The call was amply answered.[36] After 1870 Antonelli revised the collection of Peter's Pence, making it far more efficient and regular and one of the prime sources of papal income. A number of organizations pledged themselves to collect monies in France, Belgium, Spain, Germany, Ireland, and elsewhere, while the bishops assumed the responsibility of transmitting this to Rome. The cardinal secretary of state, who managed to save part of what was sent, invested this wisely, creating a substantial fund for the day when the generosity of the Catholic world might be curtailed. In this fashion Antonelli placed the Holy See upon a solid financial basis.[37]

Financially independent and certain of the righteousness of his cause, Pius did not hesitate to criticize one and all. Consequently relations between the Italian Kingdom and the Vatican remained strained. The Pope was scandalized by the opening of a number of Protestant churches in the city of the Church, the newspapers that were published, the legislation enacted, and the appearance and apparent government encouragement of Bible societies. The old Pope considered all these actions worthy of divine wrath and indicated to those who visited him that God revealed his justice by means of the various punishments inflicted upon Italy, including floods, earthquakes, and the outbreak of cholera. Two of these punishments, Pius noted, represented the two political parties of

Italy, *Destra* and *Sinistra:* cholera the first and earthquake the second.[38]

Pius continued to resist the Italian contention that the appointment of Italian bishops had to be confirmed by the civil authorities before they could be legally recognized and forbade his bishops from seeking such a confirmation. At the same time he discouraged Catholics from participating in the Italian parliament. In his speech of October 11, 1874, he again responded to a series of requests from Catholics about the propriety of sitting among the deputies in the Palazzo Montecitorio. As earlier, he declared that such participation could not be permitted under any circumstances because the selection of deputies was not truly free, and then there was the matter of the oath required of all the representatives. To take such an oath of loyalty was to accept the spoliation of the Church, the sacrileges committed, the anti-Catholic instruction in the schools, and the future iniquities that might well be committed by the Italian state. For these reasons he maintained the *non expedit.*[39]

Relations between Italy and the papacy went from bad to worse. From 1872 to 1874 some twenty-nine bishops were prosecuted in the peninsula and the bishop of Mantova was condemned to thirty-five days in jail for a sermon.[40] It is true that privately Pius recognized that times had changed. Following the loss of his trusted secretary of state, Antonelli, in November 1876, in naming his successor, Cardinal Giovanni Simeoni, he observed that now that the papacy no longer had the temporal power, a new type of secretary of state was required. Rather than occupying himself with political matters, Pio Nono indicated that Antonelli's successor would have to be primarily concerned with religious issues and with bringing souls to heaven.[41]

In November 1876 Pius was not only troubled by the loss of Antonelli, who had remained by his side since the revolution of 1848, but also by the speech of Vittorio Emanuele at the opening of the new parliament that same month. The king's speech seemed to herald a new antagonism toward the Church, reflecting the strong anticlerical bent of the *Sinistra*, the left, which replaced the *Destra* party of the right in power in 1876. The Pope's worst fears materialized as Pasquale Stanislao Mancini, the Minister of Justice, was to use violent language in referring to the clergy and even the Pope while the state increased its interference in the allocation of benefices and banned outdoor religious processions. The teaching of religion was abolished in the intermediate schools and the sector of public education was increasingly permeated by anticlericalism.[42]

The new government introduced legislation to muzzle the clergy, prescribing severe penalties with fines of up to 300 lire and two years' imprisonment for those clerics who attempted to use their influence to promote political aims. During the course of the discussion on the measure, Mancini declared that the Church and its ministers had to be held accountable for their intrusion into the political arena. The "Clerical Abuses Bill" was passed in the chamber of deputies in January 1877, promoting Pius to issue a strong allocution arguing that the much-vaunted independence of the Holy See was only a delusion. Reciting the wrongs committed by the Piedmontese government since the invasion of September 1870, he harped upon the present law which threatened to take away from the clergy their right to speak.

Pio Nono not only lashed out against the Rome government but appealed to Catholics throughout the world to influence their governments against the Italians on behalf of the Church, asserting that this legislation proved that the existence of unitary Italy was incompatible with the independence of the Holy See. When Antonelli had been directing foreign affairs, he had never so blatantly and unequivocally asserted the incompatability of the Vatican with the Italian state. "Here are the consequences of the death of Antonelli," one cardinal remarked; "here is the triumph of the party which he had always fought."[43] In a letter to the president of the Italian Catholic Youth Council the old Pope struck out against those who counseled conciliation. "We congratulate you, therefore, on the fact that although you suffer, doubtless at the defection of your brothers separated from you by the breath of perfidious teaching, you are not troubled for all that," adding, that the faithful should be stimulated by the error of those who went astray "to receive with greater willingness and to follow with more zeal not only the orders, but even the directives of the Apostolic See; and by so doing you are certain that you cannot be deceived or betrayed."[44]

CHAPTER 13

The Kulturkampf

FOLLOWING the collapse of the temporal power and the loss of Rome, Pius believed that the European powers had abandoned him, the papacy, and the Church. The Pope, who had hoped for Austrian or German intervention on behalf of the Vatican, learned quickly that such aid was not forthcoming. "Archbishop Ledochowski has really had a mandate from the Pope," Prince Hohenlohe noted in his *Journal*, November 28, 1870. "He was to obtain a protest from Prussia against the occupation of Rome, and to request a habitat for the Pope in the Prussian dominions. Bismarck and the King were unfavourable to the protest."[1] Consequently the mission ended in failure.

Count Friedrich Ferdinand von Beust, who since October 1866 had been Austria's foreign minister, let it be known that the Habsburg monarchy would steer a neutral course in the conflict between Italy and the Vatican. "It is said that Austria has done nothing; but a demonstration without force would be ineffectual, and would do nought but compromise Austria's dignity," he responded when attacked in the clerical journal *Vaterland* for his inactivity in the Roman question.[2] Beust believed that even an expression of Austrian hostility to Italy would work to restore the Italo-Prussian alliance.

The Marquis Emilio Visconti Venosta, foreign minister of Italy from 1869 to 1876, recognized that Germany's sympathy for the person of the Holy Father had its natural limit in the value Berlin attached to Italian friendship. He concluded that this would prevent the Berlin cabinet from creating difficulties for the Italian Kingdom or entering combinations hostile to her interests.[3] Rome, therefore, could expect little from the Germans. Perhaps this is why Pius urged a delegation of Catholic women from Germany, to whom he had accorded an audience in February 1871, to pray constantly for him, the Holy Church, and for Europe, which was in the midst of a terrible convulsion.[4]

The opposition to papal infallibility had been very strong in Austria-Hungary, Germany, and Switzerland so that it was not surprising that influential groups in these countries refused to follow their bishops and submit to the decrees of the Council. Furthermore the liberal legislation aganst the religious orders in Austria provoked a papal encyclical *Vix dum a Nobis* which protested the unilateral violations of the concordat of 1855.[5] France, under the leadership of Adolphe Theirs, proved to be of little comfort to the Vatican. "I am decided, for my part, not to resurrect the Roman Question, which we are in no position to bring to a happy solution," wrote the French president. "Infinite regard for the Pope, earnest entreaties that he be spared further torments—that is our natural and honorable role; but to embroil ourselves with Italy at this moment would be an imprudence and a folly."[6]

In Germany a number of priests in charge of parishes as well as teachers in the schools and universities refused to subscribe to papal infallibility, and they were not dismissed from their posts. Then, in September 1871, a conference of the opponents of the definition was held in Munich, and after Italy it was the German empire that would create the greatest difficulties for Pio Nono during the last days of his pontificate. Pointing to the persecution of the Church in Germany, the Orient, and elsewhere, Pius warned the students of the Propaganda Fide that the war against the Church was growing and urged them to prepare themselves for combat because the Church even in times of peace had to prepare for war.[7] He was particularly upset by the actions of Bismarck in Germany.

While there is evidence that Bismarck was hostile to a number of Catholic politicians, there is little to suggest that he was prejudiced against Catholics as such. In 1851 he had considered the Prussian Catholics among the most loyal subjects of the king and during the 1850s and early 1860s he viewed the Catholic clergy of the Rhineland as a bulwark against liberalism. Apparently the poor showing of the national parties in the *Zollparlament* elections of 1868 largely as a result of Catholic political action played an important part in arousing the chancellor against the Church. He prepared an analysis of the position of the Church in Germany and dispatched it to Harry von Arnim on April 12, 1868, "to enlighten the Roman Curia on the state of things." Bismarck hoped to moderate Catholic opposition "through a serious intervention of the Pope."[8] Such an intervention did not occur, and relations between Prussia and the Vatican became increasingly cool.

During the discussion of the imperial constitution no provision was made for the independence of the Church. Furthermore the Catholic department of the ministry of worship, existent since 1841 in Prussia, was suppressed. This contributed to the creation of the *Zentrumspartei Deutschlands*, or German Center party. A rebirth of the defunct *Zentrumsfraktion*, it aimed to safeguard the interests of the 16 million Catholics of the empire. At the same time the *Germania* was established to voice the sentiments of the new group.

The appearance of a party with a democratic and social program, not strictly confessional but open to all those who desired to defend Christian traditions and religious liberty against the intransigent laicism of the National Liberals, alarmed some.[9] The unhappiness intensified when in March 1871 Emperor William, escorted by the princes of the blood, appeared for the first time in the Reichstag. Rudolf von Bennigsen of the National Liberals, who drafted the response to the emperor's speech, presented it before the assembly. During the course of the discussion to the response, this liberal leader acknowledged that certain elements in the chamber looked to the empire to restore the Pope's temporal power and vehemently affirmed that Germany would not be a party to such a policy.

The deputies of the Center party found Bennigsen's attitude unacceptable, as one of them explained:

Gentlemen, my colleagues and myself are entirely willing to sign the address to the emperor. Our patriotism is second to none. But do not ask us to assent to a pretended principle which every conscientious man must reject. There is no question of the Holy Father at present. We never alluded to him here. What you propose is a theory, and a theory which is as contrary to common sense as to natural and Christian law. How long is it since the duty of helping one's neighbor when his house is on fire has been abrogated? Let us hope that we may never be required to lend such assistance, but at the same time let us not begin our work by proclaiming a policy which no statesman can honestly accept.[10]

The Chancellor of Germany, Otto von Bismarck, was disenchanted with Pio Nono and found him difficult if not impossible to deal with. While at Versailles, in accordance with the proverb "One hand washes the other," Bismarck wrote, "I proposed that reciprocity in the relations between the Pope and ourselves should be effected by bringing Papal influence to bear upon the French clergy in the interests of peace. . . ."[11] The chancellor was disturbed that these "advances had been coldly met and declined" and concluded that

Pius was unwilling to pay the price for their openly championing papal interests in regard to Rome. Small wonder that Bismarck, in a confidential diplomatic circular to German representatives abroad, warned of the power of the Pope, who by means of his infallibility was more of an absolute ruler than any other monarch in the world, and sought to influence the election of his successor. Bismarck's diplomatic mission ended in dismal failure.[12]

Pius, for his part, was less than pleased by Bismarck and developments in Germany. Speaking to a deputation from Alsace in June 1871 he expressed the hope that their new owner would leave them alone—especially regarding religion. He indicated that he had received a number of letters from the emperor promising that he wanted to adopt measures on behalf of the Holy See, but the Pope clearly remained skeptical. "Nice letters, good words," he told the Alsatians, adding, "but this is not the moment to speak." Nonetheless he did say, "It is known that it is better to be grieved by a Catholic king, even if he is not too praiseworthy, than by an emperor of another religion. But since God has permitted it in your case, resign yourselves for the time and await the day of his mercy."[13]

The Pope's obvious displeasure with the empire's absorption of Alsace-Lorraine disturbed Bismarck. The German government, on its side, did little to improve relations with the Vatican. Indeed it exacerbated the tension by showing itself sympathetic to Döllinger, who refused to submit to the declaration of infallibility and was excommunicated, and it was supportive of the Old Catholic movement, which also broke with Rome on the issue of infallibility. To make matters worse Prince Choldwig zu Hohenlohe, who distrusted the Jesuits and the Court of Rome, was elected vice-president of the first Reichstag. Soon thereafter his brother Cardinal Gustav Adolf zu Hohenlohe was selected to represent the German Empire at the Holy See.

The appointment of Cardinal Hohenlohe was a slap in the face of Pio Nono because the cardinal had been a thorn in his side during the Vatican Council, critical of the proceedings and almost always friendly to the views of Döllinger. During the Council he had written his brother the prince, "Stupidity and fanaticism hold hands here and dance the tarantella making the music of cats."[14] In addition to his adherence to the theology of the liberal school of Munich, his position as a member of the Pope's senate made it awkward for him to act as the representative of a foreign power at the papal court. For these and other reasons Pius opposed the appointment, considering it to be of immediate danger to the Church, the Holy See, to himself, and to the cardinal.[15] Following the Pope's refusal to accept Hohenlohe as German ambassador to the Holy See Bismarck spoke in the Reichstag, May 14, 1872, and warned, "There is only one sovereignty, the sovereignty of the law.... fear not, *we shall not go to Canossa, neither in body nor in spirit.*"[16] Determined to wage war against particularism, upset by what he regarded as papal pretensions, and angered that the Center party had pronounced itself on the side of the Pope on the Roman question, Bismarck determined to wage war against the Jesuits and Ultramontanes and even the Church if necessary.[17]

In alliance with the National Liberals the Iron Chancellor now launched a full-scale conflict of cultures, or *Kulturkampf*, contrasting the liberal and national ideals of modern Germany with the medieval traditionalism of the Church which had produced the Syllabus of Errors and papal infallibility. Thus was the word *Kulturkampf*, coined by the Socialist Ferdinand Lassalle, applied by Professor Rudolf Virchow, the Progressive deputy, to the campaign against the Catholics in the name of culture.

Bismarck, unlike the National Liberals who were associated with him in the struggle against the Catholics, was more concerned with political than ideological questions and hoped to use the Pope's fear of retaliation against the Church to curb the Center party.[18] He therefore instructed Count Karl von Tauffkirchen, the Bavarian who had succeeded Count Harry von Arnim as minister to the Vatican, to inform Pius of the Chancellor's anger against the Catholic party, which he claimed was hostile to the new Empire. Bismarck hoped to have Rome censure the Center party because of his antagonistic attitude in the Reichstag. Antonelli, the secretary of state, gave the impression that something might be done by uttering a few well-chosen phrases. However, once Baron Bishop Wilhelm von Ketteler went to Rome and explained the German Catholic position, Pius made it clear that he was not prepared to silence the Center. Following the interview, Antonelli issued a clear statement of support for the party, providing the full moral support of the Holy See in the defense of rights of conscience and religion.[19]

In June 1872 Pius gave an audience to a German group that had come to present its support. Visibly excited, his hand shaking, Pius observed that he had received similar sentiments from various cities in Germany and this was one way of keeping in check the persecutors of the Church in the empire. The Pope urged those before him to combat the enemies of the Church by their voice and by their writings. God wishes superiors to be obeyed, he told his German visitors, but he wants truth to prevail and false teaching to be combated. Pius let the group know that he had sent a letter to Bismarck, observing therein that until this time Catholics had been in favor of the German Empire and bishops had reported to him that they were satisfied with their relations with the government. How is it, he asked, that after the Catholics were treated so well and have long been appreciated as good citizens, they have suddenly become a threat? Noting that the Iron Chancellor had not responded to his query, the Pope speculated that he heard no word because no answer could be given to the truth.[20]

In an allocution at the end of 1872 Pius condemned not only the abominations of Catholic Italy but also the secret and public persecution of the Church in the German Empire. "It is not only with secret machinations, but with brute force that an attempt is made to eliminate Catholicism in the new German Empire," Pius said in his Christmas message to the cardinals. "Men who not only do not profess our holy religion but who do not even know it dare to arrogate to themselves the power to determine her dogmas and rights."[21]

The Pope's determination to uphold the Center encouraged the government to introduce a series of measures aimed at restricting the influence of the Church. The so-called pulpit paragraph forbade any clergyman from preaching on political matters in his office as minister, punishing violations of this law with imprisonment.[22] Shortly thereafter a bill was passed banning non-German Jesuits from the empire and seriously restricting the activities and residence of German members of the Order.[23] This virtually eliminated the Jesuits from Germany, and the Redemptorists, the Lazarists, the Fathers of the Holy Ghost, and the Sisters of the Sacred Heart were suppressed in 1873 because of their alleged close association with the Society of Jesus. Subsequent legislation was introduced which provided for obligatory civil matrimony.

If the struggle against the Church had been initiated in the Reichstag of the empire it was in the Prussian *Landtag* that it reached its culmination. Paradoxically, while the papacy was being criticized in Italy for being an enemy of nationalism and the unitary state, it was attacked in Prussia as an essentially Italian power which was based upon a college of cardinals containing an increasing number of Italians. "Now, Gentleman," said Dr. Rudolf Virchow, leader of the

Progressive party in a speech of January 1873, in the Prussian lower chamber, "this Italian Papacy from which ultramontism has emerged in its modern form, this ultramontane Papacy, has indeed shifted the bases for negotiations between even the most benevolent state and the church, inasmuch as in the Vatican decisions it has won an entirely new and up to now totally unprecedented status."[24]

In 1872 Adalbert Falk became the Prussian Minister of Ecclesiastical Affairs and Education and under his direction the constitution of 1848, which guaranteed the independence of the Church in Prussia, was amended to permit the state to pass legislation regulating education. The first of these laws, passed in May 1873—hence frequently called the "May Laws"—dealt with education of the clergy. It required that all priests or ministers who sought appointment attend a German high school and German university. The years spent in a seminary might be equivalent to those spent in the university, provided that the program of studies had been approved by the minister of education. Provision was therefore made for seminaries to be placed under state inspectors and their curriculum submitted to state authorities for approval.[25]

Under the new legislation, even if a candidate for the priesthood met the educational requirements, his appointment was no longer automatic. Prior to his appointment the bishop had to transmit his name to the civil authorities, who had a month to bring forward their objections, if any, to a particular individual. The ministry of education would decide upon the complaints and any appointment made in the face of such objections was declared invalid. Another of the May Laws declared that Catholics must not acknowledge any ecclesiastical court outside of Prussia, with part of the disciplinary authority transferred to an ecclesiastical court composed of laymen. Finally two other laws forbade the publication of Church decrees and facilitated separation from the Church. The persecution of the Church in Prussia, the Pope told a deputation from Naples, was more cruel than the one of the Church during the time of Nero because the latter was open while the present was camouflaged under the veil of law.[26]

In August 1873 Pius wrote to William I about the recent Prussian and German legislation against the Church, which he felt weakened the throne and the empire and which he had been led to believe did not meet the emperor's approval. Claiming that all those who received baptism in a way belonged to the jurisdiction of the Pope, he hoped that William would act to resolve the situation.[27] The emperor, in his response, indicated that the Pope was mistaken in his belief that he did not approve the laws in question, and the legislation in Germany was always such that he could approve. The specific laws in question, he continued, were rendered necessary by the action of his Catholic subjects who, supported by the higher clergy, had assumed a defiant position vis-à-vis the state. As a rejoinder to the Pope's assertion that whoever had received Baptism belonged to the jurisdiction of the Pope, William pointed out that the Evangelical faith which he and a majority of his subjects espoused did not permit any mediator between themselves and God but Jesus Christ.[28] William went so far as to suggest that Pius use his authority to see that the controversy was brought to an end, presumably by acquiescence to the recent legislation. Neither the Pope nor the German hierarchy was prepared to surrender on those terms.

The bishops of Germany issued an announcement that they could never acknowledge such laws or assist in their administration and were completely supported by Pius, who approved the courageous resistance of German Catholics. In his encyclical *Esti multa* of November 21, 1873, Pius bewailed at once the abolition of the monasteries in Rome and the May Laws under whose terms Catholics in Prussia were suffering. Still the Pontiff counseled courage and reminded the faithful that the Church would triumph in the end as it had previously, its enemies demolished while the Church gleamed brighter than the sun.[29]

In the face of Catholic resistance to the Prussian legislation Falk began to fine, arrest, and banish hundreds of priests and treated the bishops no better. Archbishop Ledochowski of Posen was imprisoned for resisting implementation of the laws and his property was confiscated. Bishop Brinkman of Münster was fined so often and so heavily that he had little left except his household furniture, and this was seized and sold by government agents. As before, Pius supported the hierarchy in Germany. Acknowledging that Christ wished sovereigns and princes to be respected, he added that God had armed the princes to protect, not to persecute, the Church. He praised the German episcopacy for their constancy and resistance which in his words had rendered it admirable throughout the world.[30]

The German government, in turn, increased the pressure upon the Church. In 1875 all the monastic orders except those caring for the sick were dissolved in Prussia and there was enacted the so-called Bread Basket Law, which ended subsidies to bishops and priests who refused to conform to the new ecclesiastical and educational legislation.[31] By 1876 all of the Prussian bishops had been imprisoned or forced to take refuge abroad and some one-third of Catholic parishes were without priests. The *Germania*, the organ of the Center party, faced numerous confiscations and its chief editor was arrested and imprisoned. Over 100 other Catholic editors joined him behind bars.

Although he was in his eighties, the Pope's health remained sufficiently good to allow him to fulfill all of his obligations and responsibilities,[32] and he actively combated the persecution of the Church in Germany. He responded to the measures against the Church in his encyclical *Quod nunquam* to the archbishops and bishops of Prussia, February 5, 1875, denouncing the laws issued against the rights of the Church, condemning the attempt to overthrow the God-given constitution of the Church, and attacking those provisions which sought to destroy the prerogatives of the bishops and infringed upon the freedom of believers. Pius praised the clergy of Prussia as well as all loyal German Catholics for their constancy and exhorted them to stand firm in the face of persecution, just as he stood firm in the face of the Italian revolution. At the same time he declared the bulk of the legislation aimed against the Church null and void and excommunicated those who accepted the misdeeds and obnoxious laws, noting it was necessary to obey God rather than men. Indeed he admonished the faithful to stay away from the services of those who accepted the laws, refusing to receive the sacraments from their hands, so that the corrupt not spoil the good.[33]

Distressed by developments in Italy as well as Germany, Pius felt that the Church was on trial and remained convinced that by standing by the holy laws of the fathers, Catholics were sustaining the rights of the Holy See and God. He received some consolation from the fact that the persecution of Bismarck's government, which he compared to the threat of a new Atilla, had not destroyed the faith but rather reinvigorated it. Seeing the German Catholic population remain true to its faith throughout the persecution and strong and constant in sustaining the rights of the Church increased his own courage and spirit of resistance.[34]

By the end of 1876, when Pius lost his secretary of state, Antonelli, whom Bismarck considered shrewd but powerless on the issue of the conflict with the empire,[35] the *Kulturkampf* remained in a state of suspended animation. While no new major proposals were brought forward to restrict the Church or the clergy, there was no move toward reconciliation. Bismarck was enraged in the spring of 1876 when Pius named Ledochowski, still in prison, a cardinal, and vented his anger on the Center party, which he termed revolutionary and an enemy of the state. However, the Iron Chancellor proved unable to destroy the Center, as Ludwig Windthorst, the tireless and crafty leader of the party, feared, or nationalize or undermine the Catholic Church, as Pio Nono feared.

Pius was certain that eventually the tide against the Church would turn and divine intervention would advance its cause vis-à-vis its oppressors. In the German case, the Church and the Center party were to improve their position as a result of political rather than religious factors. Among the important developments in the Empire were the deterioration of relations between Bismarck and the National Liberals, the allies of the *Kulturkampf,* and the first steps toward the creation of a coalition between the Center and the Conservatives which materialized during the elections of 1877. Confronted with this bloc, and desirous of shaking off the National Liberals, who were demanding concessions that amounted to the establishment of a liberal parliamentary regime in Prussia and the empire, Bismarck broke off the conflict with the Church. Thus during the reign of Pio Nono's successor, Leo XIII, 1878–1903, Bismarck annulled most of the measures against the Church and reconciled himself with the Center party in order to end his association with the National Liberals.

There was no comparable improvement in relations with Italy, no impending resolution of the Roman question on the horizon. Initially Pius did not believe that the Holy See could depend upon the guarantees made by the new state, placing little trust in the government which had extended the antiecclesiastical legislation introduced in Piedmont to the entire peninsula and Rome itself.[36] Later, when Pius realized that the papacy was in fact protected by the Law of Guarantees from Italian encroachment, other factors prevented him from coming to terms with the new state. The Pope was very sensitive to the concern expressed by the other Catholic powers that the Vatican would fall under the sway of Italy, and he therefore sought to make it clear by maintaining his public opposition to the new regime. Thus the Pope continued to protest against the usurpation of his rights while declaring in private that he doubted that the papal territory would be restored and admitted that he would indeed be embarrassed if his states were returned to him.[37]

In June 1877 Pius celebrated his golden episcopal jubilee, which marked fifty years of service as a bishop, as pilgrims flocked to the

The Kulturkampf

Vatican from all parts of the world. Those who went to see and hear the eighty-five-year-old Pope found his voice to be dynamic and compelling and noted the great impact that he had upon his audience.[38] Interestingly enough, on that same day, June 3, Vittorio Emanuele dutifully celebrated the thirteenth anniversary of the Piedmontese *Statuto*, which received scant attention in comparison to the golden jubilee. A few months later the king, who had not yet reached the age of fifty-eight, fell victim to malaria. The Princess Clotilde, daughter of Vittorio Emanuele II and married to Prince Jerome Napoleon, Napoleon III's cousin, as part of Cavour's Plombière agreement, had some years earlier written to the Pope and asked his permission to venture to Rome if some member of the family should fall ill. Pius granted permission for the king's daughter to enter the Italian capital, which he still regarded as his own, on the condition that she not reside in the Quirinale Palace.[39] Unfortunately her father's illness assumed a critical turn before Clotilde could return to Rome.

On January 7 Pius called upon Monsignor Francesco Marinelli and informed him that it had been brought to his attention that the king was gravely ill and he, as Vicar of Christ and universal father of all believers, wished to assist him in his spiritual needs. He therefore commanded the monsignor to go to the Quirinale and aid the king, giving him full power and authority to do so. However, before Marinelli could accomplish his mission and present himself to the dying monarch, he received word of Vittorio Emanuele's death on January 9, 1878.[40]

Pius did not long survive the death of the king with whom he had long corresponded but never met. On February 2, when the Pope spoke to a number of bishops and apostolic delegates in the throne room, it was clear to all that he was not well. In this last speech Pius thanked the prelates for the prayers and proclamations in his favor and cited the need for loyalty to the head of the Church. He ended this speech, which was quickly termed his last testament, by a benediction. "And now I bless you," he told those in the throne room. "I bless your persons, your religious houses, and all the souls that are in your care. This benediction accompanies you in all the days of your life, and let this benediction be the theme of your prayers and your praise when God chooses to call you to heaven."[41]

Early in February word spread that the condition of the Pontiff, who was almost eighty-six years old and in the thirty-second year of his pontificate, had deteriorated. Weakened by a long bronchial illness, on February 7 he received the last sacrament, and at about three o'clock in the afternoon he blessed the cardinals and prelates who attended him. Less than two hours later he was dead, succumbing to a pernicious fever complicated by a cerebral hemorrhage. The tolling of the church bells alerted those in the capital to the fact that the longest-reigning Pope was no longer with them, and crowds flocked to the Chapel of the Sacrament in Saint Peter's, where his body lay in state.

CHAPTER 14

Conclusion

FOR many the death of Pio Nono marked the end of one age and the opening of another as almost immediately an assessment of the longest-reigning Pope commenced. It was widely acknowledged that he had led an exemplary private life. Possessing an ardent piety, he almost completely abandoned himself to the will of God and the intercession of the Virgin. Even those who opposed his political stand attested his great fervor, his touching simplicity, and his serene courage in confronting adversity. He was most scrupulous in the fulfillment of his duties as a priest, and throughout his pontificate he remained devoted to pious practices and long hours of prayer and fasting. Sympathetic to the needs of others, he gave generously to various groups, orders, individuals, and worthy causes. Confident that salvation of one's soul was the central matter of life, he dedicated himself to this, to the detriment of worldly matters.[1]

The Pope's deep religious sentiments and stubborn otherworldliness, qualities most admirable in a priest, conflicted with the political and diplomatic goals of his state and the frequent need to subordinate conscience to *Realpolitik*. As early as May 1847 the Austrian representative at Rome, Count Lutzow, wrote Metternich that the greatest enemy of Pius as a sovereign was his heart, adding that the number of men in Rome who appreciated the qualities of his nature were few and far between.[2] The prince concurred, early branding Pius a good priest but a poor statesman.

While the estimates of Pius as Pope and sovereign differ substantially, almost all concur upon the importance of events which filled his thirty-two-year pontificate and the magnitude of the actions with which his name is associated. Those whose assessment of the pontificate is negative point to Pio Nono's failure to prevent Italian unification and his inability to preserve the temporal power. These critics see as his legacy the Roman question, which troubled the Church and the Italian Kingdom for half a century. Others, however, observed that Pius's interests always had been primarily spiritual rather than political and that in his heart the Pope always took precedence over the prince, and must be evaluated in this light.

The Pontifical State ceased to exist not only because of the Franco-Prussian War and the withdrawal of the remnant of French troops from Rome but also because of the total international isolation of the papacy, which resulted from the religious policies pursued by Pius from the Syllabus of Errors to the proclamation of infallibility. Despite the loss of his state, Pius considered that the Church had derived great advantage from the publication of the Syllabus and the decrees of the Vatican Council and considered these measures essential in light of the fierce and obstinate war he believed was being waged upon the Church by her enemies.[3]

The actions deemed necessary by Pius's religious perspective represented a grave political liability which alienated the few friends that Rome still possessed. It would therefore not be an exaggeration to say that the Papal State was indirectly but clearly sacrificed to the reaction provoked first by the Pope's refusal to accommodate himself to the national spirit and later the reaction unleashed by the Syllabus of Errors and the proclamation of infallibility. Thus the cause to which Cardinal Antonelli had dedicated himself without interruption from 1848 to his death in 1876 was in many ways a lost one, given the mentality of Pius—one of the least political of Popes in the modern period—and his determination to have religious preoccupations always prevail over diplomatic ones. Given these circumstances, no other secretary of state in the place of Antonelli could have avoided the inevitable and saved the temporal power.[4]

It has long been assumed that Pius commenced his career as a liberal and ended it as a reactionary. This generalization is inaccurate because Pius was never really one or the other. In fact, even in his "reformist" period, he favored administrative rather than political changes. Not adverse to improving the material position of his people, from the first he was more concerned about the welfare of their souls. Furthermore, he wished to reform the state to assure the continuation of the temporal power which he considered vital to the exercise of the spiritual power.[5] Pius was initially willing to tolerate liberalism and even nationalism as long as they did not infringe upon the position of the Church or the papacy's spiritual authority. As the head of a universal institution he could not sanction the nationalism of Italian patriots, even though he personally shared many of their sentiments. "Jesus died for all nations, without distinction," he later explained to a group of American women, "making all the beneficiaries of his suffering."[6]

The experience of 1848 was crucial because the adherents of liberalism and nationalism insisted that the Pope assume leadership in the war against Austria and the unification of the Italian peninsula, steps Pius could not support, for they endangered the Church's religious mission. His refusal to follow their scenario led to revolution, exile, and the restoration which nationalists relentlessly attacked because the continued existence of the Papal State contradicted the vision they had for Italy. The eventual triumph of the principle of nationalism at the expense of the States of the Church led Pius to brand the *Risorgimento* a moral, civil, and religious oppression.[7]

Following the loss of Rome Pius reflected on the events of the beginning of his pontificate. Initially the revolution was timid and obsequious and deceived many, including himself, although Pius did not directly admit the latter. As Pope he made all the concessions that it was permissible to accord, and these were followed by enthusiastic applause which served as the pretext for more and broader concessions. The cycle came to an end, Pius acknowledged, when it was demanded that he play the part of warrior and aggressor, which he was unwilling and unable to do. Then he was forced to withdraw from his state by barbarous threats, which in his own words, were quickly translated into action.[8]

Certainly Pius loved Italy and was not immune to the allure of an Italian state but not if this meant the abolition of the temporal power of the Popes, which had been in existence for more than a millennium, or the evolution of Italy from an aggregate of states organized along Christian principles to a unitary state based on liberal ones. Perhaps he best expressed his position during an audience granted to representatives of various Italian cities. During his talk to them, Pius denied that his benediction of Italy of some twenty-four years ago had been turned into a condemnation. The Pope stressed that he was not sorry he blessed Italy and blessed her still, but he could not bless the corrupters, the usurpers, and the enemies of religion.[9]

Count Cavour understood that Pio Nono was moved by profound religious convictions and would relent on the question of Rome and the loss of his territory only if he were convinced that he could do so without violating his conscience and the duties of his sacred ministry. The greatest affliction that it was God's will to let him endure, Pius wrote Vittorio Emanuele, did not stem from the ingratitude or bad faith of certain men, but rather from the offenses made against God and his Church.[10] To serve the Church was his only true ambition and he acted first and foremost as priest and Pope and only secondarily as prince. He was not prepared to accept the separation of Church and State because he considered it a deception and was firmly convinced that the attempt on the part of liberal Catholics to incorporate into the Church modern, secular ideas would undermine its spiritual vitality.

Pius's principal aim was to strengthen Catholic ideology and safeguard the integrity of the pontifical magistracy which he believed to be threatened by the revisionist, liberal, and heretical currents that had become diffused in Europe from 1830 onward.[11] He believed that he was held responsible before God and the Church he served for the most strenuous defense of Christian values, which he considered to be threatened by impiety, laicism, and the rationalism of the age. He deplored the rise of incredulity, which he saw emerge in the most eminent circles, where there was an attempt to believe in nothing that could not be explained by human reason. In response to their rationalism Pius cried out that there was a God, there was a God![12]

Imbued with a profound native faith and certain of divine assistance in his crusade, Pius believed in the ultimate triumph of his cause because it was the cause of the Church, religion and God. Small wonder that he was prepared to resist to the end on its behalf and openly and severely condemned whatever and whomever he considered to be in error, regardless or rank, power, or popularity. After having despoiled the Church there were those, Pius observed, who wanted to silence him as well, but he added that this would never happen. Truth and justice, outraged and offended, screamed in his conscience, and he could not but let the people know.[13]

When Pius was constrained to declare his *non possumus*, he defended the scepter because he feared that, without it, one could not sustain the cross in a society so increasingly alien and adverse to it. It was never the desire for personal sovereignty or thirst for power that motivated his action. Rather he was moved by the conviction that sovereignty was indispensable for the free and independent exercise of his spiritual power, and he continued to repeat this even after his sovereignty had been totally lost.[14]

The liberal demand for popular sovereignty and the omnipotence of parliament was bound to conflict with the Pope's assertion that he was God's representative on earth and had to control the temporal power in order to freely exercise his spiritual authority. The Church could not exist simply as an appendage to the state; Pius insisted that it had to instruct, direct, and govern the Christian world.[15] Between Pius's traditionalism and the liberal parliamentary notions there was little room for compromise and none was to be achieved until half a century later. Cardinal John Henry Newman, writing after the Pope's death, observed that he was a controversial figure who was hailed by some and condemned by others. "He claimed, he exercised, larger powers than any other Pope ever did," Newman explained, adding, "He committed himself to ecclesiastical acts bolder than those of any other Pope."[16] Unquestionably Pius had a far broader notion of papal authority than many of his contemporaries, both lay and ecclesiastic,[17] and his will prevailed. Under his inspiration the authority of the Church was further centralized in Rome and vigorously ranged itself against the contemporary political currents.

Those who expected that the collapse of the papacy would follow the death of the Pope were mistaken, in part because of the efforts of Pius. He finally understood that it was no longer possible to preserve an international Catholic order upon the forces of the various states and governments and found it increasingly necessary to rely upon the faithful.[18] Observing that the various governments of the world were to a greater or lesser degree "infected by the false principles of the revolution," Pius perforce sought support elsewhere. Above all he relied upon God. However, he also recognized that the faithful Catholic populations of the world through their contributions had assured the Church a degree of financial independence and enabled it to reject the monies offered by the Italian Kingdom. The Pope, who had earlier resented Franz Josef's request for a revision of the concordat, now saw this as the secret design of providence to free the Church from the ties which men had imposed upon it.[19]

When Pius was disillusioned by the diplomatic maneuvers of Austria, France, Germany, and even Spain, and abandoned by their governments, who were not prepared to sacrifice national for religious interests, he counted upon the Catholic masses of Europe and the New World. Thus, though the revolution had done much harm, as he never tired of saying, Pius acknowledged that one almost had to thank God for it, because it provided the occasion for thousands of Italians and foreigners to demonstrate their filial affection to the Holy See.[20]

As a result of his long life and reign and his conception of Catholic order, Pius left a Church that was more powerful and vigorous than he found it. One consequence of his crusade to spread the Gospel was the flowering of the missionary activity of the Church in the latter half of the nineteenth century. Another was the increased emphasis on the universality of the Church attested to by the erection of new Apostolic Vicariates, Prefectures and Delegations. Pius, more than any other contemporary Pope, shaped the modern papacy and compelled acceptance of his conception of the office, rendering it perhaps the strongest it had been since the Middle Ages. "The Roman Pontiff, in conformity with the office which God has entrusted to him to guide and govern the universal Church of Christ, must not only zealously watch over the observance of the laws, but also make known their true and Catholic meaning...," read the *Romanus Pontifex* of August 28, 1873, "lest they be the object of differing interpretations and the unity of ecclesiastical discipline be destroyed, to the great detriment of the government of the Church."[21]

Pius's centralization and quest for dogmatic unity provided compensation of sorts for the loss of the temporal power. Whether one approves of his design or not, one must acknowledge that Pius served as the chief architect of the modern Church prior to John XXIII and the Second Vatican Council.

Notes and References

Introduction

1. Count C. A. de Goddes de Liancourt and James A. Manning, *Pius the Ninth: The First Year of His Pontificate* (London, 1848), II, 6.
2. *Proceedings of the Public Demonstration of Sympathy with Pope Pius IX., and with Italy, in the City of New York, on Monday, November 29, A.D. 1847* (New York, 1847), *passim*.
3. Palmerston's instructions to the Earl of Minto, September 18, 1847, *British and Foreign State Papers*, XXXVI (1847-48), 1271.
4. Alexandre De Saint-Albin, *Pie IX* (Paris, 1860), p. 47.
5. *Posthumous Papers of Jessie White Mario: The Birth of Modern Italy*, ed. Duke Litta-Visconti-Arese (New York, 1909), p. 120.
6. Metternich to Apponyi, October 7, 1847 in *Mémoires, Documents et Écrits Divers laisses par le Prince de Metternich*, ed. M. A. Klinkowstroem (1883), VII, 342-343.
7. Giacomo Martina, *Pio IX (1846-1850)* (Rome, 1974), p. 3; Mario Borsa, *Carlo Cattaneo* (Cernusco sul Naviglio, 1945), p. 217.

Chapter One

1. Angelo Menucci, "La riapetura del museo 'Pio IX' in vista delle celebrazioni di Senigallia," *Pio IX. Studi e ricerche sulla vita della Chiesa dal Settecento ad oggi*, VI (January-April 1977), 117.
2. Pius to the Patricians and Nobility of Rome, June 17, 1871, Pasquale De Franciscis, *Discorsi del Sommo Pontefice Pio IX Pronunziati in Vaticano ai Fedeli di Roma e dell' Orbe dal principio della sua prigionia fino al presente* (Rome, 1872), I, 127.
3. For a series of letters sent from 1792 to 1820 to Mons. Paplino Mastai, brother of Count Girolamo, see *Fondo Particolare Pio IX, cassetta* II, *Archivio Segreto del Vaticano*.
4. Alberto Serafini, *Pio Nono. Giovanni Maria Mastai Ferretti dalla giovinezza alla morte nei suoi scritti e discorsi editi e inediti (1792-1846)* (Vatican City, 1958), p. 58.
5. Pierre Fernessole, *Pie IX Pape* (Paris, 1960), I, 15.
6. Mastai's Speech of February 2, 1833 in the Cathedral of Senigallia. *Archivio Segreto del Vaticano*, hereafter referred to as *ASV, Fondo Particolare Pio IX, cassetta* IX, busta 2, n. 75.

7. Serafini, p. 7.
8. The Correspondence of Cardinals Pacca and Gabrieli on Pope's visit to France for coronation, *ASV, Archivio Particolare Pio IX, Ogetti Vari*, n. 909, *fascicolo* 3.
9. Serafini, pp. 10-12, 168.
10. *ASV, Archivio Particolare Pio IX, Ogetti Vari*, n. 909, f. 23.
11. On the expulsion from Rome of all the English and enemies of France requested by Napoleon, *ASV, Ogetti Vari*, n. 909, f. 6.
12. Cardinal Gabrielli to Cardinal Pacca, May 14, 1808, *ASV, Archivio Particolare Pio IX, Ogetti Vari*, n. 909., f. 1.
13. *ASV, Archivio Particolare Pio IX, Ogetti Vari*, n. 909, f. 16.
14. Serafini, pp. 29-30.
15. Pius IX to the inhabitants of the Trastevere, October 13, 1872, De Franciscis, *Discorsi del Sommo Pontefice Pio IX*, II, 88.
16. Serafini, pp. 18, 25.
17. *Ibid.*, p. 172.
18. Paolo dalla Torre (ed.), *Pio IX e Vittorio Emanuele II. Dal loro carteggio private negli anni del Dilaceramento (1865-1878)* (Città di Castelli, 1972), p. 23.
19. Serafini, p. 175.
20. One of Mastai's brothers to Giovanni Maria, April 30, 1818, *ASV, Fondo Particolare Pio IX, cassetta* II.
21. *ASV, Fondo Particolare Pio IX, cassetta* IX, *busta* 1, f. 2.
22. "Celebrando il primo incruento sacrifizio nella chiesa di S. Anna di Falegnami L'Illmo Signor Canonico Giammaria de' Conti Masti-Ferretti di Senigallia," *ASV, Fondo Particolare Pio IX, cassetta* II.
23. Antonio Monti, *Pio IX nel Risorgimento Italiano con documenti inediti* (Bari, 1928), p. 23; Serafini, I, 182.
24. Serafini, p. 180.
25. *ASV, Fondo Particolare Pio IX, cassetta* IX, b. 3.
26. "Breve relazione del viaggio fatto al Chili dal Canonico Giovanni Maria Mastai-Ferretti di Sinigaglia," *Memorie. Viaggio al Chile, Biblioteca Apostolica Vaticana Latina*, n. 10190, *sala studio manoscritti*, p. 25.
27. Giulio Andreotti, *La sciarada di Papa Mastai* (Milan, 1967), p. 17.
28. *Memorie. Viaggio al Chile*, pp. 29-48.
29. *Ibid.*, p. 61.
30. Serafini, p. 307.
31. *Ibid.*, p. 290.
32. *Memorie. Viaggio al Chile*, pp. 255-56.
33. *Ibid.*, p. 334.
34. Serafini, pp. 402-403.
35. Filippo Pregno to Mastai, August 25, 1825, *ASV, Fondo Particolare Pio IX, cassetta* V, b. 1.
36. Information on the Patients in the Apostolic Hospital presided over by G. Maria Mastai 1826, *ASV, Fondo Particolare Pio IX, cassetta* VI.

37. Letters directed to G. M. Mastai while president of San Michele, *ASV, Fondo Particolare Pio IX, cassetta* V, b. 2.
38. *ASV, Fondo Particolare Pio IX, cassetta* VI.
39. Sermon to priests of San Michele, April 3, 1826, *ASV, Fondo Particolare Pio IX, cassetta* IX, b. 3, n. 25.

Chapter Two

1. Monti, *Pio IX nel Risorgimento Italiano con documenti inediti*, p. 34.
2. Outlines of Mastai's speeches, *ASV, Fondo Particolare Pio IX, cassetta* X, busta 1, *fascicoli* 1-75.
3. List of books belonging to G. M. Mastai, Archbishop of Spoleto, *ASV, Fondo Particolare Pio IX, cassetta* V, b. 1.
4. Expenses of the household of the Archbishop of Spoleto, *ASV, Fondo Particolare Pio IX, cassetta* VII.
5. Letters of Gaetano Mastai to Giovanni Maria on the administration of the affairs of Senigallia, *ASV, Fondo Particolare Pio IX, cassetta* XIII, b. 1.
6. Speech of December 25, 1828, *ASV, Fondo Particolare Pio IX, cassetta* IX, b. 1, f. 43.
7. *ASV, Fondo Particolare Pio IX, cassetta* V, b. 4.
8. Giovanni Maioli (ed.), *Pio IX da Vescovo a pontifice. Lettere al Card. Luigi Amat, Agosto 1839-Luglio 1848* (Modena, 1943), p. 7.
9. *Ibid.*, Edgar Quinet, *La questione romaine devant l'histoire, 1848-1867* (Paris, 1868), p. 16.
10. Expenses incurred to assist the inhabitants of the dioceses of Spoleto cope with the ravages of the earthquake, *ASV, Fondo Particolare Pio IX, cassetta* VII.
11. Giuseppe Chiaretti, "Una lettera di protesta per il trasferimento da Spoleto di Mons. Mastai Ferretti," *Pio IX*, VI (January-April 1977), 109-11.
12. Serafini, *Pio Nono*, pp. 597-98.
13. *ASV, Fondo Particolare Pio IX, cassetta* IX, b. 2, n. 76.
14. *ASV, Fondo Particolare Pio IX, cassetta* IX, bb. 1-2.
15. Giuseppe Pasolini, *Memorie 1815-1876*, ed. Pietro Desiderio Pasolini (3rd. ed.; Turin, 1887), p. 52.
16. *ASV, Fondo Particolare Pio IX, cassetta* XI.
17. Maioli, p. 13.
18. *Ibid.*, pp. 44-45.
19. *Ibid.*, p. 26.
20. *ASV, Fondo Particolare Pio IX, cassetta* X, b. 2.
21. G. Maria Mastai to Gregory XVI, December 16[?] 1840, *ASV, Fondo Particolare Pio IX, cassetta* IX, b. 2, f. 101.
22. Mastai's testimonial will made in Imola in 1841 and amended thereafter, *ASV, Archivio Particolare Pio IX, Ogetti Vari*, #422.
23. Monti, p. 43.
24. Angelo Filipuzzi, *Pio IX e la politica austriaca in Italia dal 1815 al*

1848 [*nella relazione di Riccardo Weiss di Starkenfels*] (Florence, 1958), pp. 100, 108-109.

25. Cavour to William Brockedon, April 16, 1832, *Lettere edite ed inedite di Camillo Cavour*, ed. Luigi Chiala (Turin, 1883-1887), V, 21-22; Quinet, p. 16.

26. Filipuzzi, p. 125.

27. Giuseppe Leti, *Roma e lo Stato Pontificio dal 1849 al 1870. Note di storia politica* (Ascoli Picenso, 1911), I, 12.

28. Maioli, pp. 16, 46.

29. Carlo Ghisalberti, "Il Consiglio di Stato di Pio IX," *Studi Romani*, II (1954), 58; "Pensieri relativi alla Amministrazione pubblica dello Stato Pontificio," in Serafini, pp. 1397-1406.

30. Maioli, p. 101.

31. *Ibid.*, p. 42.

32. Pasolini, p. 57.

33. Maioli, p. 108.

34. Metternich to Count Lutzow, June 9, 1846, *Mémoires, Documents et Ecrits Divers laisses par le Prince de Metternich*, VII, 246.

35. Expenses sustained by G. M. Mastai in trip from Imola to Rome, *ASV, Fondo Particolare Pio IX, cassetta* XXX, b. 2, f. 19.

36. *ASV, Archivio Particolare Pio IX, Ogetti Vari*, #419.

37. Giacomo Martina, *Pio IX (1846-1850)* (Rome, 1974), pp. 88-89.

38. Filipuzzi, p. 131; Metternich, *Mémoires*, VII, 248.

39. Count C. A. de Goddes de Liancourt and James A. Manning, *Pius the Ninth or the First Year of his Pontificate* (London, 1847), I, 123.

40. Bernard O'Reilly, *A Life of Pius IX Down to the Episcopal Jubilee of 1877* (8th ed.; New York, 1878), p. 82.

Chapter Three

1. Pius to the representatives of the first Italian Catholic Congress, June 21, 1874, De Franciscis, III, 270.

2. Filipuzzi, *Pio IX e la politica austriaca in Italia dal 1815 al 1848*, p. 133; Martina, *Pio IX (1846-1850)*, p. 94; Alexandre de Saint-Albin, *Pie IX* (Paris, 1860), p. 27; Andreotti, *La sciarada di Papa Mastai*, p. 37.

3. Dalla Torre, *Pio IX e Vittorio Emanuele II*, p. 20.

4. "Pubbliche beneficenze dispensate dalla Santità di nostro Signore alla occasione di sua solenne coronazione," June 20, 1846, *Atti del Sommo Pontefice Pio IX Felicemente Regnante. Parte seconda che comprende I motu proprii, chirografi editti, notifacazioni ec. per lo stato pontificio* (Rome, 1857), I, 3-4.

5. Report of Monsignor Corboli Bussi to Pope Pius on the first session of the Congregation of State, July 1, 1846, *AVS, Archivio Particolare Pio IX, Stato Pontificio*, #1.

6. Fernessole, I, 131, 151, Domenico Demarco, *Una rivoluzione sociale. La Repubblica Romana del 1849* (Naples, 1944), p. 14.

7. Dalla Torre, p. 27; R. De Cesare, *The Last Days of Papal Rome*, trans. Helen Zimmern (London, 1909), p. 117.

8. *Epistolario di Luigi Carlo Farini*, ed. Luigi Rava (Bologna, 1911), I, 471.

9. Great Britain, *British and Foreign State Papers*, XXXVI (1847-48), 1195.

10. Report of Monsignor Corboli Bussi to Pope Pius on the first session of the Congregation of State, July 1, 1846, *ASV, Archivio Particolare Pio IX, Stato Pontificio*, #1.

11. Report of Monsignor Corboli Bussi to Pope Pius on the second session of the Congregation of State, July 8, 1846, *ASV, Archivio Particolare Pio IX, Stato Pontificio* #2.

12. Maiolo, p. 56.

13. "Amnistia accordata dalla Santità di nostro Signore Pio IX nella Sua esaltazione al Pontificato," July 16, 1848, *Atti del Sommo Pontefice Pio IX*, I, 4-6; Great Britain, *British and Foreign State Papers* XXXVI (1847-48), 1197-98. Also see the List of individuals included within the terms of the amnesty of July 16, 1846 and those excluded from the same. *Archivio di Stato di Roma, Miscellanea di Carte Politiche o Riservate*, 1846, *busta* 154, *fascicolo* 1.

14. *Epistolario di Luigi Carlo Farini*, I, 507.

15. Dispatch of Apostolic Nuncio in Vienna to the Papal Secretary of State transmitting Metternich's report on Central Italy, *ASV, Archivio Particolare Pio IX, Ogetti Vari*, #412; Metternich, *Mémoires*, VII, 255.

16. Report of Monsignor Corboli Bussi to Pope Pius IX on the fifth session of the Congregation of State, September 16, 1846, *ASV, Archivio Particolare Pio IX, Stato Pontificio*, #5.

17. "Disposizioni riguardanti le esecuzione delle strade ferrate nello Stato pontificio," *Atti del Sommo Pontefice Pio IX*, I, 15; Filipuzzi, pp. 134-135.

18. Benedetto Filippani's day by day breakdown of Pope's food and household expenses for 1846, *ASV, Fondo Particolare Pio IX, cassetta* XXX.

19. "Rapporto a Sua Santità per l'Udienza del 30 Settembre 1846," *Archivio di Stato di Roma, Fondo Famiglia Antonelli, busta* 3; *United States Ministers to the Papal States: Instructions and Despatches 1848-1868*, ed. Leo Francis Stock (Washington, D.C., 1933), I, xxii.

20. "Disposizione tendente a rimuovere l'ozio come ordinaria sorgente di deletti che accadono in alcune provincie dello Stato, ed a procciare una utile e religiosa educazione nella gioventù," *Atti del Sommo Pontefice Pio IX*, I, 8-10.

21. Filippo Perfetti, *Ricordi di Roma* (Florence, 1861), p. 49; Carlo Minnocci, *Pietro Sterbini e La Rivoluzione Romana* (Rome, 1967), p. 24.

22. Romolo Quazza, *Pio IX e Massimo D'Azeglio nelle vicende romane*

del 1847. Dalle questione interne al problema nazionale (Modena, 1954), I, 14.
23. *ASV, Segreteria di Stato Esteri*, 1870, rubrica 246, *fascicolo* 3.
24. Martina, *Pio IX*, pp. 113-14; Metternich, *Mémoires*, VII, 256.
25. Pius to Carlo Alberto, September 7, 1846, *ASV, Archivio Particolare Pio IX, Sardegna, Sovrani*; Maiolo, p. 50.
26. Monti, p. 248.
27. Martina, pp. 109-10.
28. "S'insinua moderazione nelle pubbliche dimostrazioni," *Atti del Sommo Pontefice Pio IX*, I, 7; "Desideri di Sua Santità che cessino nelle manifestazioni di gioja per la sua esaltazione al Trono, e che le quote raccolte per le medesime s'impieghino in qualche lavoro di pubblica utilità," *Atti del Sommo Pontefice Pio IX*, I, 12-13.
29. Ugo Morinelli, *Pio IX e Ciceruacchio* (Rome, 1937), p. 15.
30. Marco Minghetti, *Miei Ricordi* (3rd ed.; Turin, 1888), I, 214.
31. Maiolo, p. 49; Fernessole, I, 150.
32. *Acta Pio IX. Pontificis Maximi. Pars prima acta exhibens quae ad Ecclesiam universam spectant*, Vol. I (1846-1854) (Rome, 1855), pp. 6-24. *Papal Teachings: The Church* (Boston, 1962), pp. 143-144.
33. Martina, p. 121.
34. Quazza, I, 171.
35. Viscount D'Arlincourt, *L'Italia rossa or storia delle rivoluzione dall' elezione di Pio IX al di lui ritorno in sua capitale* (Florence, 1851), p. 51; Minnocci, p. 26.
36. Joseph Jay Deiss, *The Roman Years of Margaret Fuller* (New York, 1969), p. 51.
37. Martina, p. 118.
38. Luigi Carlo Farini, *Lo Stato Romano dall'anno 1815 al 1850* (2nd ed.; Felice Le Monnier, 1853), I, 277.
39. "Disposizioni sulla revisione delle opere da pubblicarsi colla stampa," *Atti del Sommo Pontefice Pio IX*, I, 44.
40. Maiolo, p. 111.
41. Guglielmo Gajani, *The Roman Exile* (Boston, 1856), p. 351.
42. Luigi Rodelli, *La Repubblica Romana del 1849* (Pisa, 1955), p. 41.

Chapter Four

1. Quazza, *Pio IX e Massimo D'Azeglio nelle vicende romane del 1847*, I, 28, 61.
2. "Si commette ai Delegati delle provincie di proporre due o tre sogetti per isceglierne uno di ciascuna provincia ed adoprarlo nel coadjuvare la pubblica amministrazione e nel migliore ordinamento dei consigli comunali," *Atti del Sommo Pontefice Pio IX*, I, 47-48.
3. *Archivio di Stato di Roma, Consulta di Stato, busta* 1.
4. Deiss, *The Roman Years of Margaret Fuller*, p. 52.

5. "Motu-proprio della Santità di Nostro Signore concernente la istituzione del Consiglio di Ministri," *Atti del Sommo Pontefice Pio IX*, I, 52-54.
6. Émile Ollivier, *L'Empire Liberal. Études, Recits, Souvenirs* (Paris, 1895), I, 452; Metternich, *Mémoires*, VII, 412.
7. Monsignor Corboli Bussi to Pius IX, August 30, 1847, *ASV, Archivio Particolare Pio IX, Stato Pontificio*.
8. Carlo Alberto to Pius IX, December 19, 1847, *ASV, Archivio Particolare Pio IX, Sardegna, Sovrani*.
9. Quazza, I, 164-68.
10. "Desiderio di Sua Santità che sia posto termine alle insolite popolari riunioni e straordinarie manifestazioni per qualsivoglia occasione e motivo," *Atti del Sommo Pontefice Pio IX*, I, 68.
11. Quazza, I, 174.
12. Leo Wollemborg, "Lo Statuto Pontificio nel quadro costituzionale del 1848," *Rassegna Storica del Risorgimento*, anno XXII (October 1935), II, 545; Metternich, *Mémoires*, VII, 411.
13. Martina, *Pio IX (1846-1850)*, p. 141; Quazza, II, 3-5.
14. "Regolamento per la Guardia Civica nello Stato Pontificio," *Atti del Sommo Pontefice Pio IX*, I, 77-80.
15. Martina, p. 143.
16. Quazza, II, 15; Metternich, *Mémoires*, VII, 413-414.
17. Great Britain, *British and Foreign State Papers*, XXXVI (1847-48), 1226.
18. Pius to Emperor Ferdinand, September 12, 1847; Pius to Empress Maria Anna, September 12, 1847, *ASV, Archivio Particolare Pio IX, Austria, Sovrani*, nn. 1-2.
19. "Disposizioni per procedere contro gli autori dei clamori suscitatisi in Roma nelle sere dei 7 ed 8 del corrente mese di Settembre," *Atti del Sommo Pontefice Pio IX*, I, 22.
20. Great Britain, *British and Foreign State Papers*, XXXVI (1847-48), 1228-1331.
21. *Ibid.*, 1230; Filipuzzi, *Pio IX e la politica Austriaca in Italia dal 1815 al 1848*, p. 203; Metternich, *Mémoires*, VII, 414-415.
22. Great Britain, *British and Foreign State Papers*, XXXVI (1847-48), 1234.
23. Martina, p. 169.
24. Lillian Parker Wallace, "Pius IX and Lord Palmerston, 1846-1849," *Power, Public Opinion and Diplomacy* by L. P. Wallace and William C. Askew (Durham, N.C., 1959), p. 21.
25. "Motu proprio della Santità di Nostro Signore Papa Pio IX sulla organizzazione del Consiglio e Senato di Roma," *Atti del Sommo Pontefice Pio IX*, I, 124-29.
26. Martina, p. 157; Corboli Bussi to Pius, October 9, 1847, *ASV, Archivio Particolare Pio IX, Stato Pontificio*.

27. Corboli Bussi to Pius, October 17, 1847, *ASV, Archivio Particolare Pio IX, Stato Pontificio.*
28. Filipuzzi, pp. 168-69; Corboli Bussi to Pius, November 14, 1847, *ASV, Archivio Particolare Pio IX, Stato Pontificio.*
29. "Motu-proprio della Santità di Nostro Signore sulla Consulta di Stato," *Atti del Sommo Pontefice Pio IX,* I, 150-65.
30. *Archivio di Stato di Roma, Consulta di Stato, busta* 2, *fascicoli* 30-58; Carlo Ghisalberti, "Il Consiglio di Stato di Pio IX," *Studi Romani, anno* II (1954), 62.
31. Maiolo, p. 114.
32. Secretary of State to Giacomo Antonelli, November 3, 1847, *Archivio di Stato di Roma, Consulta di Stato,* b. 1, f. 5.
33. Great Britain, *British and Foreign State Papers,* XXXVI (1847-48), 1348.
34. Arturo De Grandeffe, *Pio IX e L'Italia* (Turin, 1859), p. 37.
35. Minghetti, *Ricordi,* I, 297-98.
36. Martina, pp. 194-95.
37. *Posthumous Papers of Jessie White Mario: The Birth of Modern Italy,* edited with an introduction by Duke Letta-Visconti-Arese (New York, 1909), p. 127.
38. Deiss, *The Roman Years of Margaret Fuller,* p. 101.
39. "Motu-proprio della Santità di Nostro Signore sul Consiglio dei Ministri," *Atti del Sommo Pontefice Pio IX,* I, 204-205.

Chapter Five

1. Monti, *Pio IX nel Risorgimento Italiano con Documenti Inediti,* p. 79.
2. Pius to Carlo Alberto, January 2, 1848, *ASV, Archivio Particolare Pio IX, Sardegna, Sovrani.*
3. Morinelli, *Pio IX e Ciceruacchio,* pp. 20-21.
4. Minghetti, *Miei Ricordi,* I, 327.
5. Martina, *Pio IX (1846-1850),* pp. 142-43.
6. Pius to Cardinal Amat, February 7, 1848, in Maiolo, *Pio IX da Vescovo a Pontefice,* p. 116.
7. De Grandeffe, *Pio IX e L'Italia,* p. 44; Pasolini, *Memorie, 1815-1876,* p. 77; Filipuzzi, *Pio IX e la politica austriaca in Italia dal 1815 al 1848,* pp. 235-37.
8. Wollemborg, *Rassegna Storica del Risorgimento,* anno XXII (October 1935), II, 557.
9. Monti, p. 89.
10. Martina, pp. 209-212; Gajani, p. 377.
11. Pasolini, *Memorie,* p. 83; Minnocci, *Pietro Sterbini e la Rivoluzione Romana,* p. 58.
12. Giuseppe Massari, *Diario dalle cento voci* (Bologna: Cappelli, 1959), p. 63.

13. Cardinal Bofondi to Giacomo Antonelli, *Archivio di Stato di Roma, Fondo Famiglia Antonelli*, b. 2, f. 1.
14. Martina, p. 229.
15. "Statuto fondamentale del governo temporale degli Stati di S. Chiesa," *Atti del Sommo Pontefice Pio IX*, I, 223-24.
16. *Ibid.*, I, 232.
17. *Ibid.*, I, 223-24; Luigi Rodelli, *La Repubblica Romana del 1849* (Pisa, 1955), pp. 45-46.
18. *Posthumous Papers of Jessie White Mario*, p. 148.
19. Martina, p. 199.
20. Morinelli, p. 24.
21. Martina, p. 230.
22. Great Britain, *British and Foreign State Papers*, XXXVII (1848-49), 981.
23. Corboli Bussi to Giacomo Antonelli, April 9, 1848, *Archivio di Stato di Roma, Fondo Famiglia Antonelli, busta* 1; Pier Silverio Leicht, "Memorie di Michele Leicht," *Rassegna Storica del Risorgimento*, anno XXII (July 1935), II, 84.
24. Farini, *Lo Stato Romano dall' anno 1815 al 1850*, II, 84.
25. Pietro Palazzini, "Spiritualità di Pio IX il Papa della Croce," *Pio IX*, VI (January-April 1977), 11; Metternich, *Mémoires*, VII, 556.
26. Great Britain, *Hansard's Parliamentary Debates*, XCII (1848), 144-45.
27. G. F. Berkeley and J. Berkeley, *Italy in the Making: January 1st 1848 to November 16, 1848* (Cambridge, England, 1940), III, 158-59.
28. Martina, p. 237.
29. Minghetti, I, 367.
30. Carlo Alberto to Pius, April 18, 1848, *ASV, Archivio Particolare Pio IX, Sardegna, Sovrani*, #11.
31. Maiolo, p. 117.
32. Pius to Corboli Bussi, April 27, 1848, *ASV, Archivio Particolare Pio IX, Stato Pontificio*.
33. Great Britain, *British and Foreign State Papers*, XXXVII (1848-49), 1065. Papal Teachings: The Church (Boston, 1962), p. 150.
34. Martina, p. 244.
35. Farini to Pius, May 7, 1848, *ASV, Archivio Particolare Pio IX, Stato Pontificio*.
36. Cardinal Amat to Pius IX, May 5, 1848, *ASV, Archivio Particolare Pio IX, Stato Pontificio*.
37. Pasolini, *Memorie*, pp. 102-103; R. Aubert, *Le pontificat de Pie IX (1846-1878)* (Paris, 1952), p. 31.
38. Frank J. Coppa, "Cardinal Antonelli, the Papal States and the Counter-Risorgimento," *The Journal of Church and State*, XVI (Autumn 1974), 460-61.

Chapter Six

1. Luigi Settembrini, *Ricordanze della mia vita* (Milan, 1961), p. 173.
2. Martina, *Pio IX (1846-1850)*, p. 200.
3. Corboli Bussi to Pius, April 27, 1848, *ASV, Archivio Particolare Pio IX, Stato Pontificio*, #33.
4. Martina, p. 265.
5. Maiolo, p. 118.
6. *Epistolario di Luigi Carlo Farini*, II, 215.
7. *ASV, Archivio Particolare Pio IX, Ogetti Vari*, n. 415.
8. Martina, p. 248.
9. Maiolo, p. 118.
10. *Il Risorgimento*, July 17, 1848; De Grandeffe, *Pio IX e L'Italia*, p. 51.
11. Pius to Carlo Alberto, August 1, 1848, *ASV, Archivio Particolare Pio IX, Sardegna, Sovrani*.
12. Pius to General Cavaignac, August 10, 1848, *ASV, Archivio Particolare Pio IX, Francia, Particolari*, #3.
13. Aubert, *Le pontificat de Pie IX*, p. 33; Deiss, *The Roman Years of Margaret Fuller*, p. 169.
14. Gianfranco Radice, *Pio IX e Antonio Rosmini* (Città del Vaticano, 1974), p. 65; *Il Contemporaneo*, November 12, 1848.
15. De Saint-Albin, *Pie IX*, p. 239.
16. Morinelli, *Pio IX e Ciceruacchio*, p. 33.
17. *Il Risorgimento*, November 21, 1848.
18. *Archivio di Stato di Roma, Miscellanea di Carte Politiche o Riservate*, November 16, 1848, *busta* 124, *fascicolo* 4345.
19. Martina, p. 291.
20. *Archivio di Stato di Roma, Miscellanea di Carte Politiche o Riservate, busta* 124, f. 4345; *Il Risorgimento*, November 22, 1848.
21. *ASV, Archivio Particolare Pio IX, Ogetti Vari*, n. 515.
22. *Ibid.*
23. Narration of events of November 16, 1848, and Considerations Leading Pius to Abandon Rome, *ASV, Archivio Particolare Pio IX; Stato Pontificio*, #19.
24. Filippo to Angelo Antonelli, November 19, 1848, *Archivio di Stato di Roma, Fondo Famiglia Antonelli*, b. 6, f. 3.
25. "Allontamamento temporaneo del S. Padre dai suoi Stati, protesta per le violenze usate e creazione di una commissione governativa," *Atti del Sommo Pontefice Pio IX*, I, 252.
26. *ASV, Fondo Particolare Pio IX, cassetta* n. 30.
27. "Proroga dell' annuale sessione dell' alto Consiglio e del Consiglio dei Deputati, *Atti del Sommo Pontefice Pio IX*, I, 255-57.
28. Pius to Corboli Bussi, December 28, 1848, *ASV, Archivio Particolare Pio IX, Stato Pontificio*.

29. *ASV, Segreteria di Stato Esteri, Corrispondenza di Gaeta e Portici 1848-50, Rubrica* 247, *sotto fascicoli* 85-86.
30. Carlo Alberto to Pius, December 17, 1848, *ASV, Archivio Particolare Pio IX, Sardegna, Sovrani.*
31. Letter of Pius, December 23, 1848, *Archivio di Stato di Roma, Fondo Famiglia Antonelli,* b. 2, f. 22; *Il Risorgimento,* December 9, 1848; *L'Opinione,* December 21, 1848.
32. Pius to Carlo Alberto, December 28, 1848, *ASV, Archivio Particolare Pio IX, Sardegna, Sovrani,* #18.
33. "Si deplorara l'ulteriore atto di smascherata fellonia nella convocazione di una sedicente Assemblea generale nazionale dello stato romano, e si ricorda l'incorso della scomunica," *Atti del Sommo Pontefice Pio IX,* I, 258-60.
34. Martina, *Pio IX,* pp. 337-38.
35. Radice, *Pio IX e Antonio Rosmini,* p. 78.
36. Carlo Alberto to Pius, December 24, 1848, *ASV, Archivio Particolare Pio IX, Sardegna, Sovrani,* n. 17.
37. Count E. Martina to Antonelli, January 12, 1849, and Papal response, *ASV, Segreteria di Stato Esteri, Corrispondenza da Gaeta e Portici, 1848-50, Rubrica* 267, *sottofascicoli* 4-7.
38. Radice, p. 76.
39. Antonelli to Austrian Foreign Minister, February 9, 1849, *ASV, Segreteria di Stato Esteri, Corrispondenza da Gaeta e Portici, 1848-50, Rubrica* 247, s.f. 13.
40. *ASV, Archivio Particolare Pio IX, Ogetti Vari,* n. 515.
41. *Archivio di Stato di Roma, Repubblica Romana, 1849,* b. 1, f. 3; *Il Risorgimento,* February 15, 1849, n. 352.

Chapter Seven

1. "Protesta fatta in Gaeta da Sua Santità Pio PP. IX contro l'atto del sedicente assemblea costituente romana in data 9 Febbrajo corrente," *Atti del Sommo Pontefice Pio IX,* I, 262-63.
2. Vittorio Emanuele to Pius, March 30, 1849, *ASV, Segreteria di Stato Esteri, Corrispondenza di Gaeta e Portici, Rubrica* 267, *sottofascicolo* 19.
3. Ollivier, *L'Empire Libéral,* II, 220.
4. Great Britain, *Hansard's Parliamentary Debates,* CV (1849), 376.
5. Martina, *Pio IX,* pp. 347-48.
6. The Apostolic Nuncio at Turin to Antonelli, May 21, 1849, *ASV, Segreteria di Stato Esteri, Corrispondenza di Gaeta e Portici, 1848-50, Rubrica* 257, *sotto fascicolo* 55.
7. Emile Bourgeois and E. Cleremont, *Rome et Napoleone III (1849-1870)* (Paris, 1907), pp. 91-93.
8. Massimo D'Azeglio to Cardinal Antonelli, May 14, 1849; Vittorio Emanuele to Pius IX, May 15, 1849, *ASV, Segreteria di Stato Esteri,*

Corrispondenza di Gaeta e Portici, 1848-1850, Rubrica 267, s.f. 50-52; Nicomede Bianchi, *La politica di Massimo D'Azeglio dal 1848 al 1859* (Turin, 1884), pp. 69-70.

9. Massimo D'Azeglio to Antonelli, 1849, *ASV, Segreteria di Stato Esteri, Corrispondenza di Gaeta e Portici, 1848-1850, Rubrica* 267, s.f. 54.

10. Radice, *Pio IX e Antonio Rosmini*, p. 80; Martina, *Pio IX*, pp. 364-65.

11. French Memorandum on Reforms the Pope should concede to his people, July 30, 1849, *ASV, Archivio Particolare Pio IX, Francia, Sovrani*, #24.

12. Pius to Franz Josef, August 2, 1849, *ASV, Archivio Particolare Pio IX, Austria, Sovrani*, #8.

13. Pius to his subjects, July 17, 1849, *Atti del Sommo Pontefice Pio IX*, I, 269-70.

14. Antonelli to the Commission of Cardinals, 1849, *Archivio di Stato di Roma, Fondo Famiglia Antonelli*, b. 1.

15. Cardinals della Genga, Vannicelli and Altieri to Antonelli, August 3, 1849, *ASV, Archivio Particolare Pio IX, Francia, Particolari*, #25.

16. General Oudinot to Pius, August 5, 1849, *ASV, Archivio Particolare Pio IX, Francia, Particolari*, #25.

17. *Atti del Sommo Pontefice Pio IX*, I, 272, 279-80.

18. Martina, pp. 360-61; 381-84.

19. Ollivier, *L'Empire Libéral*, II, 247.

20. *ASV, Segreteria di Stato Esteri, Corrispondenza di Gaeta e Portici, 1849 Rubrica* 242, s.f. 57; Aubert, *Le pontificat de Pie IX*, p. 37.

21. Gregorio Antonelli to brother Filippo at Terracina, September 15, 1849, *Archivio di Stato di Roma, Fondo Famiglia Antonelli*, b. 7, f. 9.

22. Consul General in Marseilles to Apostolic Nuncio in Paris, September 9, 1849, *ASV, Archivio Nunziatura Parigi, 1849*, n. 77, b. 4.

23. General Rostolan to President of the Council of Ministers, September 14, 1849, *ASV, Archivio Particolare Pio IX, Francia, Particolari*, #31.

24. Pius to Louis Napoleon, July 31, 1849, *ASV, Archivio Particolare Pio IX, Francia, Sovrani*, #7.

25. *ASV, Segreteria di Stato Esteri, Corrispondenza di Gaeta e Portici, 1848-1850, Rubrica* 220, f. 2.

26. "Motu-proprio di Sua Santità sulla istituzione del consiglio di Stato e della Consulta di Stato per le Finanze," *Atti del Sommo Pontefice Pio IX*, I, 287-89.

27. Pius to De Corcelles, October 22, 1849, *ASV, Archivio Particolare Pio IX, Francia, Partocolari*, #32.

28. "Notifacazione della Commissione governativa di Stato colla quale si annuncia il perdono accordato da Sua Santità con alcune riserve a coloro che presero parte nella cessata rivoluzione negli Stati Pontifici, *Atti del Sommo Pontefice Pio IX*, I, 293.

29. Micaud to Antonelli, December 31, 1849, *ASV, Segreteria di Stato Esteri, Corrispondenza di Gaeta e Portici, Rubrica* 248, s.f. 133.
30. General Rostolan to Pius, November 14, 1849, *ASV, Archivio Particolare Pio IX, Francia, Sovrani,* #34.
31. Antonelli to Cardinals of the Commission in Rome, December 4, 1849, *ASV, Segreteria di Stato Esteri, Corrispondenza di Gaeta e Portici,* 1849, *Rubrica* 242, s.f. 177.
32. Giacomo Antonelli to brother Gregorio Antonelli, January 3, 1850, *Archivio di Stato di Roma, Busta* 1, n. 247.
33. Martina, *Pio IX*, pp. 409-12.
34. Monsignor Ferrari to Antonelli, August 14, 1849, *ASV, Segreteria di Stato Esteri, Corrispondenza di Gaeta e Portici, 1849, Rubrica* 283, f. 2.
35. *Il Risorgimento,* August 13, 1849.
36. Antonelli to Apostolic Nuncio in Turin, June 8, 1849, *ASV, Segreteria di Stato Esteri, Corrispondenza di Gaeta e Portici, 1848-1850, Rubrica* 257, s.f. 64.
37. Apostolic Nuncio in Turin to Antonelli, September 2, 1849, *ASV, Segreteria di Stato Esteri, Corrispondenza di Gaeta e Portici, Rubrica* 267, s.f. 60-61.
38. Pius to Vittorio Emanuele, November 9, 1849, *ASV, Archivio Particolare Pio IX, Sardegna, Sovrani,* #22.
39. Apostolic Nuncio at Turin to Antonelli, *ASV, Segreteria di Stato Esteri, Corrispondenza di Gaeta e Portici, 1848-1850, Rubrica* 257, s.f. 9.
40. ASV, *Segreteria di Stato Esteri, Corrispondenza di Gaeta e Portici, 1848-1850, Rubrica* 267, s.f. 62-65; Arturo Carlo Jemolo, *Chiesa e Stato in Italia negli ultimi cento anni* (Turin, 1952), p. 145.
41. Antonelli to Apostolic Nuncio in Turin, December 10, 1849, *ASV, Segreteria di Stato Esteri, Corrispondenza di Gaeta e Portici, 1848-1850, Rubrica* 257, s.f. 181-82.
42. Pius to the Bishop of Vercelli, September 4, 1850, *ASV, Archivio Particolare Pio IX, Sardegna, Sovrani,* #31; "Il Ritorno del Cav. Pinelli da Roma," *Il Risorgimento,* October 17, 1850.
43. Raffaele de Cesare, *Roma e lo Stato del Papa* (Milan, 1970), p. 15.
44. *Atti del Sommo Pontefice Pio IX*, I, 594; Deiss, *The Roman Years of Margaret Fuller,* p. 301.
45. Antonelli to Apostolic Nuncio in Paris, April 21, 1850, *ASV, Archivio Nunziatura Parigi,* 1850, n. 78.
46. Allocution to the Consistory, May 20, 1850 in *Papal Teachings: The Church,* p. 152.

Chapter Eight

1. Ernesto Vercesi, *Pio IX* (Milan, 1930), pp. 248-50.
2. "Editto della Segreteria di Stato sulla istituzione di un consiglio di Stato," *Atti del Sommo Pontefice Pio IX*, I, 607-10.

3. "Editto della Segreteria di Stato sull' ordinamento dei ministri," *Atti del Sommo Pontefice Pio IX*, I, 613-14, 623-25.

4. "Editto della Segreteria di Stato sulla istituzione della Consulta di Stato per le finanze," October 28, 1850, *Atti del Sommo Pontefice Pio IX*, I, 643-48.

5. "Editto della Segreteria di Stato sul governo delle province ed amministrazione provinciale," November 22, 1850, *Atti del Sommo Pontefice Pio IX*, I, 652-56.

6. Director General of Police to Antonelli, April 3, 1850, *ASV, Segreteria di Stato Esteri, Corrispondenza di Gaeta e Portici, 1848-1850, Rubrica* 155, f. 2.

7. De Cesare, *Roma e lo Stato del Papa*, p. 236.

8. Franz-Josef to Pius IX, August 25, 1855, *ASV, Archivio Particolare Pio IX, Austria, Sovrani*.

9. Vittorio Emanuele to Pius IX, February 13, 1852, *ASV, Archivio Particolare Pio IX, Sardegna, Sovrani*, #33.

10. Nuncio at Turin to G. Antonelli, February 8, 1850, *ASV, Segreteria di Stato Esteri, Corrispondenza di Gaeta e Portici, 1848-1850, Rubrica* 257, s.f. 194.

11. Anonymous letter from Turin to G. Antonelli, May 8, 1850, *ASV, Segreteria di Stato Esteri, Rubrica* 258, s.f. 77.

12. Antonelli to the Charge d'affaires of Sardinian King, May 14, 1850, *ASV, Archivio Nunziatura Parigi*, 1850, #78.

13. "Editto della Segreteria di Stato sulla rappresentanza e sull' amministrazione del commune di Roma," January 25, 1851, *Atti del Sommo Pontefice Pio IX*, II, 3-6.

14. Report from the Count de Rayneval, the French Envoy at Rome, to the French Minister for Foreign Affairs, May 14, 1856 in John Francis Maguire, *Rome: Its Rulers and Its Institutions* (London, 1857), p. 444.

15. Minghetti, *Miei Ricordi*, III, 14.

16. Nuncio in Paris to G. Antonelli [1852], *ASV, Segreteria di Stato*, 1853, *Rubrica* 242, f. 6, s.f. 9.

17. Ollivier, *L'Empire Libéral*, III, 140; Minghetti, III, 84.

18. Report of January 20, 1852, *Archivio di Stato di Roma, Miscellanea di Carte Politiche o Riservate*, b. 121, f. 4214; Memorandum of June 23, 1852, *Archivio di Stato di Roma, Miscellanea di Carte Politiche o Riservate*, b. 121, f. 4213; *L'Osservatore Ligure-Subalpino*, June 25, 1852.

19. Vittorio Emanuele to Pius, November 2, 1851, *ASV, Archivio Particolare Pio IX, Sardegna, Sovrani*, #24.

20. Pius to Vittorio Emanuele, July 2, 1852, *ASV, Archivio Particolare Pio IX, Sardegna, Sovrani*; Pietro Pirri, *La laicizzazione dello stato sardo, 1848-1856* (Rome, 1944), pp. 79-80.

21. Pirri, p. 89.

22. Luigi Chiala (ed.), *Il Conte di Cavour. Ricordi di Michelangelo Castelli* (Turin, 1886), pp. 181-82.

23. Louis Napoleon to Pius IX, May 8, 1853, and response of Pius to Louis Napoleon, June 1, 1853, *ASV, Archivio Particolare Pio IX, Francia, Sovrani*, #22.
24. Rayneval to Antonelli, December 9, 1852, *ASV, Segreteria di Stato, 1853, Rubrica* 242, f. 6, s.f. 196–97.
25. Nuncio to Antonelli, January 20, 1853, *ASV, Segreteria di Stato Esteri, Rubrica* 242, f. 6, s.f. 40.
26. Pius to Franz-Josef, March 7, 1853, *ASV, Archivio Particolare Pio IX, Austria, Sovrani*, #11.
27. Nuncio at Vienna to Antonelli, January 17, 1853, *ASV, Segreteria di Stato*, 1853, *Rubrica* 246, f. 6, s.f. 122.
28. Pius to Cardinal Deacon, December 10, 1853, *ASV, Archivio Particolare Pio IX, Stato Pontificio*, #46.
29. Minghetti, *Ricordi*, III, 26.
30. Maguire, p. 446.
31. Antonelli to Nuncio at Paris, June 9, 1853, *ASV, Segreteria di Stato Esteri*, 1853, *Rubrica* 242, f. 3, s.f. 23.
32. Vercesi, p. 251; Denzinger, *The Sources of Catholic Dogma*, pp. 413–414.
33. *L'Opinione*, August 13, 1855.
34. Pius to Vittorio Emanuele, January 26, 1855, *ASV, Archivio Particolare Pio IX, Sardegna, Sovrani*, #44.
35. Vittorio Emanuele to Pius, March 22, 1855, *ASV, Archivio Particolare Pio IX, Sardegna, Sovrani*, #47.
36. Pius to the Youth Club of Saint Peter's, April 12, 1875, De Franciscis, *Discorsi del Sommo Pontefice Pio IX*, III, 466–67.
37. Franz-Josef to Pius, April 24, 1855, *ASV, Archivio Particolare Pio IX, Austria, Sovrani*, #13; General Rostolan to Pius, April 24, 1855, *ASV, Archivio Particolare Pio IX, Francia, Particolari*, #77.
38. Giuseppe Massari, *Il Conte di Cavour. Ricordi biografici* (Turin, 1873), pp. 129–31; Edmondo Mayor, *Nuove Lettere inedite del Conte Camillo di Cavour* (Turin, 1895), p. 319; Princess Caroline Murat, *My Memoirs* (New York, 1910), p. 128.
39. Mayor, p. 372.
40. Pius to Franz Josef, February 8, 1856, and the Emperor's response to the Pope, February 25, 1856, *ASV, Archivio Particolare Pio IX, Austria, Sovrani*, #19 and #20.
41. Frank J. Coppa, *Camillo di Cavour* (New York, 1973), pp. 127–28.
42. Pius to Count Gabriele Mastai, July 15, [1859], Monti, *Pio IX nel Risorgimento Italiano con Documenti Inediti*, p. 260.

Chapter Nine

1. *Pio Nono ed i suoi Popoli nel MDCCCLVII ossia memoria Intorno al viaggio della Santità di N.S. per L'Italia centrale* (Rome, 1860), I, 2.

2. Report to G. Antonelli on the Progress and Events of the Pope's trip, May 4, 1857, *ASV, Segreteria di Stato*, 1858, *Rubrica* lc, f. 1.

3. Cardinal Patrizi to Pius, July 23, 1857, *ASV, Archivio Particolare Pio IX, Stato Pontificio*, #106.

4. De Cesare, *Roma e lo Stato del Papa*, p. 236.

5. *Ibid.*, p. 238.

6. Minghetti, *Miei Ricordi*, p. 177.

7. Giuseppe Pasolini, *Memorie, 1815–1876*, p. 214.

8. *The Roman Journals of Ferdinand Gregorovius, 1852–1874*, ed. Friedrich Althaus, trans. Mrs. Gustavus W. Hamilton (London, 1907), p. 38.

9. General Goyon's Report on Pontifical Troops, June 16, 1857, *ASV, Archivio Particolare Pio IX, Francia, Particolari*, #111.

10. Minghetti, III, 165.

11. Mariano Gabriele (ed.), *Il Carteggio Antonelli-Sacconi (1858–1860)* (Rome, 1962), I, 5; Giuseppe Massari, *Diario dalle cento voci* (Bologna, 1959), pp. 84, 93.

12. "Breve Cenni e reflessione . . . relative al Battesimo conferito in Bologna al fanciullo Edgardo figlio degli Ebrei Salomone e Mariana Mortara," *ASV, Archivio Particolare Pio IX, Ogetti Vari*, n. 1433.

13. Massari, *Diario dalle cento voci*, p. 67; Gabriele, I, xiii.

14. Gabriele, I, 26.

15. Noel Blakiston (ed.), *The Roman Question: Extracts from the Despatches of Odo Russell from Rome, 1858–1870* (London, 1962), p. 2.

16. *Ibid.*

17. *Ibid.*, p. 16.

18. Napoleon III to Pius, May 1, 1859, *ASV, Archivio Particolare Pio IX, Francia, Sovrani*, #42.

19. Vittorio Emanuele to Pius, May 29, 1859, *ASV, Archivio Particolare Pio IX, Sardegna, Sovrani*.

20. Maioli, *Pio IX da vescovo a pontefice*, p. 55.

21. Pius to Vittorio Emanuele, January 1859, *ASV, Archivio Particolare Pio IX, Sardegna, Sovrani*, #53.

22. Massari, p. 239.

23. Blakiston, pp. 26–27; Gabriele, p. 139.

24. *Posthumous Papers of Jessie White Mario: The Birth of Modern Italy*, p. 283.

25. Pius to the Archbishop of Rouen, June 5, 1859, *ASV, Archivio Particolare Pio IX, Francia, Particolari*, #128.

26. Gabriele, I, 149, 173.

27. Napoleon to Pius, July 14, 1859, *ASV, Archivio Particolare Pio IX, Francia, Sovrani*, #44.

28. Blakiston, p. 32.

29. Draft of Antonelli's note protesting Piedmontese invasion of the Romagna, December 1859, *ASV, Segreteria di Stato*, 1860, *Rubrica* 165, f. 70, s.f. 9–10.

30. Federigo Sclopis di Salerano, *Diario Segreto (1859-1878)*, ed. Pietro P. Pirri (Turin, 1959), p. 174; Blakiston, pp. 34-35.

31. Pius to Count Gabriele Mastai, September 19, 1859, in Monti, *Pio IX nel Risorgimento Italiano con Documenti Inediti*, p. 261.

32. *Archivio di Stato di Roma, Miscellanea di Carte Politiche o Riservate*, b. 132; Giovanni Orioli (ed.), *Memorie romane dell' ottocento* (Rome, 1963), pp. 84-85.

33. Mack Walker (ed.), *Plombieres: Secret Diplomacy and the Rebirth of Italy* (New York, 1968), p. 244.

34. Napoleon to Pius, December 31, 1859, *Archivio di Stato di Roma, Miscellanea di Carte Politiche o Riservate*, b. 137, f. 4789.

35. *The Roman Journals of Ferdinand Gregorovius*, p. 78; Monti, *Pio IX nel Risorgimento Italiano con Documenti Inediti*, p. 146; Quinet, p. 323.

36. *Archivio di Stato di Roma, Miscellanea di Carte Politiche o Riservate*, b. 137, f. 4913.

37. Blakiston, p. 77.

38. Orioli, *Memorie romane dell' ottocento*, p. 90; Papal *Teachings: The Church*, p. 160.

39. Vittorio Emanuele to Pius, February 7, 1860, *ASV, Archivio Particolare Pio IX, Sardegna, Sovrani*, #57.

40. Nicomede Bianchi, *Storia documentata della diplomazia in Italia dall' anno 1814 all' anno 1861* (Turin, 1872), VIII, 401.

41. Pius to Vittorio Emanuele, February 14, 1860, *ASV, Archivio Particolare Pio IX, Sardegna, Sovrani*, #58.

42. "Un dispaccio del Cardinale Segretario di Stato a Mons. Nunzio in Parigi in risposta a due scritti del Ministro degli Affari Stranieri in Francia intorno alla quistione romana," *ASV, Segreteria di Stato*, 1860, Rubrica 165, f. 70, s.f. 85.

43. Report from Bologna, March 12, 1860, *Archivio di Stato di Roma, Miscellanea di Carte Politiche o riservate, busta* 134, f. 4811.

44. Antonelli's circular note to the diplomatic corps, November 4, 1860, *ASV, Segreteria di Stato*, 1860, Rubrica 165, f. 71, s.f. 221-24.

45. Pius to Vittorio Emanuele, April 2, 1860, *ASV, Archivio Particolare Pio IX, Sardegna, Sovrani*, #60.

46. Blakiston, p. 118.

47. Leo Francis Stock (ed.), *Consular Relations between the United States and the Papal States: Instructions and Despatches* (Washington, D.C., 1945), II, 251.

48. Walker, p. 259.

49. Cavour's Instructions to General Fanti, September 7, 1860, *Archivio Centrale dello Stato, E.U.R., Carte Fanti, Scatola* 1.

50. Cavour to Antonelli, September 7, 1860, *Archivio di Stato di Roma, Miscellanea di Carte Politiche o Riservate, Busta* 134, f. 4809.

51. *Archivio di Stato di Roma, Miscellanea di Carte Politiche o Riservate*, 1860, b. 134, f. 4815.

52. *Le Secret de L'Empereur. Correspondance confidentielle et inédite exchangée entre M. Thouvenel Le Duc de Gramont et le Général Comte de Flahualt, 1860-1863* (Paris, 1889), I, 161-63; Frank J. Coppa, "Italy, the Papal States and the American Civil War," *La Parola del Popolo* (November-December, 1976), 364-67.

Chapter Ten

1. Blakiston, *The Roman Question*, pp. 129-33, 142-43; *Le Secret de L'Empereur*, I, 182.
2. Giacomo Martina, *Pio IX e Leopold II* (Rome, 1967), p. 48; Passerin D'Entreves, "Appunti sull' impostazione delle ultime trattative del governo cavouriano colla S. Sede per una soluzione della quistione romana (novembre 1860-marzo 1861)," in *Chiesa e Stato nell' ottocento. Miscellanea in onore di Pietro Pirri*, ed. R. Aubert et. al. (Padua, 1962), II, 569-70; *ASV, Segreteria di Stato*, 1860, Rubrica 165, f. 80.
3. Blakiston, pp. 168-71; E. E. Y. Hales, *Pio Nono* (Garden City, New York, 1962), pp. 228-29; *Le Secret de L'Empereur*, I, 492-93.
4. "Allucuzione di N.S. Papa Pio IX nel concistorio segreto del 18 Marzo 1861," *Civiltà Cattolica* (1861), series iv, X, 5-12.
5. *The Roman Journals of Ferdinand Gregorovius 1852-1874*, pp. 129, 133; Blakiston, p. 172, *Le Secret de L'Empereur. Correspondance confidentielle et inédite . . . 1860-1863* (Paris, 1889), II, 34.
6. Franz Josef to Pius IX, August 31, 1861, *ASV, Archivio Particolare Pio IX, Austria, Sovrani*, #38; *Le Secret de L'Empereur*, II, 132.
7. Fiorella Bartoccini, *La "Roma dei Romani"* (Rome, 1971), p. 248; Andreotti, *La sciarada di Papa Mastai*, p. 15; Blakiston, p. 248.
8. Gabriele, *Il Carteggio-Antonelli-Sacconi (1858-1860)*, I, 45.
9. Antonio Monti, *La Politica degli Stati Italiani durante il Risorgimento* (Milan, 1948), pp. 222-23; Glorney Bolton, *Roman Century: A Portrait of Rome as the Capital of Italy, 1870-1970* (New York, 1970), p. 42.
10. Pius to Maria Pia, September 11, 1862, *ASV, Archivio Particolare Pio IX, Sardegna, Sovrani*.
11. Blakiston, p. 281.
12. Monti, *Pio IX nel Risorgimento Italiano con Documenti Inediti*, p. 267.
13. Blakiston, p. 268.
14. Report of the Supreme Sacred Congregation of the Holy Office on the propositions containing the 70 principal errors of the time, *ASV, Archivio Particolare Pio IX, Ogetti Vari*, n. 1779.
15. Eighth session of the Supreme Sacred Congregation of the Holy Office on the issue of the principal errors of the times, April 8, 1862, *ASV, Archivio Particolare Pio IX, Ogetti Vari*, n. 1779.
16. *Ibid*.

17. Emile Bourgeois and E. Clermont, *Rome et Napoleon III (1849-1870)* (Paris, 1907), p. 212.

18. R. Aubert, "Antonelli, Giacomo," *Dizionario Biografico degli Italiani* (Rome, 1961), III, 490; Blakiston, p. 320.

19. "The Syllabus of the principal errors of our times which are stigmatized in the Consistorial Allocutions, Encyclicals, and other Apostolic Letters of the Most Holy Father, Pope Pius IX," *Documents in the Political History of the European Continent*, ed. C. A. Kertesz (Oxford, 1968), pp. 237, 241; Aubert, *Le pontificat de Pie IX*, pp. 254-55. *The Papal Encyclicals in their Historical Context*, ed. A. Freemantle (New York, 1956), p. 152.

20. Blakiston, p. 299.

21. *Ibid.*, p. 307.

22. Fernand Mourret, *A History of the Catholic Church: Period of the Early Nineteenth Century (1823-1878)*, trans. Newton Thomspon (New York, 1957), VIII, 572, 627.

23. Pius to Vittorio Emanuele, March 10, 1865, *ASV, Archivio Particolare Pio IX, Sardegna, Sovrani,* #66.

24. Vittorio Emanuele to Pius, April 5, 1865, *ASV, Archivio Particolare Pio IX, Sardegna, Sovrani,* #67.

25. Dalla Torre, pp. 38-39.

26. Vittorio Emanuele to Pius, December 6, 1866, *ASV, Archivio Particolare Pio IX, Sardegna, Sovrani,* #68.

27. Nippold, p. 145.

28. Blakiston, pp. 330-31.

29. *The Roman Journals of Ferdinand Gregorovius 1852-1874*, pp. 260-61.

30. Kenneth Bourne, "The British Government and the proposed Roman Conference of 1867," *Rassegna Storica del Risorgimento*, anno XLIII (October-December 1956), IV, 761.

31. Pius to Cardinal Bonnechose, Archbishop of Rouen, November 10, 1866, *ASV, Archivio Particolare Pio IX, Francia, Particolari,* #183.

32. Stock, *United States Ministers to the Papal States*, I, 403.

33. Cardinal Bonnechose to Pius, July 28, 1867, *ASV, Archivio Particolare Pio IX, Francia, Particolari,* #188.

34. Andreotti, p. 59.

35. Filippo Crispolti, *Pio IX, Leone XII, Pio X, Benedetti XV. Ricordi Personali* (Milan, 1932), p. 10.

36. *The Roman Journals of Ferdinand Gregorovius*, p. 301.

37. Pius to Monsignor Luciano Bonaparte, November 8, 1867, *ASV, Archivio Particolare Pio IX, Stato Pontificio,* #163A.

Chapter Eleven

1. Blakiston, *The Roman Question*, p. 347.

2. Eugenio Cecconi, *Storia del Concilio Ecumenico Vaticano scritta sui Documenti originali* (Rome: Tipografia Vaticana, 1872), I, 3–8; Cuthbert Butler, *The Vatican Council: The Story Told from Inside in Bishop Ullathorne's Letters* (New York, 1930), I, 81.

3. Michele Maccarrone, *Il Concilio Vaticano I e il "Giornale" di Mons. Arrigoni* (Padua, 1966), p. 135.

4. *Ibid.*, p. 137; Cecconi, I, 57–63.

5. Blakiston, p. 352.

6. Count Alessandro Adorni to Antonelli, March 1, 1869, *ASV, Segreteria di Stato,* 1869, *Rubrica* 284, f. 1; Johann Joseph Ignaz von Döllinger, *Letters from Rome on the Council by Quirinus* (New York, 1973), I, 14–16.

7. Vercesi, *Pio IX*, pp. 254–55.

8. *The Roman Journals of Ferdinand Gregorovius*, p. 325.

9. Pius to Archbishop of Paris, December 1, 1852, *ASV, Francia, Particolari,* #55.

10. Maccarrone, pp. 267–68.

11. Butler, I, 88.

12. Andreotti, pp. 21–22; Cecconi, I, 82–85.

13. Maccarrone, p. 220; *Letters from Rome on the Council by Quirinus*, I, 26.

14. *The Roman Journals of Ferdinand Gregorovius*, p. 351.

15. Letters of Count Alessandro Adorni to Cardinal Antonelli, March 14, 1869, and May 20, 1869, *ASV, Segreteria di Stato,* 1869, *Rubrica* 284, f. 1.

16. Andreotti, p. 22; Maccarrone, p. 242.

17. Giacomo Martina, *Pio IX. Chiesa e mondo moderno* (Rome, 1976), p. 151; *Letters from Rome on the Council by Quirinus*, I, 35–36.

18. Butler, I, 97.

19. Maccarrone, p. 228; George O. Kent, *Arnim and Bismarck* (Oxford, 1968), pp. 24–25.

20. Maccarrone, p. 160.

21. Rev. Thomas Mozley, *Letters from Rome on the Occasion of the Oecumenical Council 1869–1870* (London, 1891), I, 43–44.

22. De Cesare, *Roma e lo Stato del Papa,* p. 697; Cecconi, I, 288–89.

23. Maccarrone, p. 163.

24. Butler, I, 166.

25. Alessandro Adorni to Antonelli, December 8, 1869, *ASV, Segreteria di Stato,* 1869, *Rubrica* 284, f. 1.

26. Mozley, I, 155; Jacques Gadille, *Albert du Boÿs. Ses "Souvenirs du Concile du Vatican, 1869–1870"* (Louvain, 1968), pp. 112–15.

27. James Hennesey, *The First Council of the Vatican: The American Experience* (New York, 1963), p. 174.

28. Mozley, I, 155, 283.

29. Hennesey, pp. 121–22.

30. Andreotti, p. 46; J. B. Bury, *History of the Papacy in the 19th Century*

Notes and References

(1864-1878) (London, 1930), p. 103; *Albert du Boÿs,* pp. 136, 140.
   31. Mourret, *A History of the Catholic Church,* VIII, 658.
   32. Mozley, II, 172.
   33. Butler, II, 35.
   34. Hennesey, p. 182.
   35. Martina, *Pio IX. Chiesa e mondo moderno,* p. 160; *Albert du Boÿs. Ses "Souvenirs du Concile du Vatican, 1869-1870,"* p. 84; Lillian Parker Wallace, *The Papacy and European Diplomacy* (Chapel Hill, 1948), p. 99.
   36. Hales, Pio Nono, p. 315.
   37. De Cesare, *Roma e lo stato del Papa,* p. 695; *Letters from Rome on the Council by Quirinus,* II, 713.
   38. *ASV, Archivio Particolare Pio IX, Ogetti Vari,* n. 2152.
   39. De Cesare, p. 696.
   40. Butler, II, 115.
   41. *Ibid.,* II, 149.
   42. Martina, *Pio IX. Chiesa e mondo moderno,* p. 164.
   43. Butler, II, 164.
   44. John Henry Newman to Madame J. Blumenthal, July 30, 1870, *The Letters and Diaries of John Henry Newman,* edited by Charles Stephen Dessain and Thomas Gornall. Volume XXV: *The Vatican Council, January 1870 to December 1871,* p. 169.
   45. Butler, II, 295; *Dogmatic Canons and Decrees* (New York, 1912), 256-57.
   46. Louis Napoleon to Pius, July 27, 1870, *ASV, Archivio Particolare Pio IX, Francia, Sovrani,* #86.
   47. Bury, p. 147.

Chapter Twelve

   1. Andreotti, *La sciarada di Papa Mastai,* pp. 72-73; Kent, *Arnim and Bismarck,* p. 39.
   2. Vittorio Emanuele to Pius IX, September 8, 1870, *ASV, Archivio Particolare Pio IX, Sardegna, Sovrani,* #82.
   3. Monti, *La Politica degli Stati Italiani durante Il Risorgimento,* p. 226.
   4. Pius to Vittorio Emanuele, September 11, 1870, *ASV, Archivio Particolare Pio IX, Sardegna, Sovrani,* #83.
   5. Monti, *Pio IX nel Risorgimento Italiano con Documenti Inediti,* p. 194.
   6. Pius to General Kanzler, September 19, 1870, *ASV, Archivio Particolare Pio IX, Stato Pontificio,* #180.
   7. Dalla Torre, *Pio IX e Vittorio Emanuele II,* pp. 154-55.
   8. Monti, *Pio IX nel Risorgimento Italiano con Documenti Inediti,* p. 196.
   9. Vercesi, *Pio IX,* p. 257.

10. Speech of Pius to the Delegation from Ecuador, June 16, 1871, De Franciscis, *Discorsi del Sommo Pontefice Pio IX in Vaticano ai Fedeli di Roma e dell' orbe dal principio della sua prigionia fino al presente*, I, 113.

11. P. Pietro Pirri, "Il Cardinale Antonelli tra il mito e la storia," *Rivista di Storia della Chiesa in Italia*, XII (1958), 99-100.

12. Monti, *Pio IX nel Risorgimento Italiano con Documenti Inediti*, p. 167.

13. Monsignor Mermilliod to Pius, October 12, 1870, *ASV, Archivio Particolare Pio IX, Stato Pontificio*, #181.

14. Fernand Mourret, *Le concile du Vatican d'apres des Documents inédits* (Paris, 1919), pp. 312-13.

15. Great Britain, *British and Foreign State Papers*, LXV (1873-74), 638-42.

16. Monti, *Pio IX nel Risorgimento Italiano con Documenti Inediti*, p. 203.

17. Consistorial Allocution to the Sacred College of Cardinals, October 27, 1871, De Franciscis, I, 248. *Papal Teachings: The Church* (Boston, 1962), p. 220.

18. Monti, *La Politica degli Stati Italiani durante Il Risorgimento*, p. 230.

19. Speech of Pius to a Deputation of Romans from various parishes, De Franciscis, I, 298-99.

20. Speech of Pius to an Austrian Delegation, May 16, 1871, De Franciscis, I, 89.

21. Draft of Letter from Pius to Vittorio Emanuele, August 1871, *ASV, Archivio Particolare Pio IX, Sardegna, Sovrani*, n. 90.

22. Pius to Comte de Chambord, April 15, 1872, *ASV, Archivio Particolare Pio IX, Francia, Sovrani*, #109.

23. Hubert Bastgen, *Die Romische Frage: Dokumente und Stimmen* (Freiburg, 1919), III, 98.

24. Pius to a number of foreign women, March 9, 1871, De Franciscis, I, 72.

25. Speech of Pius to Deputation of Catholics from various countries, April 13, 1872, De Franciscis, I, 396.

26. Lillian Parker Wallace, *The Papacy and European Diplomacy* (Chapel Hill, N.C., 1948), p. 287.

27. Pius to Maria Teresa, Countess of Chambord, July 25, 1871, *ASV, Archivio Particolare Pio IX, Francia, Sovrani*, # 92.

28. Napoleon III to Pius, June 13, 1871, *ASV, Archivio Particolare Pio IX, Francia, Sovrani*, #95.

29. Pius to Vittorio Emanuele, August 21, 1871, *ASV, Archivio Particolare Pio IX, Sardegna, Sovrani*, #89.

30. Pius to an Italian Delegation, June 19, 1871, De Franciscis, I, 142.

31. Pius to Vittorio Emanuele, July 18, 1872, *ASV, Archivio Particolare Pio IX, Sardegna, Sovrani*, #91.

32. Pius to the Roman Society for Catholic Interests, May 30, 1872, De Franciscis, I, 428-29.
33. Monti, *Pio IX nel Risorgimento Italiano con Documenti Inediti*, p. 6.
34. De Franciscis, I, 283-84.
35. Dalla Torre, *Pio IX e Vittorio Emanuele II*, p. 26.
36. Notes of Cardinal Villecourt on Peters' Pence [1860?], *ASV, Archivio Particolare Pio IX, Francia, Particolari.*
37. Roger Aubert, "Antonelli, Giacomo," *Dizionario Biografico degli Italiani*, III, 491.
38. De Franciscis, II, 371.
39. Speech of Pius to two women's religious clubs, October 11, 1874, De Franciscis, III, 334-35.
40. Dalla Torre, p. 71.
41. Pietro Pirri, "Il Cardinale Antonelli tra il mito e la storia," *Rivista di Storia della Chiesa in Italia*, XII (1958), 119-20.
42. Dalla Torre, p. 73.
43. Samuel William Halperin, *Italy and the Vatican at War* (Chicago, 1939), p. 417.
44. *Didicimus, non sine dolore*, January 21, 1878 in *Papal Teachings: The Church*, p. 249.

Chapter Thirteen

1. *Memoirs of Prince Chlodwig of Hohenlohe-Schillingsfuerst*, ed. Friedrich Curtius (New York, 1906), II, 27.
2. Herbert Bastgen, *Die Römische Frage. Dokumente und Stimmen* (Freiburg, 1917-19), II, 796.
3. *Ibid.*, II, 803.
4. Pius to a delegation of Catholic Women of Germany, February 10, 1871, De Franciscis, *Discorsi del Sommo Pontefice Pio IX*, I, 53.
5. Encyclical letter of Pius IX to the Archbishops and Bishops of the Austrian Empire, March 7, 1874, De Franciscis, III, 566-72.
6. William S. Halperin, *Italy and the Vatican at War* (Chicago, 1939), p. 189.
7. Speech of Pius IX to the Students of the Propaganda Fide, April 12, 1874; De Franciscis, III, 218.
8. George G. Windell, *The Catholics and German Unity 1866-1871* (Minneapolis, 1954), pp. 197, 198.
9. Aubert, *Le pontificat de Pie IX*, p. 385. Stewart A. Stehlin, *Bismarck and the Guelph Problem, 1866-1890* (The Hague, 1973), pp. 112-113.
10. "The Impregnable Fortress: Prince Bismarck and the Centre Party," *American Catholic Quarterly Review*, XV (July 1890), 406.
11. Otto von Bismarck, *Reflections and Reminiscences*, ed. Theodore S. Hamerow (New York, 1968), p. 211.

12. Bismarck's confidential diplomatic circular to German representatives abroad, May 14, 1872, *Bismarck*, ed. Frederic M. Hollyday (Englewood Cliffs, N.J., 1970), p. 43; Kent, *Arnim and Bismarck*, p. 87.

13. Speech of Pius IX to a deputation from Alsace, June 20, 1871, De Franciscis, I, 146.

14. Andreotti, p. 29.

15. Pius IX to Cardinal Hohenlohe, April 26, 1872, *ASV, Archivio Particolare Pio IX, Stato Pontificio* #203.

16. *American Catholic Quarterly Review*, XV (July 1890), 416.

17. Brunero Gherardine, "Pio IX, episcopato e *Kulturkampf*," *Pio IX*, anno vi, n. 1 (January-April 1977), 35-36.

18. *Ibid.*; Aubert, *Le pontificat de Pie IX*, pp. 385-86; *Bismarck: Some Secret Pages of His History* (New York, 1970), II, 248-49.

19. *American Catholic Quarterly Review*, XV (July 1890), 407; Edward Husgen, *Ludwig Windhorst* (Cologne, 1907), p. 94; Erich Eyck, *Bismarck and the German Empire* (New York, 1964), p. 205.

20. Speech of Pius IX to the German Club of Catholic Literature in Rome, June 24, 1872, De Franciscis, I, 457.

21. Allocution of Pius to the Cardinals, December 23, 1872, De Franciscis, II, 130.

22. Aubert, *Le pontificat de Pie IX*, p. 387; Ross, *Beleaguered Tower*, p. 30.

23. "Imperial Law concerning Jesuits," July 4, 1872, *Documents in the Political History of the European Continent 1815-1939*, p. 246.

24. "Excerpts from a speech on the Education and Appointment of Clergy in the Prussian Lower Chamber," January 17, 1873, *A Free Church in a Free State?*, ed. Ernst Helmreich (Boston, 1964), p. 67.

25. "Law concerning the Education and Appointment of Priests," May 11, 1873, *Documents in the Political History of the European Continent 1815-1939*, p. 247; Ronald J. Ross, *Beleaguered Tower: The Dilemma of Political Catholicism in Wilhelmine Germany* (Notre Dame, 1976), pp. 16-17.

26. Speech of Pius to a deputation from the Archdioceses of Naples, January 18, 1873, De Franciscis, II, 216.

27. Pius to William of Prussia, August 7, 1873, De Franciscis, III, 573.

28. William of Prussia to Pius, September 3, 1873, De Franciscis, III, 574.

29. Encyclical letter of Pius to all the Patriarchs, Primates, Archbishops and Bishops, De Franciscis, III, 543-56; *Papal Teachings: The Church*, 239-40.

30. Speech of Pius to the German Club of Catholic literature in Rome, January 12, 1873, De Franciscis, II, 198; Speech of Pius to the same group, January 4, 1874, De Franciscis, III, 107.

31. Aubert, *Le pontificast de Pie IX*, pp. 390-92; Ross, *Beleaguered Tower: The Dilemma of Political Catholicism in Wilhelmine Germany*, p. 16.

32. Pius to the Prince Imperial Louis Napoleon, January 4, 1875, *ASV, Archivio Particolare Pio IX, Francia, Sovrani,* #127.

33. Encyclical letter of Pius to the Archbishops and Bishops of Prussia, February 5, 1875, De Franciscis, III, 562-65. Henry Denzinger, *The Sources of Catholic Dogma* (London, 1957), p. 458.

34. Pius to the German Club of Catholic Literature in Rome, January 18, 1875, De Franciscis, III, 419-21.

35. Bismarck's speech in the Prussian Chamber of Peers, April 12, 1886, *Bismarck,* ed. B. M. Hollyday, p. 47.

36. Bastgen, *Die Römische Frage,* III, 101.

37. Federico Chabod, *Storia della politica estera in Italia dal 1870 al 1896. Le promesse* (Bari, 1951), I, 417.

38. Crispolti, *Pio IX, Leone XII, Pio X, Benedetto XV. Ricordi Personali,* pp. 5-6.

39. Princess Clotilde of Savoy to Pius, March 4, 1872; Pius to Princess Clotilde, March 20, 1872, *ASV, Archivio Particolare Pio IX, Francia, Sovrani,* #106, #107.

40. Dalla Torre, pp. 178-81.

41. Monti, *Pio IX nel Risorgimento Italiano con Documenti Inediti,* p. 222.

Chapter Fourteen

1. Pius IX to Prince Imperial, Louis Napoleon, January 18, 1873, *ASV, Archivio Particolare Pio IX, Francia, Sovrani,* #115.

2. Count Lutzow to Prince Metternich, May 15, 1847, Quazza, *Pio IX e Massimo D'Azeglio nelle vicende romane del 1847,* I, 130.

3. Pius to the College of Cardinals, June 17, 1872, De Franciscis, I, 441.

4. Dalla Torre, *Pio IX e Vittorio Emanuele II,* pp. 33, 55-58.

5. Farini, *Lo Stato Romano dall' anno 1815 al 1850,* II, 59.

6. Speech of Pius IX to a great number of foreign women, mainly from America, March 3, 1871, De Franciscis, I, 65.

7. Speech of Pius to young Romans of various Catholic associations, October 2, 1872, De Franciscis, II, 77.

8. Speech of Pius IX to the youth of the club of St. Peter, October 29, 1870, Monti, *Pio IX nel Risorgimento Italiano con Documenti Inediti,* p. 175.

9. Speech of Pius to the representatives of various Italian cities, June 21, 1872, De Franciscis, I, 450-51.

10. Pius to Vittorio Emanuele II, September 29, 1859, *ASV, Archivio Particolare Pio IX, Sardegna, Sovrani,* #55.

11. Dalla Torre, p. 33. *Quartus supra,* January 6, 1873 in *Papal Teachings: The Church,* p. 391.

12. Speech of Pius to the representatives of a number of Roman parishes, April 28, 1872, De Franciscis, I, 408.

13. Speech of Pius to a group of his former employees, July 2, 1873, De Franciscis, II, 366.

14. Speech of Pius to the representatives of the faithful youth of Rome, October 2, 1874, De Franciscis, III, 330.

15. Pius to a deputation of young English Catholics, June 16, 1871, De Franciscis, I, 115.

16. Wilfrid Ward, *The Life of John Henry Cardinal Newman Based on his Private Journals and Correspondence* (New York: Longmans, Green and Co., 1913), II, 301.

17. Pius to the Cardinal Archbishop of Besanzone, March 6, 1855 and Pius to the Archbishop of Paris, November 24, 1864, *ASV, Archivio Particolare Pio IX, Francia, Particolari,* #75, #168.

18. Speech of Pius to the heads of a number of religious orders, December 15, 1873, De Franciscis, III, 68.

19. Pius to Franz-Josef, May 21, 1868, *ASV, Archivio Particolare Pio IX, Austria, Sovrani,* #59.

20. Speech of Pius to the youth of the club of St. Peter, October 29, 1870, De Franciscis, I, 37.

21. Apost. Const. *Romanus Pontifex*, August 28, 1873 in *Papal Teachings: The Church*, p. 239.

Selected Bibliography

ARCHIVAL SOURCES

1. *L'Archivio Segreto del Vaticano*

The papers of the pontificate of Pio Nono in the Vatican Archives were made available to scholars in 1967. Included therein are a number of collections important for a study of the longest reigning Pope. Among the most useful are *L'Archivio Particolare Pio IX*, which is subdivided into *Sovrani* and *Particolari* catalogued by State, and the *Ogetti Vari*, catalogued by number and containing papers upon a wide series of events and issues.

The *Fondo Particolare Pio IX* contains many of the letters and sermons of Mastai-Ferretti and a number of his personal papers before his accession to the papal throne as well as household information and expenses upon assuming the papal office. There are catalogs for the *Archivio Particolare* and the *Ogetti Vari*, although that for the former is far more detailed and useful than the catalog for the latter. The inventory for the *Fondo Particolare Pio IX* is sketchy at best and one must call for a *cassetta* to determine the importance of the papers therein.

A good deal can be learned of papal foreign as well as domestic policy from the *Archivio della Segretia di Stato* and the *Archivii delle Nunziature*, especially the *Fondo Archivio della Nunziatura di Firenze, Fondo Archivio della Nunziatura di Vienna* and the *Fondo Archivio della Nunziatura di Parigi*. Since the opening of the *Archivio Segreto del Vaticano* for the pontificate of Pio Nono some of the papers have been published including the correspondence between Antonelli and the Apostolic Nuncio at Madrid, Monsignor Lorenzo Barili, which is drawn primarily from the *Archivio della Segreteria di Stato* and the *Archivio della Nunziatura di Madrid*. This correspondence is edited by Carla Meneguzzi Rostagni, *Il Carteggio Antonelli-Barili, 1859-1861* (Rome: Istituto per la Storia del Risorgimento Italiano, 1973).

The *Archivio degli Affari Ecclesiastici* contains the documentation regarding the various concordats. The papers of the *Fondo del Concilio Vaticano* are in the process of being reorganized.

2. L'Archivio di Stato di Roma

This is another rich source for a study of the pontificate of Pio Nono. Just recently the *Archivio di Stato di Roma* acquired the *Fondo Lettere Inedite di Monsignor Giovanni Maria Mastai Ferretti*, a series of 295 letters written by the future Pope when he was first Archbishop of Spoleto and then Bishop of Imola. The correspondence, which dates from May 1827 to December 1837, is a private one with almost all of the letters of Mastai addressed to Matteo Chiocca, his agent in Rome. They reveal much about the personal state of mind and the affairs of Mastai.

The *Archivio di Stato di Roma* also contains much material concerning the governance and administration of the Pontifical States during the first half of the nineteenth century. Particularly useful are the *Carte Miscellanea Politiche o Riservate*, arranged chronologically and containing a wide variety of political papers, the documents of the *Fondo Repubblica Romana*, invaluable for an understanding of developments in Rome in 1849, and the reports of the *Consiglio di Stato* as well as the *Consulta di Stato*.

The *Archivio di Stato di Roma* is also the repository of the papers of the friend, advisor, and Secretary of State of the Pope, Cardinal Giacomo Antonelli. Included in the *Fondo Famiglia Antonelli* are some of the public as well as the private papers of the Cardinal, the correspondence and records of various members of his immediate family—especially his father and brothers—as well as some of the papers of a number of his ancestors. The correspondence between Antonelli and the Nuncio at Paris, Carlo Sacconi, found in this archive was edited by Mariano Gabriele and published as *Il Carteggio Antonelli-Sacconi (1850-1860)* (Rome: Istituto per la Storia del *Risorgimento* Italiano, 1962).

3. Fondi Archivistici del Museo Centrale del Risorgimento

These are rich in material for a study of the pontificate of Pio Nono. Included herein are the papers of Nicola Roncalli and his *Cronaca di Roma*, some fifty-one bound volumes of his chronicle of events in the Papal States from 1844 to 1870. This newsletter, based on what the author saw, heard, or read about events in the capital, presents quite a range of information about Papal Rome during these years. The archives of the Museo *Centrale del Risorgimento* also contain part of the correspondence of Michelangelo Caetani, Duke of Sermoneta, Garibaldi, Callimaco Zambianchi, Luigi Carlo Farini, and others. The miscellaneous volume on the Stato Pontificio numbered 114 contains a number of apostolic letters, encyclicals and circulars regarding the Roman state from 1814 to 1871.

Selected Bibliography

4. *L'Archivio Centrale dello Stato, E.U.R.*

This central archive of the Italian State contains the papers of the various ministries of unitary Italy and contains a number of archives that are useful for the earlier period as well as the years from 1861 to 1878. Among the most useful for this particular study are some of the papers of the *Archivio Depretis*, those of the *Famiglia Benso di Cavour*, and those of the *Archivio Fanti*.

ADDITIONAL MANUSCRIPT MATERIAL

1. *Biblioteca Apostolica Vatican Latina*

In the *Sala Studio Manoscritti* of the Apostolic Vatican Library there is a hand-written copy of Mastai-Ferretti's journal kept while in Chile entitled *Memorie. Viaggio al Chili*, which forms part of the larger *Breve relazione del Viaggio fatto al Chile dal Canonico Giovanni Mastai-Ferretti di Sinigaglia*. It is useful not only for assessing Mastai-Ferretti's attitudes toward missionary work and the Latin American Church but also for tracing the young prelate's religious and political evolution.

PRINTED WORKS OF POPE PIUS IX

1. *Allocutions, Encyclicals, Statements and Acts*

Atti del Sommo Pontefice Pio Nono Felicemente Regnante. Parte seconda che comprende i mutu-proprii, chirografi, editti, Notifacazioni, ec. per lo stato pontificio. Rome: Tipografia delle Belle Arti, 1857. This is particularly useful for a study of the first two years of the pontificate and for understanding the institutions provided by Pio Nono and Antonelli for the Papal States following the restoration of 1849. Included within these two volumes are a number of edicts of the early 1850s.

Discorsi del Sommo Pontefice Pio IX Pronciati in Vaticano ai Fedeli di Roma e dell' Orbe dal principio della sua prigionia fino al presente. 4 vols. Rome: Tipografia di G. Aurelj, 1872–78. Within these four volumes edited by Pasquale de Franciscis are the speeches and encyclicals of Pius following the loss of Rome during the years of his "imprisonment" in the Vatican.

Pii IX Pontificis Maxima Acta . . . . Rome: Artium, 1854–75. Contains the Pope's allocutions and encyclicals. Whereas the *Atti* is a compilation of Pius's secular acts—decrees, notifications, edits, motu-propri, etc.—the *Acta* includes those documents of an ecclesiastical nature. His encyclicals can also be found in *Tutte le Encicliche dei Sommi Pontifici*. Milan: Dall' Oglio, 1959. A number of Pius's encyclicals and allocutions are available in English in *Papal Teachings: The Church*. Selected and arranged by the Benedictine Monks of Solesmes and translated by Mother E. O'Gorman. Boston: Daughters of St. Paul, 1962. Another important source in English is Roy J. Deferrari's translation of Henry Denzinger's *Enchiridion Symboloroum*, 13th edition, which is published under the title *The Sources of Catholic Dogma* (St. Louis: B. Herder Book Co., 1957). Also see *Dogmatic Canons and Decrees* (of the Catholic Church) (New York: The Devin-Adair Co., 1912), and *The Papal Encyclicals in their Historical Context*. Edited by Anne Fremantle with an introduction by Gustave Weigel (New York: G.P. Putnam's Sons, 1956).

2. *Correspondence: Personal and Public*

DALLA TORRE, PAOLO. *Pio IX e Vittorio Emanuele II. Dal Loro Carteggio privato negli anni del dilaceramento (1865-1878)*. Rome: Istituto di Studi Romani Editori, 1972. Includes the last years of the correspondence of Pius and the Italian king, not included by Father Pirri in his more extensive work on the correspondence of the two. Although the title emphasizes their private correspondence, attention is given to the Pope's correspondence with a number of other sovereigns, particularly Napoleon III.

MAIOLI, GIOVANNI. *Pio IX da vescovo a Pontefice. Lettere al Card. Luigi Amat. agosto 1839-luglio 1848*. Modena: Società Tipografico Modenese, 1943. Includes the correspondence of Mastai-Ferretti while Bishop of Imola with his friend Card. Amat. This provides the best printed account of the pastoral work of the future Pope as well as a good source of Pius's reaction to the main problems he had to confront during the first months of his pontificate.

MARTINA, GIACOMO. *Pio IX e Leopold II*. Rome: Pontifica Università Gregoriana, 1967. This twenty-eighth volume of the *Miscellanea Historiae Pontificiae* gathers the correspondence of the grand duke of Tuscany and Pius and reveals the humanity of the Pope, his religious preoccupations, and his firm adherence to a confessional state not encumbered by parliamentary rule.

OLSZAMOWSKA-SKOWRONSKA. *La correspondance des Papes et des Empereurs de Russie (1814-1878) selon le documents authentiques*. Rome: Pontifica Università Gregoriana, 1970.

PIRRI, PIETRO. *Pio IX e Vittorio Emanuele II dal loro carteggio privato. I. La laicizzazione dello Stato Sardo, 1848-1856*. Rome: Università Gregoriana, 1944. *Pio IX e Vittorio Emanuele II dal loro carteggio privato. II. La questione romana, 1856-1864. Parte I: Testo, Parte II: I Documenti*. Rome: Università Gregoriana, 1951. These volumes in the series *Miscellanea Historiae Pontificiae* are invaluable for an understanding of the diplomacy and the war which led to the collapse of the Papal State and the creation of the rump state which disappeared in 1870. Father Pirri was allowed access to the Vatican Archives prior to its opening to the scholarly community in order to publish this work, to which he brought his preoccupation with exact documentation, a moderation of judgment, and a remarkable objectivity.

CONTEMPORARY ACCOUNTS

1. *Observations of Contemporaries before the Accession of Pio Nono*

BALBO, CESARE. *Della Speranza d'Italia.* 2nd ed. Paris, 1844.
D'AZEGLIO, MASSIMO. *Degli ultimi casi di Romagna.* Florence, 1846.
———. *I Miei Ricordi.* First published posthumously, 1868. Translated into English by Count Maffei. *Recollections of Massimo D'Azeglio.* London: Chapman and Hall, 1868.
GIOBERTI, VINCENZO. *Del primato morale e civile degli Italiani.* Brussels, 1843. The 1932 edition was published in Turin by Unione Tipografico Editrice Torinese.
MAZZINI, JOSEPH. *Italy, Austria and the Pope: A Letter to Sir James Bart.* London: Albanesi, 1845.

2. *Memoirs, Diaries, Studies, and Correspondence of Those Who Had Access to Pio Nono*

There is a surprising amount of consensus about events in Rome before and following the revolution of 1848 by those who had access to Pio Nono. By and large one finds the tendency to be critical of the political acumen of the Pope and more often than not criticism of his Secretary of State, Cardinal Giacomo Antonelli. Important light is shed on the period by such works as:

BIANCHI, NICOMEDE. *La politica di Massimo D'Azeglio dal 1848 al 1859. I Documenti.* Turin: Roux e Favale, 1884.
BLAKISTON, NOEL. "Con Odo Russell a Roma nel 1860," *Rassegna Storica del Risorgimento, anno* XLVII (January-March 1960), 61-68.
BRAZÃO, E. *L'Unificazione Italiana vista dai diplomatici portoghesi.* Rome: Istituto per la Storia del Risorgimento Italiano, 1962.
DE LIEDEKERKE DE BEAUFORT, AUGUSTO. *Rapporti delle cose di Roma* [1846-1849]. Edited by A. M. Ghisalberti. Rome: Istituto per la Storia del Risorgimento Italiano, 1949. The correspondence of the Dutch ambassador at Rome during these years, an acute observer of the problems confronting Pio Nono and the individuals surrounding him, forms one of the sources for the first years of the pontificate. This Protestant representative of a Protestant power was a critic of the papal government but a warm admirer of Pius IX.
Della missione a Roma di Antonio Serbati Rosmini negli anni 1848-1849. Turin: Paravia, 1881. Published posthumously. Rosmini in this work

accounts for both the failure of his mission to Rome as well as the increasingly conservative policy pursued by Pius after 1849. If the first could in part be explained by the bad faith of those Piedmontese ministers who had entrusted him with the assignment, the latter he tended to explain in terms of the increasing influence that Antonelli had upon Pius and the affairs of state.

Epistolario di Luigi Carlo Farini. Edited by Luigi Rava. Bologna: Zanichelli, 1911.

FARINI, LUIGI CARLO. *Lo Stato Romano dall'anno 1815 al 1850*. 3rd ed. 4 vols. Florence: Felice Le Monnier, 1853. This is a well-documented work even though Farini often does not indicate the sources he has employed. This Romagnol openly reveals his constitutionalist and federalist bias in the work, giving it a marked political tone. Farini holds the democrats mainly responsible for the failure of the constitutional experiment in the Papal States and presents an interesting picture of the Pope. Stressing the absolute moral integrity of Pius, he nonetheless notes the religious basis for his political outlook. He also makes clear the limitations of Pius, as he sees them, including his emotionalism, his inability to resist the applause and condemnation of the crowd, and his indecision and uncertainty during difficult times. Farini, like others in the moderate school, does not interpret the Allocution of April 29, 1848, as a betrayal, but as a clarification of his position.

FRANCO, GIOVANNI GIUSEPPE. *Appunti storici sopra il Concilio Vaticano*. Edited by Giacomo Martina. Rome: Università Gregoriana Editrice, 1972. Provides the almost daily observations of one of the writers of the *Civiltà Cattolica* from the days before the opening of the Council through the declaration of infallibility. The volume draws heavily upon the observations of Carlo Piccirillo who as director of the journal had regular audiences with Pius. The picture of the Pope that emerges from Piccirillo's audiences shows him to be usually informal and at times impulsive. As regards the Council the Pope's initial policy of noninterference is shown to be gradually altered in favor of increasing intervention, especially on the question of infallibility which this work shows he decidedly wanted decreed.

HUDRY, MARIUS. "Correspondance de Manfredo Bertone, Comte de Sambuy, Ministre plénipotentiare du gouvernement Sarde après du Saint Seige (Nov. 1851–Nov. 1852) à monsigneur Andre Charvaz, ancien precepteur du Roi Victor Emmanuel II," in *Chiesa e stato nell' ottocento. Miscellanea in onore di Pietro Pirri*. Edited by R. Aubert *et al.* Padua: Antinore, 1962, I, 327–54.

Lettere di Michelangelo Caetani duca di Sermoneta. Cultura e politica nella Roma di Pio IX. Edited by Fiorella Bartoccini. Rome: Istituto di Studi Romani, 1974. This part of the Duke of Sermoneta's vast correspondence from 1859 to 1874 tends to coincide with the collapse of the temporal power and reveals the attitude of this liberal aristocrat to what emerges clearly as an inevitable end.

MANNO, ANTONIO (ed.). *L'Opinione religiosa e conservatrice in Italia dal 1830 al 1850 ricercata nelle corrispondenze di Monsignor Giovanni Corboli Bussi.* Turin: 1910. This is one of the most important sources for an understanding of the early years of the pontificate because Mons. Bussi was one of the closest and most listened to collaborators of the Pope in this period. The young prelate, who shared the Pope's piety and desire to serve the Church, inspired many of the early reforms and often sustained an uncertain Pius. His correspondence is crucial not only for an understanding of the forces that impinged upon the Pope and a clear picture of the nature of the difficulties he confronted, but also important for an understanding of the Roman ambience and the mentality of Pius.

MANZOTTI, FERNANDO. "Il problema italiano nella corrispondenza di Luigi Carlo Farini sulla *Presse,* sulla *Morning Post* e sulla *Continental Review, Rassegna Storica del Risorgimento, anno* IL (1959), 43-60.

Memorie biografiche di S. Giovanni Bosco. Turin, 1898 ff. These memoirs are not always historical, and more often than not concentrate upon religious matters. However, they are important for an understanding of relations between Pius and Don Bosco—the Saint died ten years after the Pontiff. The religious beliefs of Pius, often ignored in other works, clearly emerge in the memoirs of Bosco.

ROSMINI, ANTONIO. *Epistolario Completo.* 13 vols. Casale: Pane, 1887-92. Within these volumes one finds the basic Rosminian position sympathetic to the piety of Pius but somewhat critical of his political approach.

THOUVENEL, L. (ed.). *Le Secret de L'Empereur. Correspondance confidentielle et inédite éxchangée entre M. Thouvenel, Le Duc de Gramont et Le Général Comte de Flahault 1860-1863.* 2vv. 2nd ed. Paris: Calmann-Levy, 1889. Provides insights into the position of France and Napoleon III towards the Papacy and the remnant of Papal State during these critical years.

3. *Memoirs, Diaries, Studies, and Correspondence of Contemporaries of Pio Nono*

ACTON, LORD. *Historical Essays and Studies.* Edited by John N. Figgis and R. V. Laurence. London: Macmillan and Co., 1908.

ADAMOLI, G. *Da San Martino a Mentana. Ricordi di un voluntario.* Milan: Treves, 1892. An account by one of the volunteers of the events of Mentana.

Antologia degli scritti politici di Carlo Cattaneo. Edited by Giuseppe Galazzo. Bologna: Società editrice il Mulino, 1962. The references of this federalist to Pius and Roman developments tend to be somewhat less fiery than the radicals and even other moderate liberals, but they are nonetheless critical.

ASPRONI, GIORGIO. *Diario politico 1855–1876.* Introduction and notes by Carlino Sole and Tito Orrù. Milan: Giuffrè, 1974. The first volume of this religious turned democrat covers the years from 1855 to 1857. A polemical spirit, Asproni is almost as critical of Cavour as he is of papal policy.

BARRILI, A. G. *Con Garibaldi alle porte di Roma (1867). Ricordi e note de A. G. Barrili.* Milan: Treves, 1895. Mentana seen from a Garibaldian perspective.

BEUST, COMTE DE. *Trois-quarts de siecle. Memoires du comte de Beust.* Paris: L. Westhausser, 1888.

BIANCHI, NICOMEDE (ed.). *Il Conte Camillo di Cavour. Documenti editi e inediti.* Turin: Unione Tipografico Editrice, 1863. Within these pages as well as in Cavour's diary, correspondence, and the columns of his newspaper *Il Risorgimento* one finds a generally hostile attitude toward Rome and Pio Nono after 1848. This reflects in part Cavour's own sentiments, the needs of his domestic policies in Piedmont, particularly his alliance with the Center-Left of Urbano Rattazzi, the secularization of the state as well as his anti-Austrian orientation and his ambitions for expansion in the Italian peninsula.

BISMARCK, OTTO VON. *Reflections and Reminiscences.* Edited by Theodore S. Hamerow. New York: Harper and Row, Publishers, 1968.

Carteggio di Bettino Ricasoli. Edited by Sergio Camerani. Volume XXVI: *12 aprile 1867–27 dicembre 1869.* Rome: Istituto storica italiano per l'età contemporanea, 1972. The documents published in this volume are important for clarifying a number of the earlier ministerial activities and positions of the Iron Baron and his colleagues and even more important for an understanding of the Italian political crisis of 1867–1869 during the ministries of Rattazzi and Menabrea.

Carteggi di Camillo Cavour. La liberazione del Mezzogiorno e la formazione del Regno d'Italia. 5 volumes. Edited by the Commission for the publication of the correspondence of Camillo Cavour. Bologna: Nicola Zanichelli, 1949–54.

COSTA, EMILIO. "Le carte di Francesco Balbi Senarega," *Rassegna Storica del Risorgimento, anno* LXV (April–June, 1978), pp. 207–217.

Count Cavour and Madame de Circourt. Some Unpublished Correspondence. Edited by Costantino Nigra. Translated by Arthur John Butler. London: Cassell and Co., 1894. Contains a series of critical references to Rome and Papal policy.

CRAVEN, A. *Lord Palmerston, sa correspondance intime pour servir à l'histoire diplomatique de l'Europe de 1830 à 1865.* Paris: Didier, 1879.

CRISPI, FRANCESCO. *L'Italia e il Papa ed altri scritti.* Milan: Istituto Editoriale Italiano, 1917.

CRISPOLTI, FILIPPO. *Pio IX, Leone XIII, Pio X, Benedetto XV. Ricordi Personali.* Milan: Treves, 1932. Presents a short but interesting picture of Pius IX.

DEISS, JOSEPH JAY. *The Roman Years of Margaret Fuller.* New York: Thomas Y. Crowell, 1969. Although sympathetic to the person of Pope Pius, Fuller's writing from Rome during the troubled days preceding the revolution and during the Republican period reflect the Mazzinian beliefs on the question of temporal power.

Diario di Nicola Roncalli dal anno 1849 al 1870. Edited by R. Ambrosi de Magistris and I Ghiron. Turin: Bocca, 1884. It includes selections from the *Cronaca di Roma* and sheds considerable light on the counter-*Risorgimento* and the final days of Papal Rome.

FEO, FRANCESCO DE. *Carteggi di Cesare Guasti. Il Carteggio con Enrico Bindi.* Florence: Leo Olschki Editore, 1972.

FILIPUZZI, ANGELO. *Pio IX e la politica austriaca in Italia dal 1815 al 1848* [nella relazione di Riccardo Weiss di Starkenfels]. Florence: Felice Le Monnier, 1958.

GAJANI, GUGLIELMO. *The Roman Exile.* Boston: John P. Jewett and Co., 1856. An account of events in the Papal States, the Roman Republic, and the fall of the Republic told by a member of the Roman Constituent Assembly.

GARIBALDI, GIUSEPPE. *Autobiography of Giuseppe Garibaldi.* 3 vols. Translated by A. Werner with a supplement by Jessie White Mario. London: Walter Smith and Innes, 1889.

GIOBERTI, VINCENZO. *Del Rinnovamento civile d'Italia.* Turin: G. Bocca, 1851. Within these pages Gioberti places the responsibility for the failure of the program he had envisioned in his *Primato morale e civile degli Italiani* upon the shoulders of the statesmen of Piedmont, the democrats, and the Pope. He holds the Piedmontese accountable for not being able to transcend their own immediate, narrow goals and for placing obstacles in the way of the political league of Italian states. The democrats he accuses of obstinancy in pursuing utopian goals that could not be realized and thus impeding that which was possible at the time. As regards Pio Nono, Gioberti recognizes that his actions had provided the *Risorgimento* with momentum but accuses him of later destroying the work he had initiated. He attributes the Pope's actions not only to political inexperience and uncertainty but also to his fear of weakening the Church by provoking a schism in the German speaking countries. Gioberti believes that Pius might have joined in the war as an Italian prince rather than as Pope, noting that there were historical precedents for such action. The failure to do so he attributes in part to his unfortunate choice of advisors and above all his movement away from Rosmini and his increasing reliance upon Antonelli. This Gioberti considered a grave error which compromised the temporal power.

GREGOROVIUS, FERDINAND. *The Ghetto and the Jews of Rome.* Trans. Moses Hadas. New York: Schocken Books, 1948. An analysis of the Jews of Rome by this historian of the medieval period who resided in Italy from 1852 to 1874.

HUBNER, COUNT JOSEPH. *Neuf ans de souvenirs d'un ambassadeur d'Autriche à Paris sous le Second Empire, 1851-59.* Paris: Plon, 1904.

Il Carteggio Cavour-Nigra dal 1858 al 1861. Edited by the National Commission for the Publication of the Papers of Count Cavour. Bologna: Zanichelli, 1961.

Il Conte di Cavour. Ricordi di Michelangelo Castelli. Edited by Luigi Chiala. Turin: Roux e Favale, 1886.

Il Regno di Sardegna nel 1848-49 nei carteggi di Domenico Buffa. Edited by Emilio Costa. Volume III: *20 febbraio 1848-29 novembre 1849.* Rome: Istituto per la Storia del Risorgimento Italiano, 1970. This is the third volume of the correspondence of the political moderate Buffa, friend of Rattazzi, Castelli and Cavour and Minister of Agriculture. The letters included herein are important for an understanding of two crucial years in the Piedmont of Carlo Alberto and decisive for the history of Italy.

KANZLER, HERMANN. *La campagna romana dell' esercito pontificio nel 1867 descritta dal gen. Kanzler e documentata.* Bologna. Libreria della Immacolata, 1861. The Commander of the papal forces describes the events of 1867 and the campaign.

LECCISOTTI, TOMMASO. "La corrisondenza fra Don Luigi Tosti e l'ambasciatore d'Harcourt nel periodo della Repubblica Romana (1849)," *Pio IX,* anno V (September-December 1976), 312-39.

LEICHT, PIER SILVERIO. "Memorie di Michele Leicht," *Rassegna Storica del Risorgimento,* anno XXII (July 1935), 56-109.

Lettere edite ed inedite di Camillo di Cavour. Edited by Luigi Chiala. Turin: Roux e Favale, 1882-87.

LEZZANI, MARIO. "Noterelle epistolari di un Romano dei Mille," *Rassegna Storica del Risorgimento,* anno XXII (December 1935), 928-31.

MARTINI, FERDINANDO (ed.). *Due dell' estrema. Il Guerrazzi e il Brofferio. Carteggi inediti (1859-1866).* Florence: Felice Le Monnier, 1920. Within this correspondence one finds expression of their radical anti-clerical sentiments and their opposition to the Rome of Pius IX.

Memoirs of Prince Chlodwig of Hohenlohe-Schillingsfuerst. Edited by Friedrich Vurtius. New York: The Macmillan Co., 1906. Provides some insights into events that led to the *Kulturkampf.*

MASSARI, GIUSEPPE. *Diario dalle cento voce.* Bologna: Cappelli, 1959.

MAZZINI, GIUSEPPE. *Scritti editi ed inediti.* 18 volumes. Milan and Rome: G. Daelli, 1861-91. The first seven volumes include Mazzini's own *Autobiographical Notes.* Within them as well as Mazzini's other works one finds perhaps the clearest expression of the democratic and radical attitude toward Rome and the papacy. This stresses the incompatibility between the papacy and liberty and views the Roman Curia and the temporal power as major obstacles to Italian unification.

MENABREA, LUIGI FEDERICO. *Memorie.* Edited by Letterio Briguglio and Luigi Bulferettii. Florence: Giunti-Barbera, 1971. Has a number of things to say about the events of 1848 and the myth of Pio Nono.

METTERNICH, KLEMENS VON. *Mémoires, documents et écrits divers laissés par le prince de Metternich.* Edited by Prince Richard Metternich with the papers being arranged and classified by M. A. de Klinkowstroem. 8 vols. Paris, 1880-84. The seventh volume is particularly important for assessing the doubts that the Austrian Chancellor had about the new Pope who oscillated in his tendencies.

OLLIVIER, ÉMILE. *Journal, 1861-1869.* Edited by Theodore Zedlin and Anne Troisier de Diaz. Paris: Julliard, 1961. Vol. I: 1846-1860; Vol. II: 1861-1869. In this and other of his works Ollivier takes a balanced view of events in Rome.

──────. *L'Eglise et l'etat au Concile du Vatican.* Paris, 1879. 2 vols. This work does not restrict itself to the Council and in the first volume concentrates upon the personality of the Pope, providing a picture of Pius drawn primarily from the memoirs of the Princess Caroline de Sayn Wittgenstein, who lived for many years in the Eternal City.

Ozanam in his Correspondence. Edited by Reverend Monsignor Baunard. New York: Benzinger Brothers, 1925. By and large sympathetic to the efforts made by Pius as Pope and Prince.

PALLAVICINO, GIORGIO. *Memorie di Giorgio Pallavicino. Pubblicate per cura della figlia.* Turin: Roux, Frassati and Co., 1895.

PERRAUD, CARDINAL. *Mes relations personnelles avec les deux derniers Papes Pie IX et Leon XIII.* Souvenirs, notes, lettres (1856-1903). Edited by Francois-Leon Gauthey. Paris: Pierre Tequi, 1917.

PERFETTI, FILIPPO. *Ricordi Di Roma.* Florence: G. Barbera, 1861.

Pio Nono ed i suoi Popoli nel MDCCCLVII ossia Memorie intorno al viaggio della Santita di N.S. per L'Italia Centrale. Rome: Tipografia degli SS Palazzi Apostolici, 1860. A detailed account of the Pope's visit to the northern parts of his state in 1857. While it tends to emphasize the warm reception he received as a manifestation of the love of his people and its objectivity is suspect, it is useful for an itinerary of the trip.

Posthumous Papers of Jessie White Mario: The Birth of Modern Italy. Edited with an introduction by the Duke Litta-Visconti-Arese. New York: Charles Scribners Sons, 1909. Devoted to Garibaldi and Mazzini, her papers reflect their attitude toward Rome and Papal policy.

Proceedings of the Public Demonstration of Sympathy with Pope Pius IX, and with Italy, in the City of New York, on Monday, November 29 A.D. 1847. New York: William Van Norden, 1847. The interest and approval that Pius evoked during the first year of his Pontificate transcended the Atlantic and in the early part of November, 1847, steps were taken to convene an assembly of American citizens in New York to give public expression of their sentiments and a Committee of Arrangements was created for this purpose. Under their auspices a meeting was held on November 29 and the proceedings are included in this work. Among the documents of interest are letters from Martin van Buren, George M.

Dallas, ex-vice-president of the United States, James Buchanan, Secretary of State, William H. Seward, and Albert Gallatin. It also includes the address to the Pope.

Ricordi di Michelangelo Castelli, 1847-1875. Edited by Luigi Chiala. Turin: L. Rous, 1888. The views of this political moderate approximate those of Cavour as regards attitude toward Rome.

RONCALLI, NICOLA. *Cronaca di Roma. Volume I: (1844-1848).* Edited by Maria Luisa Trebiliani. Rome: Istituto per la Storia del Risorgimento Italiano, 1972. The Institute for the History of the Risorgimento hopes to eventually publish the entire vast literature of the *Cronaca di Roma* of Roncalli. The first volume throws considerable light on the Rome of the last days of Gregory XVI and the first two years of the pontificate of Pio Nono.

SCLOPIS DI SALERANO, FEDERIGO. *Diario segreto (1859-1878).* Edited by Pietro Pirri. Turin: Deputazione subalpine di storia patria, 1959. Although profoundly Catholic Sclopis tends to be objective and balanced in his assessment of events in Rome, relations between Church and state in Piedmont first and then Italy, and in his evaluation of Pio Nono and Antonelli.

SETTEMBRINI, LUIGI. *Ricordanze della mia vita.* Milan: Feltrinelli, 1961.

STEFANUTTI, J. A. *La Lega Italiana promossa da Pio IX. Il '49 romano negli scritti editi e inediti di mons. Corboli Bussi.* Tarcento: Grafiche D. Stefanutti, 1951.

The Memoirs of Francesco Crispi. Edited by Thomas Palamenghi-Crispi. Translated by Mary Prichard-Agnetti. New York: Hodder and Stoughton, 1912.

The Roman Journals of Ferdinand Gregorovius, 1852-1875. Edited by Freidrich Althaus. Translated by Mrs. Gustavus W. Hamilton. London: George Bell and Sons, 1907. Although the author is hostile to the papacy, he reports a number of amusing incidents that occurred in Papal Rome which he enjoyed despite his antipathy to the papacy. Present in Rome during the Vatican Council he portrays Pius as alternately weak and vacillating one moment, and dictatorial and imposing his will upon the assembly the next. The same dichotomy is found in his view of Antonelli, though he is more favorable to the Cardinal than most other critics.

VISCONTI-VENOSTA, GIOVANNI. *Ricordi di gioventù. Cose vedute e sapute, 1847-1860.* Milan: Rizzoli Editore, 1959. Translated by William Prall from third edition as *Memoirs of Youth: Things Seen and Known, 1847-1860.* Boston: Houghton Mifflin Co., 1914. Extremely hostile to the papal government following the restoration without attacking Pio Nono personally.

ZANICHELLI, NICOLA (ed.). *La questione romana negli anni 1860-61. Carteggio del Conte di Cavour con D. Pantaleoni, C. Passaglia, O. Vimercati.* Bologna: Commissione Reale Editrice, 1929.

_____. *Cavour e L'Inghilterra: Carteggio con V. E. D'Azeglio.* Bologna: Commissione Reale Editrice, 1933.

4. *Contemporary Accounts of Pio Nono and the Papal Regime*

ABOUT, EDMUND. *The Roman Question.* Translated by H. C. Coape. New York: Appleton and Co., 1859. Originally published in French as *La question romaine* this work is critical of Pius, the papal monarchy, and even more so of Cardinal Antonelli, who is presented as a minister grafted on a savage and held responsible for many of the abuses in Rome.

BIANCHI-GIOVINI, A. *Quadro dei costumi della corte di Roma.* 3rd ed. Libreria speciale della novita, 1861. This short work is political and polemical and ultra critical of the papal regime following the second restoration. While there are few kind words for the Pope, the Antonelli family is especially criticized with the Secretary of State depicted as the real power in Rome and the cause of many of its problems.

BOERO, GIUSEPPE. *La rivoluzione romana al giudizio degli imparziali.* Florence: 1850. Although Catholic and conservative in its inspiration this is more than an apologetic work and is based upon some sound sources.

BRENNAN, RICHARD. *A Popular Life of our Holy Father Pope Pius IX Drawn from the Most Reliable Authorities.* New York: Benzinger Brothers, 1877. An apologetic, popular, clerical biography which makes no attempt to be critical or to assess objectively the life of the Pope or the events of his pontificate. Having neither footnotes nor bibliography, it is difficult to assess just how reliable his sources are.

D'ARLINCOURT, VISCOUNT. *L'Italia Rossa o Storia delle rivoluzioni dall' elezione di Pio IX al di lui ritorno in sua capitale.* Translated by Francesco Giuntini. Florence: Published by the author, 1851. This work, inspired by conservative, clerical sentiments believes the revolution to be inspired by the diffusion of incredulity whose ultimate aim is to undermine the temporal power and destroy religion. Pius is depicted as the sovereign whose desire to improve the lot of his people was abused to achieve ends he had never intended.

DE BONI, FILIPPO. *La congiura di Roma e Pio IX.* Lausanne, 1847. This work is a typical expression of the early enthusiasm the reformism of Pius inspired as the author praised the anti-Austrian, liberal course that the Pontiff seemed to pursue. He was to alter his opinion following the allocution of April 1848, the revolution, and the Pope's flight to Gaeta. This is his work *Il Papa Pio IX*, which appeared in 1849. De Boni declared that Pius was more detrimental to Italian aspirations than Gregory XVI.

DE GODDES DE LIANCOURT, COUNT C. A. and JAMES A. MANNING. *Pius the Ninth: The First Year of His Pontificate.* 2 vols. London: Thomas Cautley Newby Publishers, 1847. A flattering interpretation that borders on adulation.

DE GRANDEFFE, ARTURO. *Pio IX e L'Italia.* Turin: Reviglio, 1859.

D'IDEVILLE, H. *Pie IX, sa vie, sa mort. Souvenirs personnels.* Paris: Palme-Albanel, 1878.

GOURARD, CARLO. *L'Italia: Sue ultime rivoluzioni e suo stato presente.* Edited by Mario Carletti. Florence, 1852.

HASSARD, JOHN R. G. *Life of Pope Pius IX.* New York: Catholic Publication Society Co., 1878. Another apologetic account.

LIVERANI, FRANCESCO. *Il Papato, L'Impero e il Regno d'Italia.* Florence: Barbera, 1861.

MAGUIRE, JOHN FRANCIS. *Pontificate of Pius the Ninth.* London: Longmans, Green and Co., 1870. This is the third edition of *Rome: Its Rulers and Its Institutions*, originally published in 1857, and carries the history of the pontificate through the Vatican Council. Like the earlier volumes it tends to be clerical in its orientation but is factually accurate in most instances. In its appendix is the important "Report from the Count de Rayneval the French Envoy at Rome to the French Minister for Foreign Affairs" of May 14, 1856, on conditions in the Papal States and its assessment of that government.

O'REILLY, BERNARD. *A Life of Pius IX Down to the Episcopal Jubilee of 1877.* 8th ed. New York: P. F. Collier, Publisher, 1878. An apologetic, clerical biography which has few notes and lacks a bibliography.

QUINET, EDGAR. *La question romaine devant l'histoire, 1848-1867.* Paris: Armand Le Chevalier, 1868. Tends to be critical of Papal policy and especially harsh on the Jesuits.

SHEA, JOHN GILMARY. *The Life of Pope Pius IX and the Great Events in the History of the Church during his Pontificate.* New York: Thomas Kelly, 1878. Among the better of the apologetic biographies of Pius IX written in English.

SPADA, GIUSEPPE. *Storia della Rivoluzione di Roma e della restaurazione del governo pontificio dal 1 giugno al 15 luglio 1849.* Florence: 1868-69. 3 vols. This antirevolutionary history is very well documented and the author's ideological preconceptions and his attachment to the papacy do not mar his objective account of events.

VEILLOT, LOUIS. *Vita di S.S. Pio IX.* Translated by L. Gibelli. Paris, 1863. An apologetic study by one of the leading ultramontanes.

DIPLOMATIC DISPATCHES AND DOCUMENTS

Confederate States of America. *The Messages and Papers of Jefferson Davis and the Confederacy Including Diplomatic Correspondence 1861-1865.* Introduction by Allan Nevins. Edited and compiled by James D. Richardson. New York: Chelsea House—Robert Hector, Publishers, 1966. Includes information about the appointment and mission of Dudly Mann as envoy of the Confederate States of America to Pope Pius IX in 1863.

ELLIOT, SIR HENRY. *Some revolutions and other diplomatic experience.* London: J.M. Murray, 1922. Recollections of the English Minister at Naples and Turin.

Great Britain. *British and Foreign State Papers*, XXXVI (1847–48); XXXVII (1848–49); LXV (1873–74).

Italia. Commissione per la pubblicazione dei Documenti diplomatici. *I Documenti Diplomatic Italiani. Prima serie* (1861–1870). Rome: La Libreria dello Stato, 1952.

La diplomazia del Regno di Sardegna durante la prima guerra d'indipendenza. II: *Relazioni con lo Stato Pontificio (marzo 1848–luglio 1849).* Edited by Carlo Baudi di Vesme. Turin: Istituto per la Storia del Risorgimento Italiano, 1951.

La relazioni diplomatiche fra il governo provvisorio siciliano e la Gran Bretagna. III *serie*: 1848–1860. Volume unico (14 aprile 1848–10 aprile 1849). Edited by Federico Curato. Rome: Istituto storico italiano per l'età moderna e contemporanea, 1971.

Le relazioni diplomatiche fra L'Austria e il Granducato di Toscana. III *serie*: 1848–1860. Volume III: 10 maggio 1851–30 dicembre 1852. Edited by Angelo Filipuzzi. Rome: Istituto storico italiano per l'età moderna a contemporanea, 1968. Volume V: 19 maggio 1856–12 maggio 1859. Rome, 1969. This covers the last years of the dynasty and state and includes the visit of Pio Nono to Florence.

Le relazioni diplomatiche fra L'Austria e il Regno di Sardegna e la guerra del 1848–49. III *serie*: 1848–1860. Vol. I: 24 marzo 1848–11 aprile 1849. Edited by Angelo Filipuzzi. Rome: Istituto storico italiano per l'età moderna e contemporanea, 1961.

Le relazioni diplomatiche fra L'Austria e lo Stato Pontificio. III *serie*: 1848–1860. I: 28 novembre 1848–28 dicembre 1849. Edited by Richard Blaas. Rome: Istituto storico italiano per l'età moderna e contemporanea, 1973. Included herein are the Austrian documents on relations between Austria and the Pontifical State for the period between the flight of Pius to Gaeta and the restoration of papal power at the end of 1849. Together they reveal the differences between Vienna and Paris on matters concerning the Papal States, the nature and consequences of papal diplomacy and the impact of the events of 1849 upon Austrian policy. Although Austria had withdrawn its ambassador from the papal court, there is an excellent documentation in the instructions and despatches of Prince Schwarzenberg and in the letters of Count Esterhazy sent to Gaeta for the conference of the powers.

Le relazioni diplomatiche fra la Gran Bretagna e il Regno di Sardegna. III *serie*: 1848–1860. Vol. IV: gennaio 1852–10 gennaio 1855. Edited by Federico Curato. Rome: Istituto per l'età moderna e contemporanea, 1968. Examines the first phase of the diplomatic activity of the Cavourian and antipapal James Hudson in Piedmont.

Le relazioni diplomatiche fra lo Stato Pontificio e la Francia. III *serie*: 1848–1860. Vol. I: 4 gennaio 1848–18 febbraio 1849. Edited by Michele Fatica. Rome: Istituto storico italiano per l'età moderna e contemporanea, 1971. Throws light upon the critical situation faced by the Papal States during this revolutionary period and the attempts of Pio IX to secure French support. The correspondence ends on the eve of the Conference of Gaeta.

Le relazioni diplomatiche fra lo Stato Pontificio e la Francia. III *serie*: 1848–1860. Volume II: 19 febbraio 1849–15 aprile 1850. Rome, 1972. Much of the correspondence in this volume concerns the French attempt to make their intervention against the Roman Republic contingent upon certain prescribed reforms to be given by the Pope to his subjects, and the failure of the French to achieve their objective.

L'Unificazione italiana vista dei diplomatic statunitensi. Volume IV: 1861–1866. Edited by Howard Marraro. Rome: Istituto per la storia del Risorgimento Italiano, 1971. This volume of diplomatic documents of the first minister of the United States to the new Kingdom of Italy George P. Marsh, includes corespondence from April 1861 to the end of 1866. The comments of Marsh are interesting and tinged with an extreme anti-clericalism but provide no new insights.

STOCK, LEO FRANCIS (ed.). *Consular Relations between the United States and the Papal States: Instructions and Despatches.* Washington: American Catholic Historical Association, 1945.

———. *United States Ministers to the Papal States: Instructions and Despathes, 1848–1868.* Washington: American Catholic Historical Association, 1933. As early as 1797 the United States commissioned a consul to represent them in the Papal States and in 1848 opened formal diplomatic relations with the papal dominion and supported a minister at the court of Pius until 1867. The reports of these ministers, though long neglected, provide invaluable and surprisingly objective accounts of developments in Rome and the Papal States.

The Roman Question: Extracts from the Despatches of Odo Russell from Rome, 1858–1870. Edited by Noel Blakiston. London: Chapman and Hall, L'td, 1962. The most important sections of Odo Russell's despatches from Rome while serving as the unofficial English representative there, are available in this volume. These despatches culled from the Public Record Office, the Clarendon Papers in Oxford and the private Russell Papers provide an eyewitness view of the final struggle to preserve the temporal power. They are also important for revealing the preparations for the first Vatican Council and the divisions that developed therein. Written by a Protestant who could not shed his bias and who believed that no satisfactory solution to Italian affairs could be attained so long as the temporal power continued, some insight is provided into the character of the Pope and his Secretary of State, Antonelli.

STUDIES OF PAPAL ROME, ITS INSTITUTIONS AND ADMINISTRATION

AMMINISTRAZIONE PROVINCIALE DI ROMA. *Studi in occasione del Centenario.* I—*Scritti sull' amministrazione del territorio romano prima del Unità.* Milan: A. Giuffrè, Editore, 1970.

ANDRIEUX, MAURICE. *Rome.* Translated by Charles Lam Markmann. New York: Funk and Wagnalls, 1968. Chapter XXXI entitled "The Stormy Years" is pertinent for the Pontificate of Pio Nono.

BARTOCCINI, FIORELLA. *La "Roma dei Romani."* Rome: Istituto per la Storia del Risorgimento Italiano, 1971. This work concentrates upon the Italian attempts to acquire Rome 1859-70 and the failure of the Romans to take the initiative for their inclusion in the unitary state. The author's description of the capital's population and ambience is perceptive and she suggests that the Romans' obvious satisfaction with their own institutions and way of life was instrumental in the failures of the revolutionary groups to overturn papal rule.

BERKELEY, G. F. H. and J. BERKELEY. *The Irish Battalion in the Papal Army of 1860.* Dublin: Talbot Press, 1929. Contains much valuable information about the makeup of the Papal force and examines events leading up to the defeat of the Papal army at Castelfiardo.

BIAGINI, ANTONELLO F. MAURIZIO. "La riorganizzazione dell' esercito pontificio e gli arruolamenti in Umbria tra il 1815 e il 1848-49," *Rassegna Storica del Risorgimento, anno* LXI (April-June 1974), 214-25.

BOLTON, GLORNEY. *Roman Century: A Portrait of Rome as Capital of Italy, 1870-1970.* New York: The Viking Press, 1970. A number of the early chapters deal with the Rome of Pio Nono.

DE CESARE, RAFFAELE. *Roma e lo stato del Papa. Dal Ritorno di Pio IX al XX settembre, 1850-1870.* Milan: Longanesi and Co., 1970. Abridged and translated into English under the title *The Last Days of Papal Rome, 1850-1870.* Translated by Hellen Zimmern. London: Archibald Constable and Co., 1909. This study of the Papal States concentrates on the period that commences with the return of Pius to his capital and concludes with the fall of Rome. Long considered a classic, its reputation rests not only on its own merit but on the scarcity of objective studies of Papal Rome, Pio Nono and Cardinal Antonelli. In the work the author uses a series of anecdotes, memorabilia and a host of oral reports to create a study which is far more social than political. In fact those pages which describe the atmosphere of old Rome, its customs, institutions, religious life and social climate are the best in the book. By combining testimony from a host of eyewitnesses he presents an almost photographic view of a world long since lost.

GHISALBERTI, ALBERTO M. *Momenti e figure del Risorgimento Romano.* Milan: A. Giuffrè, 1965.

———. *Roma da Mazzini a Pio IX. Ricerche sulla restaurazione papale del 1849-50.* Milan: A. Giuffrè, 1958.

GHISALBERTI, CARLO. "Il Consiglio di Stato di Pio IX," *Studi Romani, anno* II (1954), 165-75.

———. "Lo Stato Pontificio dal 1849 al 1870," in *Studi in occasione del Centenario*, 3-11.

LETI, GIUSEPPE. *Roma e lo Stato Pontificio dal 1849 al 1870. Note di storia politica*. 2 vols. Ascoli Picenso: Giuseppe Cesari Editore, 1911. Despite the use of some important documents this presents a caricature of Papal Rome and from time to time degenerates into a bitter verbal attack upon Pio Nono.

MONSAGRATI, GIUSEPPE. "Un episodio della Seconda Restaurazione pontificia: il caso Calendrelli," *Rassegna Storica del Risorgimento, anno* LIX (October-December 1972), 531-62.

MORI, RENATO. *Il tramonto del potere temporale, 1866-1870*. Rome: Edizione di storia e letteratura, 1967.

Roma capitale d'Italia nel primo centenario. Put out by the Ministry of Public Instruction in Italy. Milan: Mondadori, 1971. This volume published on the centennial of Rome as Italy's capital is superficial in its history of Rome in general, but provides a good treatment of the decade 1860-1870.

SILVAGNI, DAVID. *La corte e la societa romana nei secoli XVIII e XIX*. Naples: Arturo Berisio Editore, 1967.

STUDIES OF PIO NONO

ANDREOTTI, GIULIO. *La sciarada di Papa Mastai*. Rizzoli: Milan, 1967. Provides some interesting anecdotes about the pontificate and Pope.

AUBERT, ROGER. *Le Pontificat de Pie IX*. Paris: Bloud and Gay, 1952. This remains the best study of the pontificate of Pio Nono. It includes an excellent general bibliography of the history of the Church during his reign.

CANI, A. *Processo romano per la causa di beatificazione e canonizzazione del Servo di Dio Papa Pio IX, articoli presentati da ecc*. Torre del Greco: Palomba, 1908. Apologetic and not always trustworthy.

CASE, LYNN M. "Anticipating the Death of Pius IX in 1861," *Catholic Historical Review*, XLIII (January 1958), 309-23.

CHIARETTI, GIUSEPPE. "Una lettera di protesta per is trasferimento da Spoleto di Mons. Mastai Ferretti," *Pio IX*, VI (January-April 1977), 117-23.

CLERICI, E. *Pio IX. Vita e pontificato*. Milan: Federazione Giovanile diocesana milanese, 1928. A work inspired by conciliatory sentiments.

FERNESSOLE, PIERRE. *Pie IX Pape*. Vol. I, 1792-1855; II, 1855-1878. Paris: P. Lethielleux, 1960-63. Despite the fact that the author was allowed access to the Vatican Archives prior to their opening to the scholarly community this study suffers from a number of shortcomings. It is one sided in its attitude toward the pontificate and fails to place the events of

Pius's reign within the broader context of nineteenth-century Church history.

GORDINI, GIAN DOMENICO. "Giudizi ed opinioni di Pio IX prima del pontificato," *Pio IX, anno* I (1972), 130–56. The quarterly review *Pio IX. Studi e ricerche sulla vita della Chiesa dal Settecento ad oggi* has since 1972 appeared under the editorship of Antonio Piolanti and has provided a constant stream of articles on Pius and his pontificate.

HALES, E. E. Y. *Pio Nono: A Study in European Politics and Religion in the Nineteenth Century.* Garden City, N.J.: Doubleday and Co., 1954. This short work, written before the opening of the Vatican Archives and so sympathetic to the papacy and the Pope as to call into question its objectivity, is important because it is the first biography of Pio Nono written in the twentieth century in English.

HAYWARD, FERNAND. *Pie IX et son temps.* Paris: Plon, 1948. Follows De Cesare in its anecdotal format and like De Cesare does not provide references.

MARTINA, GIACOMO. *Pio IX (1846-1850).* Rome: Università Gregoriana Editrice, 1974. This is the first volume of a three volume projected biography. It begins where the excellent study of Serafini ends and includes some very important documents in the text and the appendixes. In chapter I Martina provides a comprehensive survey of much of the printed material dealing with the life and pontificate. The volume is objective, scholarly, and well written.

———. *Pio IX. Chiesa e mondo moderno.* Rome: Edizioni Studium, 1976. While completing research for his larger work, Martina has produced this very brief synthesis of the history of the Church during his pontificate. It includes a good annotated bibliography.

MENUCCI, ANGELO. "La riapertura del museo 'Pio IX' in vista delle celebrazione di Senigallia," *Pio IX,* VI (January–April 1977), 117–23.

MONTI, ANTONIO. *Pio IX nel Risorgimento Italiano con Documenti Inediti.* Bari: Laterza, 1928. Included in this volume is part of the correspondence between Pius IX and his brother the Count Gabriele Mastai in the years from 1830 to 1867 as well as other letters of interest. They are printed as an appendix to the volume.

PALAZZINI, CARDINAL PIETRO. "Spiritualità di Pio IX, il Papa della Croce," *Pio IX,* VI (January–April 1977), 3–21.

RADICE, GIANFRANCO. *Pio IX e Antonio Rosmini.* Città del Vaticano: Libreria Editrice del Vaticano, 1974. This revisionist study examines the relationship between Pope Pius IX and the priest and philosopher Antonio Rosmini. Radice attempts to disprove the commonly held notions that the relationship between the two churchmen was determined essentially by the political events of 1848–49 and that Pius was not consistent in his treatment of Rosmini. Despite his wide range of primary and secondary sources, Radice does not completely dispel the traditional interpretation of their relationship.

SENCOURT, R. "Rosmini and Pius IX," *Contemporary Review*, CXIIC (1955), 387–89.
SERAFINI, ALBERTO. *Pio IX, Giovanni Maria Mastai Ferretti dalla giovinezza alla morte nei suoi scritti e discorsi editi e inediti.* I: *Le vie della Divina Provvidenza (1792–1846).* Unfortunately the author was able to produce only the first volume of this study before death interrupted his work. Città del Vaticano: Tipografia Poliglotta Vaticana, 1958. The biographical study of Pio Nono is currently being completed by Giacomo Martina. Serafini's volume is the most important printed source for the early years of Mastai-Ferretti in terms of the hitherto unpublished documentation employed and the objectivity of the author. Indeed some have criticized it on the grounds that it is more a collection of documents than a biography. However, in a field that is filled with controversy, this work is an important contribution and must be seen by all who would understand the early life of the future Pope as well as conditions in the Papal States during the early years of the nineteenth century.
TAMBORRA, ANGELO. "Pio IX, la lettera agli Orientali 'In suprema Petri Apostoli Sede' del 1848 e il mondo ortodosso," *Rassegna Storica del Risorgimento, anno* LVI (July–September 1969), 347–67.
THORNTON, FRANCIS BEAUCHESNE. *Cross upon Cross: The Life of Pope Pius IX.* New York: Benzinger Brothers, Inc., 1955. An apologetic biography, without footnotes, with a number of stories and anecdotes that cannot be substantiated.
PELCZAR, GIUSEPPE SEBASTIANO. *Pio IX ed il suo Pontificato.* 3 vols. Turin: 1911. The best of the older apologetic biographies.
VERCESI, ERNESTO. *Pio IX.* Milan: Edizioni Corbaccio, 1930. Provides some insights into the personal life and thoughts of Pio Nono.

STUDIES OF CARDINAL ANTONELLI

AUBERT, ROGER. "Antonelli, Giacomo," *Dizionario Biografico degli Italiani.* Vol. III, 484–93. A good, and generally objective, account of the Cardinal Secretary's background and career.
"Cardinal Antonelli," *Dublin Review*, XXVIII (January 1877), 74–84. One of the few favorable accounts of the activities of Antonelli.
CASTILLE, HIPPOLYTE. *Le Cardinal Antonelli.* Paris: E. Dentu, 1859. A short, polemical, and critical study of the Cardinal which stresses the unfortunate influence he allegedly had upon Pius and the governance of the states of the Church.
COPPA, FRANK J. "Cardinal Antonelli, the Papal States and the Counter-Risorgimento," *Journal of Church and State*, XVI (Autumn 1974), 453–71.
———. "Giacomo Antonelli," *Clio* (of Rome), IX (April–June 1973), 183–210.

Selected Bibliography 245

GENNARELLI, ACHILLE. "Giacomo Antonelli," in *Il Risorgimento Italiano. Biografie storico-politico d'illustri Italiani contemporanei*. Edited by Leone Carpi. Milan: Antica Casa Editrice, 1886. II, 223-36.

JOURDAN, LOUIS, and TAXILE DELORD. *Les Célebrités du jour, 1860-61*. Paris: Aux bureau du journal Le Siècle, n.d. Presents a less than flattering picture of Cardinal Antonelli.

LODOLINI, ARMANDO. "Un archivio segreto del Cardinale Antonelli-I," *Studi Romani*, anno I (July-August 1953), 410-24; Part II, *Studi Romani*, anno I (September-October 1953), 510-20.

OMODEO, A. "Fonti e memorie. Antonelli, Giacomo, Cardinale," *Rassegna Storica del Risorgimento*, anno XLVII (July-September 1960), 319-24.

PIRRI, PIETRO. "Il Cardinale Antonelli tra il mito e la storia," *Rivista di Storia della Chiesa in Italia*, XII (1958), 81-120. Although apologetic in part—perhaps as a reaction to much of the literature on the Cardinal which is polemical—this is the best single study of Antonelli and dispels many generalizations about the character and life of the Secretary of State of Pio Nono.

SILVAGNI, DAVID. "Il Cardinale Antonelli," in *La corte e la società romana nei secoli XVIII e XIX*. Naples: Arturo Berisio Editore, 1967. III, 490-534.

VETERE, VETURIO. *I ventidue anni di governo del Cardinale Antonelli*. Rome: Stabilamento di Giuseppe Civelli, 1871. A critical assessment.

DIPLOMATIC STUDIES AND THE ROLE OF OTHER STATES
DURING THE RISORGIMENTO

ACTON, HAROLD. *The Last Bourbons of Naples (1825-1861)*. New York: St. Martin's Press, Inc., 1961.

BARRIÉ, OTTAVIO. *L'Inghilterra e il problema italiano nel 1848-49*. Milan: Giuffrè, 1965.

BIANCHI, NICOMEDE. *Storia documentata della diplomazia in Italia dall' anno 1814 all' anno 1861*. 8 vols. Turin: Unione Tipografico, 1872.

BLUMBERG, ARNOLD. "George Bancroft, France, and the Vatican: Some Aspects of American, French and Vatican Diplomacy: 1866-1870," *Catholic Historical Review*, L (January 1965), 475-93.

BOURGEOIS, EMILE and E. CLERMONT. *Rome et Napoleon III (1849-1870)*. Paris: Librairie Armand Colen, 1907.

BOURNE, KENNETH. "The British Government and the Proposed Roman Conference of 1867," *Rassegna Storica del Risorgimento*, anno XLIII (October-December 1956), 759-63.

CASE, LYNN M. *Franco-Italian Relations, 1860-65: The Roman Question and the Convention of September*. Philadelphia: University of Pennsylvania Press, 1932.

COPPA, FRANK J. "Italy, the Papal States, and the American Civil War," *La Parola del Popolo* (November-December 1976), 364-67.
DI NOLFO, ENNIO. "Austria e Roma nel 1870," *Rassegna Storica del Risorgimento, anno* LVIII (July-September 1971), 409-36.
ENGEL-JANOSI, FRIEDRICH. "French and Austrian Political Advice to Pius IX, 1846-1848," *Catholic Historical Review*, XXXVIII (April 1952), 1-20.
HEARDER, HARRY. "La politica di Lord Malmesbury verso l'Italia nella primavera del 1859," *Rassegna Storica del Risorgimento, anno* XLIII (January-March 1956), 35-58.
MONTI, ANTONIO. *La politica degli Stati Italiani durante il Risorgimento.* Milan: Casa Editrice Francesco Vallardi, 1948.
ROBERT, ROGERS L. *"Jeff" Davis and the Pope: A Sketch of Confederate History.* Aurora, Missouri: Parker Publishing Co., 1925.
SAINT-ARMAND, IMBERT DE. *France and Italy.* Translated by Elizabeth Gilbert Martin. New York: Charles Scribner's Sons, 1899.
SCOTT, IVAN. *The Roman Question and the Powers, 1848-1865.* The Hague: Martinus Nijhoff, 1969.
SIMON, ALOIS. "Palmerston et les Etats Pontificaux en 1849," *Rassegna Storica del Risorgimento, anno* XLIII (July-September 1956), 539-46.
TAYLOR, A. J. P. *The Italian Problem in European Diplomacy, 1847-1849.* Manchester: Manchester University Press, 1934.
UGOLINI, ROMANO. *Cavour e Napoleone III nell' Italia Centrale.* Rome: Istituto per la Storia del Risorgimento Italiano, 1973. Perhaps the definitive account of the revolt in Perugia and its suppression by the Pope's Swiss forces in 1859.
URBAN, MIRIAM B. *British Opinion and Policy on the Unification of Italy, 1856-1861.* Scottdale, Pa.: Mennonite Press, 1938.
WALLACE, LILLIAN PARKER. "Pius IX and Lord Palmerston, 1846-1849," in Wallace, Lillian Parker, and William C. Askew, *Power, Public Opinion and Diplomacy.* Durham, N.C.: Duke University Press, 1959.
———. *The Papacy and European Diplomacy, 1869-1878.* Chapel Hill, N.C.: University of North Carolina Press, 1948.

REVOLUTIONARY 1848 AND ITS AFTERMATH

ANDRISANI, GAETANO. "Il viaggio di Pio IX da Roma a Gaeta," *Gazzetta di Gaeta, anno* V (1977), 1-6.
ARA, ANGELO. *Lo statuto fondamentale dello Stato della Chiesa (14 marzo 1848).* Milan: Giuffrè, 1966.
BERKELEY, GEORGE F., and J. BERKELEY. *Italy in the Making: January 1st 1848 to November 16, 1848.* Cambridge: University Press, 1940. This work is important because it is the first to have used the Florentine archives for an understanding of the genesis of the Allocution of April

29, 1848. It also provides a balanced picture of the general political situation in the Papal States prior to the revolutionary outburst.

BERRA, LUIGI FRANCESCO. "La fuga di Pio IX a Gaeta e il racconto del suo scalco segreto," *Studi Romani, anno* V (1957), 672-86.

BOYER, FERDINAND. "Pie IX à Gaète et l'amiral Baudin," *Rassegna Storica del Risorgimento, anno* XLIII (April-June 1956), 244-51.

CANDIDO, SALVATORE. "Giuseppe Garibaldi sulla via del ritorno in Italia (aprile 1848)," *Rassegna Storica del Risorgimento, anno* LV (October-December 1968), 548-72.

DEMARCO, DOMENICO. *Pio IX e la rivoluzione romana del 1848. Saggio di Storia economico-sociale.* Modena, 1947. Stresses the social aspects of the revolution.

GIOVANGINI, LUIGI ARMANDO. *Dalla Elezione di Pio IX alla caduta della Repubblica Romana.* Genoa: Lanterna, n.d.

MALVEZZI, NINO. "Pellegrino Rossi, Marco Minghetti e Carlo de Mazade," *Nuova Antologia, anno* LXI (October 1926), 437-53.

MIGLIORI, F. (ed.). *Roma nel 1848-49.* Florence: La nuova Italia, 1968.

MORINELLI, UGO. *Pio IX e Ciceruacchio.* Rome: Tipografia "La Precisa," 1937.

PERINI-BEMBO, A. "Brevi considerazioni demodossa-logiche sull'allucuzione pontificia del 20 aprile 1848," *Rassegna Storica del Risorgimento, anno* XLIII (July-September 1956), 525-32.

QUARRA, ALBERTO. *"Nonno Toto" e le vicende risorgimentali romane.* Rome: S. T. Pinto, 1973.

ROTA, ETTORE (ed.). *Il 1848 nella storia italiana ed europea.* 2 vols. Milan: Vallardi, 1948.

TUPPUTI, CARLA LODOLINI. "Ricerche sul Consiglio di Stato pontificio (1848-1849)," *Archivio della Società Romana di Storia patria, anno* XCV (1972), 237-315.

WOLLEMBORG, LEO. "Lo Statuto Pontificio nel guadro costituzionale del 1848," *Rassegna Storica del Risorgimento, anno* XXII (October 1935), 527-94.

THE ROMAN REPUBLIC

BONOMI, IVANOE. "Ricordi della Repubblica Romana del 1849," in *Strenna dei Romanisti,* 3-9.

COLONNA, GUSTAVO BRIGANTE. "Mazzini al Quirinale," in *Strenna dei Romanisti,* 146-49.

DEMARCO, DOMENICO. *Una rivoluzione sociale, la repubblica romana del 1849.* Naples: M. Fiorentino, 1944.

JOHNSTON, R. M. *The Roman Theocracy and the Republic 1846-1849.* London: Macmillan and Co., 1901.

LAUREANO, EDOARDO. "Il plauso del clero alla Repubblica romana del 1849,"

Rassegna Storica del Risorgimento, anno LVII (April-June 1970), 226-32.

MINOCCI, CARLO. *Pietro Sterbini e la rivoluzione romana (1846-1849).* Naples (Marcianise): Edizioni "La Diana," 1967. Provides a clear and fairly comprehensive account of the events that led to the proclamation of the Republic and Sterbini's part in bringing this about.

PENNACCHINI, LUIGI ENRICO. "Dopo la caduta della repubblica romana," *Rassegna Storica del Risorgimento,* anno XXII (July 1935), II, 161-73.

PIVANO, LIVIO. "Mazzini Dittatore (1849)," *Nuova Antologia,* anno LXI (February 1926), 265-69.

ROBERTSON, PRISCILLA. *Revolutions of 1848: A Social History.* New York: Harper and Row, 1960.

RODELLI, LUIGI. *La Repubblica Romana del 1849.* Pisa: "Domus Mazziniana," 1955.

SELVAGGI, CARLO. "La costituzione della Repubblica Romana," in *Studi in occasione del Centenario.* Edited by amministrazione provinciale di Roma. Milan: Giuffrè, 1970, 37-93.

Strenna dei Romanisti. Edited by Giuseppe Romani. Roma: Staderini Editore, 1947.

THAYER, WILLIAM ROSCOE. *The Dawn of Italian Independence: Italy from the Congress of Vienna, 1814 to the Fall of Venice, 1849.* 2 vols. Boston and New York: Houghton Mifflin Co., 1893.

TREVELYAN, GEORGE MACAULAY. *Garibaldi's Defense of the Roman Republic 1848-49.* London: Longmans, Green and Co., 1914.

TUPPUTI, CARLA LODOLINI. *La commissione governativa di Stato nella Restaurazione pontificia (17 luglio 1849-12 aprile 1850).* Milan: Giuffrè, 1970.

THE SYLLABUS OF ERRORS

"A Text of the Syllabus." Translated into English by George J. McHugh and Clement J. McNaspy, both of the Society of Jesus. Found in Raymond Corrigan's *The Church and the Nineteenth Century.* Milwaukee: Bruce Publishing Co., 1938.

AUBERT, ROGER. "Mgr. Dupanloup et le Syllabus," *Revue d'histoire Ecclésiastique,* LI (1956), 79-142.

GUZZETTI, GIOVANNI BATTISTA. "Il Sillabo di Pio IX nel suo contesto storico-dottrinale," *Pio IX,* anno V (September-December 1976), 366-81.

I documenti citati nel Syllabus edito per ordine del Sommo Pontefice Pio IX preceduti da analoghe avvertenze. Florence: Tipografia S. Antonino, 1865.

MANNING, HENRY EDWARD. "The Syllabus," Characteristics: Political, Philosophical and Religious from the Writings of Henry Edward. Edited by William Samuel Lilly. London: Burns and Oates, 1885.

MARTINA, GIACOMO. "Osservanzioni sulle varie redazioni del 'Sillabo,'" in *Chiesa e Stato nell' Ottocento*. Padua: Antenore, 1962, pp. 419-523.

———. "Nuovi documenti sulla genesi del Sillabo," *Archivum Historiae Pontificiae*, VI (1968), 319-69.

MCELRATH, DAMIAN. *The Syllabus of Pius IX. Some Reactions in England*. Louvain: Editions Nauwelaerts, 1964.

PAPA, EGIDIO. *Il Sillabo di Pio IX e la stampa francese, inglese e italiana*. Rome: Casa Editrice Cinque lune, 1968.

PETRONCELLI, M. *Il Sillabo, encicliche ed altri documenti di Pio IX*. Florence, 1927.

RINALDI, G. *Il valore del Sillabo*. Rome, 1888.

ROSSI, ERNESTO. *Il Sillabo*. Florence: Parenti Editore, 1957.

"The Syllabus of the Principal Errors of our times, which are stigmatized in the Consistorial Allocutions, Encyclicals and other Apostolic Letters of our Most Holy Father, Pope Pius IX," in *Documents in the Political History of the European Continent*. Edited by C. A. Kertesz. Oxford: Clarendon Press, 1968, 233-44.

CHURCH-STATE RELATIONS

AUBERT, R., A. M. GHISALBERTI, E. PASSERIN D'ENTRÈVES (eds.). 2 vols. *Chiesa e Stato nell' ottocento. Miscellanea in onore di Pietro Pirri*. Padua: Editrice Antenore, 1962.

AMABILE, G. *La legge delle guarnatigie*. Catania: Giannotta, 1897.

BELARDINELLI, MARIO. *Il conflitto per gli exequatur (1871-1878)*. Rome: Edizioni dell' Atteneo, 1971.

———. "L''exequatur' ai vescovi italiani dalla legge delle guarentigie al 1878," in *Chiesa e religiosità in Italia* dopo l'Unità, *Communicazioni* I, 5-42.

CADORNA. C. *Illustrazione giuridica della formula del Conte di Cavour, "Libera Chiesa in Libero Stato."* Rome: Tipografia Badoniana, 1882.

Chiesa e religiosità in Italia dopo l'unità (1861-1878). Atti del quarto Convengo di Storia della Chiesa, La Mendola 31 agosto-5 settembre 1971. Relazioni I and II; *Communicazioni* I and II. 4 vols. Milan: Universita Cattolicà del Sacre Cuore, 1973.

COPPA, FRANK J. "Realpolitik and Conviction in the Conflict between Piedmont and the Papacy during the Risorgimento," *Catholic Historical Review*, LIV (January 1969), 579-612.

GORRESIO, VITTORIO. *Risorgimento scomunicato*. Florence: Parenti Editore, 1958.

HALPERIN, SAMUEL WILLIAM. *The Separation of Church and State in Italian Thought from Cavour to Mussolini*. Chicago: University of Chicago Press, 1937.

JACINI, STEFANO. *La crisi religiosa del Risorgimento. La politica ecclesiastica italiana da Villafranca a Porta Pia*. Bari: Laterza, 1938.

JEMOLO, ARTURO CARLO. *Chiesa e stato in Italia negli ultimi cento anni.* Turin: G. Einaudi, 1952. David Moore has abridged and translated this into English as *Church and State in Italy, 1850-1950.* Oxford: Basil Blackwell, 1960.

———. "Libera Chiesa in Libero Stato," in *Cavour 1861-1966. Circolo di Conferenza di Einaudi, Grosso, Peryon, Jemolo e Pella.* Turin: Bottega D'Erasmo, 1962.

MELLANO, MARIA FRANCA. *Il caso Fransoni e la politica ecclesiastica piemontese (1848-1850).* Rome: Pontificia Università Gregoriana, 1964.

MINGHETTI, MARCO. *Stato e Chiesa.* Milan: Hoepli, 1878.

PASSERIN D'ENTREVES, ETTORE. "Appunti sull' impostazione delle ultime trattative del governo cavouriano colla S. Sede per una solutzione della questione romana (novembre 1860–marzo 1861)," in Aubert *et al., Chiesa e Stato nell' ottocento,* II, 563-95.

THE ROMAN QUESTION

BASTGEN, HUBERT. *Die Romische Frage: Dokumente und Stimmen.* 3 vols. Freiburg: Herder, 1917-19.

BOGGIO, P. C. *La questione romana studiata in Roma. Impressioni, reminiscenze, proposte.* Turin, 1865.

BONFANTI, GIUSEPPE. *Roma Capitale e la questione romana. Documenti e testamonianze di storia contemporanea.* Brescia: Editrice La Scuola, 1977. A good survey of the Roman question which includes text and documents.

BONGHI, RUGGERO. *Pio IX e il Papa futuro.* 3rd ed. Milan: Treves, 1877.

CARACCIOLO, ALBERTO. *Roma capitale: Dal Risorgimento alla crisi dello stato liberale.* Rome: Edizioni Rinascita, 1956.

DALLA TORRE, PAOLO. *L'Anno di Mentana.* Milan: A. Martello Editore, 1967.

DE FEO, ITALO. *Roma 1870. L'Italia dalla morte di Cavour a Porta Pia.* Turin: U. Mursia, 1970.

DEL CERRO, E. *Cospirazioni romane (1817-1868).* Rivelazioni storiche. Rome: E. Voghera, 1899.

"F. Curci and the Roman Question," *Dublin Review,* XXX (January 1878), 1-32.

HALPERIN, WILLIAM S. "Catholic Journalism in Italy and the Italo-Papal Conflict of the 1870's," *Catholic Historical Review,* LIX (January 1974), 587-601.

———. *Italy and the Vatican at War.* Chicago: University of Chicago Press, 1939.

JEMOLO, ARTURO CARLO. *La questione romana.* Milan: Istituto per gli studi di publica internazionale, 1938.

MOLLAT, G. *La Question Romaine de Pie VI à Pie XI.* Paris: Librairie Lecoffre, 1932.

MORI, RENATO. *La questione romana, 1861-1865.* Vol. I. Florence: Felice Le Monnier, 1963.

QUINTAVALLE, FERRUCCIO. *La questione romana negli opuscoli liberali fra il 1859 e il 1870.* Bologna: Forni Editore, 1972.

RELIGION IN THE RISORGIMENTO

BERSELLI, ALDO. "Il problema della libertà religiosa nel pensiero di Marco Minghetti," *Rassegna Storica del Risorgimento*, XLIII (1956), 234-43.

CAMIANI, PIER GIORGIO. "Motivi e riflessi religiosi della questione romana," in *Chiesa e religiosita in Italia dopo l'Unità.* Relazioni II, 65-128.

COPPA, FRANK J. "The Religious Basis of Giuseppe Mazzini's Political Thought," *Journal of Church and State*, XII (Spring 1970), 237-53.

JEMOLO, ARTURO CARLO. "I Cattolici e la formazione dello stato nazionale unitario," in *Partecipazione dei Cattolici alla vita dello stato Italiano.* Edited by E. Clerici. Rome: Editrice Studium, 1958.

MASSE, DOMENICO. *Cattolici e Risorgimento.* Rome: Edizione Paoline, 1961.

MONTALE, BIANCA. "Gustavo di Cavour e l'Armonia," *Rassegna Storica del Risorgimento*, XLI (1956), 456-66.

PELLEGRINO, BRUNO. "Nicola Caputa (1774-1862) tra religione e politica," *Rassegna Storica del Risorgimento*, anno LXIII (January-March 1976), 8-35.

PITOCCO, FRANCESCO. *Utopia e riforma religiosa nel Risorgimento.* Bari: Laterza, 1972.

SALVATORELLI, LUIGI. "Il problema religioso nel Risorgimento," *Rassegna Storica del Risorgimento*, XLIII (1956), 193-216.

SANTINI, LUIGI. *Alessandro Gavazzi: Aspetti del problema religioso del Risorgimento.* Modena: Società Tipografica Editrice, 1955.

SCOPPOLA, PIETRO. *Dal neoguelfismo alla democrazia cristiana.* Rome: Editrice Studium, 1957.

SINI, AURELIA. "Il movimento cattolico liberale nelle province pontificie (in particolare sui profili giuridici del pensiero religioso di Terenzio Mamiani)," in *Studi in occasione del Centenario*, pp. 13-36.

SUARDO, DINO SECCO. "Liberali e cattolic nel Risorgimento," *Civitas*, anno XXVI (1975), 45-59.

TRANIELLO, FRANCESCO. *Cattolicesimo conciliatorista. Religione e cultura nella tradizione rosminiana lombardo-piemontese, 1825-1870.* Milan: Marzorati, 1970.

THE VATICAN COUNCIL

ADRIANYI, GABRIEL. *Ungarn und das I. Vaticanum.* Cologne: Böhlau Verlag, 1975. Concentrates upon the role of the Hungarian and Rumanian Bishops at the Council and their opposition to papal infallibility.

ALTHOLZ, JOSEF L. "The Vatican Decrees Controversy, 1874–1875," *Catholic Historical Review*, LVII (January 1972), 593–605.

AUBERT, ROGER. "Il primo Concilio Vaticano," *Studi Romani*, anno XVIII (1970), 318–39.

―――. "L'Eglise en Italie avant et après Vatican I," in *Chiesa e religiosità in Italia dopo L'Unità*, Relazioni, I, 3–31.

BUTLER, CUTHBERT. *The Vatican Council: The Story Told from inside in Bishop Ullathorne's Letters*. 2 vols. New York: Longmans, Green and Co., 1930. Provides a clear analysis of the work of the Council based upon the diary kept by Bishop William Bernard Ullathorne of Birmingham as well as a number of other sources. It was written to refute the attacks of Dollinger and other hostile critics of the Council and is one of the most important works available in English on the subject.

CATTA, ETIENNE. "Mgr. Edouard Pie, Pie IX, le Syllabus et le Premier Concile du Vatican d'après les oeuvres de l'Evéque de Poitiers. IV—Le Concile," *Pio IX*, anno VI (January–April 1977), 60–93.

CECCONI, EUGENIO. *Storia del Concilio Ecumenico Vaticana scritta sui Documenti originali*. 4 vols. Rome: Tipografia Vaticano, 1878. These volumes published soon after the Pope's death are primarily concerned with the preliminaries of the Council and in many ways represent more an official collection of documents than a history of the Council proper.

CECCUTI, COSIMO. *Il Concilio Vaticano I nella stampa italiana (1868–1870)*. Rome: Edizioni Conque Lune, 1970.

CWIEKOWSKI, FREDERICK J. *The English Bishops and the First Vatican Council*. Louvain: Publications Universitaires de Louvain, 1971. This is an amply documented study of the English participation in the First Vatican Council. It is not restricted to the role of the Bishops and also considers the activities of men such as Acton and probes the concerns of the liberal Gladstone government.

DÖLLINGER, VON JOHANN JOSEPH IGNAZ. *Letters from Rome on the Council by Quirinus*. 2vv. New York: Da Capo Press, 1973. In addition to the 69 letters in these two volumes there is a preliminary history of the Council and a series of speeches and other documents in the appendices. All of the material in this work has a strong bias against infallibility, is critical of the Council and its majority, and presents a less than flattering picture of Pius IX.

FESSLER, MONSIGNOR JOSEPH. *Le Concile du Vatican. Son Caractère et ses Actes*. Paris: E. Plon, 1877. An apologetic, pro-papal work.

FRANCO, GIOVANNI GIUSEPPE. *Appunti storici sopra il Concilio Vaticano*. Edited by Giacomo Martina. Rome: Università Gregoriana, 1972. Reveals that Pius was not a passive instrument of the majority of the Council but shows him to be independent and decisive on a number of issues and above all that of infallibility. The diary also makes clear that although Pius made clear his wishes on a number of issues, he by and large respected the liberty of the assembly.

FRIEDRICH, JOHANN. *Geschichtedes Vatikanischen Konzils.* 3 vols. Nordlingen, 1877-87. This work by Dollinger's disciple attacks both the work of the Council and its majority which favored infallibility. The first volume is really a history of ultramontism under Pius IX.

GADILLE, JACQUES. *Albert du Boÿs. Ses "Souvenirs du Concile du Vatican, 1869-1870." L'intervention du gouvernement impérial a Vatican I.* Preface by Roger Aubert. Louvain: Publications Universitaires de Louvain, 1968.

GLADSTONE, W. E. *The Vatican Decrees in their Bearing on Civil Allegiance: A Political Expostulation.* New York: Harper and Brothers, 1875.

GRANDERATH, THEODOR. *Geschichte des Vatikanischen Konzils.* 3 vols. Freiburg. Translated into French as *Histoire du Concile du Vatican.* 5 vols. Brussels, 1907-13. This work is solidly based upon sources available in the Vatican Archives which were opened to Father Granderath of the Society of Jesus. It offers a good account of the various problems and controversies in the Council and offers considerable insights into the role of the Pope. However, it is at times apologetic and sometimes fails to appreciate the role and view of the minority in the Council.

HENNESEY, JAMES. *The First Council of the Vatican: The American Experience.* Herder and Herder: New York, 1963.

HERGENRÖTHER, DR. *Anti-Janus: An Historico-Theological Criticism of the work entitled "The Pope and the Council by Janus,"* trans. by J.B. Robertson. Dublin: W.B. Kelley, 1870.

Ignaz von Döllinger Briefwechsel, 1820-1890. Volume II: *Ignaz von Döllinger-Lord Acton Briefwechsel, 1869-1870.* Edited by Victor Conzemius. Munich: "C. H. Beck," 1965. Provides some insights into the events that shaped the history of the Church in the years from 1869-70 and is especially important for the First Vatican Council.

Lord Acton and the First Vatican Council: A Journal. Edited by Edmund Campion. Sydney: Catholic Theological Faculty, 1975. The volume contains some journal notes of Acton from 1870 and 1871 and provides insights into his contacts with the political figures in Rome at the time as well as the attempt to thwart the majority of the Council on the issue of infallibility.

MACCARRONE, MICHELE. *Il Concilio Vaticano I e il "giornale" di Mons. Arrigoni.* 2 vols. Padua: Editrice Antenore, 1966. This is a solid piece of work which covers more than the title might indicate. It concentrates primarily upon the relations between the Council and the Italian government, on the attitude of the Italian Bishops, and on the conduct of Pius during the Council. On this last issue it has made an important contribution in correcting the impression left by Dollinger and Friedrich that the Jesuits directed Council. Maccarrone notes the important role played by Pius, especially on the question of infallibility.

MANNING, HENRY EDWARD. *The Vatican Council and its Definitions.* New York: P.J. Kenedy, 1905. An ultra apologetic work by one of the chiefs of the infallibilist party in the Council.

———. *The Vatican Decrees in their Bearing on Civil Allegiance.* 2nd ed. London: Longmans, Green and Co., 1975.

MANSI, JOHANNES. *Amplissima Conciliorum Collectio.* 5 vols are important for Vatican I (vols 49–53). Paris, 1923–27.

MOURRET, FERNAND. *Le Concile du Vatican d'après des Documents inédits.* Paris: Bloud & Gay, 1919. One of the first of the more objective, scholarly studies of the Council. It is based upon the Journal of Mons. Icard, Director of the Seminary of St. Sulpice, Paris, who was in Rome throughout the sessions of the Council.

MOZLEY, THOMAS. *Letters from Rome on the Occasion of the Oecumenical Council, 1869–1870.* London: Longmans, Green and Co., 1891. Provides an eyewitness account of Rome at the opening and early days of the Council. Rather critical of the goings on.

TAMBORRA, ANGELO. "Il Concilio Vaticano I e gli orientali 'ortodossi. Illusioni e disinganni (1868–1870)," *Rassegna Storica Italiana, anno* LVII (October–December 1970), 507–19.

VEUILLOT, LOUIS. *Rome pendant le concile.* Paris, 1872.

VITELLESCHI-NOBILI, FRANCESCO. *Il Papa Infallibile. Cronaca del Concilio ecumenico vaticano primo.* Milan: Giordano editore, 1963.

The Letters and Diaries of John Henry Newman. Edited by Charles Stephen Dessain and Thomas Gornall. Volume XXV: *The Vatican Council, January 1870 to December 1871.* New York: Oxford University Press, 1973.

THE KULTURKAMPF

ALEXANDER, EDGAR. "Church and Society in Germany: Social and Political Movements and Ideas in German and Austrian Catholicism, 1789–1950," in *Church and Society: Catholic Social and Political Thoughts and Movements, 1789–1950.* Edited by Joseph N. Moody. New York: Arts, Inc., 1953.

Bismarck and Europe. Edited by W.N. Medlicott and Dorothy K. Coveney. New York: St. Martin's Press, 1971. The chapter "France and the Catholic Question, 1871–1875" provides insights into Bismarck's fears of a Catholic conspiracy and the internal and international factors that prompted the *Kulturkampf.*

Bismarck: Some Secret Pages of his History—Being a Diary kept by Dr. Moritz Busch. New York: AMS Press, 1970. Volume II is the more useful for an understanding of Bismarck's attitude toward the Center party.

GHERARDINI, BRUNNERO. "Pio IX, episcopato e 'Kulturkampf,'" *Pio IX* (January–April 1977), 22–59.

GOYAU, G. *Bismarck et l'Eglise. Le Kulturkampf, 1870–1887.* 4 vols. Paris, 1911–13. Though dated in part, this is still a very solid and useful work for understanding the *Kulturkampf.*

HELMREICH, ERNST. *A Free Church in a Free State?* Boston: D. C. Heath and Co., 1964.
HUSGEN, EDWARD. *Ludwig Windhorst*. Cologne: Bachem Verlog, 1907.
KENT, GEORGE O. *Arnim and Bismarck*. Oxford: Oxford University Press, 1968. In addition to delving into Prussia's policies during the course of the Vatican Council this work provides insight into the impact of the "diplomatic revelations" of Arnim on the *Kulturkampf*.
ROSS, RONALD J. *Beleaguered Tower: The Dilemma of Political Catholicism in Wilhelmine Germany*. Notre Dame: University of Notre Dame Press, 1976. Although it concentrates on the post Bismarckian period, the first chapter provides insight into the *Kulturkampf*.
"The Impregnable Fortress: Prince Bismarck and the Centre Party," *American Catholic Quarterly Review*, XV (July 1890), 390-421.
SCHMIDT, ERICH. *Bismarcks Kampf mit dem Katholizismus. Teil* I: *Pius der IX und die Zeit der Rüstung*, 1848-1879. 2nd ed. Hamburg: Hanseatische Verlagsanstalt, 1942.
SCHMIDT-VOLKMAR, ERICH. *Der Kulturkampf in Deutschland, 1871-1890*. Gottingen: Musterschmidt, 1962. Based on an impressive documentation it disagrees with those historians such as Heinrich Bornkamm and Erich Eyck who believe that Bismarck made a sudden decision to enter the *Kulturkampf*. While it sees the conflict emerging as a consequence of the Catholic minority's reluctance to reconcile itself to Prussian leadership in Germany, it stresses that Bismarck decided to cross swords with the Church when Rome refused to support his government against the Centre party which opposed some of his policies.
STEHLIN, STEWART A. *Bismarck and the Guelph Problem, 1866-1890: A Study in Particularist Opposition to National Unity*. The Hague: Martinus Nijhoff, 1973. Places Bismarck's fear of the Center and the *Kulturkampf* within the context of the chancellor's broader fear of particularism after unification.
WINDELL, GEORGE G. *The Catholics and German Unity, 1866-1871*. Minneapolis: University of Minnesota Press, 1954. Provides a good account of the Catholic reaction to emerging Prussian leadership in Germany. It is an excellent source for the background of the *Kulturkampf*.

CHURCH AND THE PAPACY

BURY, J. B. *History of the Papacy in the 19th Century (1864-1878)*. Edited with a memoir by Rev. F. H. Murray. London: Macmillan and Co., 1930.
Chiesa e religiosità in Italia dopo l'Unità (1861-1878). Atti del quarto Convengo di storia della Chiesa, La Mendola 31 agosto-5 settembre 1971. Relazioni I and II; *Comunicazioni* I and II. Milan: Catholic University of the Sacred Heart, 1973. This four-volume work includes the acts of the fourth congress of the history of the Church held in La

Mendola in 1971. The various papers concentrate upon the Church and religion in the peninsula from the creation of the Kingdom in 1861 to the death of Pius in 1878. The thirty-eight included therein are indispensable for those interested in the post-unification Church, neglected by much of the older historiography, which dwelt upon the Roman Question. The various articles agree that during Pio Nono's long pontificate the Italian bishops increasingly gathered around the Chair of Peter and ironically their unity in opposition to the Italian liberal state played an important part in the emergence of the Italian Church.

CORRIGAN, RAYMOND. *The Church and the Nineteenth Century.* Milwaukee: Bruce Publishing Co., 1938.

DANIEL-ROPS, HENRI. *The Church in an Age of Revolution.* 2 vols. Translated by John Warrington. Garden City, New York: Image Books, 1967.

Del potere temporale dei Papi: Opuscoli e documenti. 3 vols. Turin: Tipografia De Agostini, 1859.

MACCAFFREY, JAMES. *History of the Catholic Church in the Nineteenth Century.* 2 vols. Dublin: M. H. Gill and Son, 1909.

MANNING, HENRY EDWARD. *Miscellanies and Independence of the Holy See.* New York: The Catholic Publication Society, n.d.

———. *The Temporal Power of the Vicar of Jesus Christ.* 3rd. ed. London: Burns and Oates, 1880.

MARTIN, MICHAEL. *The Roman Curia as it Now Exists: An Account of its Departments: Sacred Congregations, Tribunals, Offices, Competence of each; Mode of Procedure; how to hold Communication with the latest Legislation.* New York: Benzinger Brothers, 1913.

MISNER, PAUL. *Papacy and Development: Newman and the Primacy of the Pope.* Leiden, New York: E.J. Brill, 1976.

MORI, RENATO. *Il Tramonto del Potere Temporale 1866-1870.* Rome: Edizioni di Storia e Letteratura, 1967.

MOURRET, FERNAND. *A History of the Catholic Church.* Volume Eight. *Period of the Early Nineteenth Century (1823-1878).* Translated by Newton Thompson. New York: Herder Book Co., 1957.

NIELSEN, FREDRIK. *The History of the Papacy in the XIXth Century.* Translated by Arthur James Mason. London: John Murray, 1906.

NIPPOLD, FRIEDRICH. *The Papacy in the 19th Century.* Translated by Laurence Henry Schwab. New York: G. P. Putnam's Sons, 1900.

VIDLER, ALEC R. *The Church in an Age of Revolution.* Baltimore: Penguin Books, 1961.

STUDIES OF CONTEMPORARIES OF PIO NONO

ADAMS-DANIELS, ELIZABETH. *Jessie White Mario, Risorgimento Revolutionary.* Athens: Ohio University Press, 1972.

ANZILOTTI, ANTONIO. *Gioberti.* Florence: Vallecchi, 1922.

AUBRY, OCTAVE. *Eugénie, Empress of the French.* Translated by F. M. Atkinson. Philadelphia: Lippincott, 1931.

BARKER, NANCY NICHOLS. *Distaff Diplomacy: The Empress Eugénie and the Foreign Policy of the Second Empire.* Austin: University of Texas Press, 1967.

BIAGGINI, CARLO ALBERTO. *Il pensiero politico di Pellegrino Rossi di fronte ai problemi del Risorgimento Italiano.* Rome: Vittoriano, 1937.

Bismarck. Edited by Frederick M. Hollyday. Englewood Cliffs, New Jersey: Prentice-Hall, Inc., 1970.

CAPPELLETTI, LICURGO. *Storia di Vittorio Emanuele II.* 3 vols. Rome: Enrico Voghera, 1892-93.

COGNASSO, FRANCESCO. *Vittorio Emanuele II.* Turin: Unione tip. Editrice Torinese, 1942.

COLLODI, C. *Biografie del Risorgimento.* Florence: Casa Editrice Marzocco, 1941.

COPPA, FRANK J. *Camillo di Cavour.* New York: Twayne Publishers, Inc., 1973.

GASQUET, ABBOT (ed.). *Lord Acton and his Circle.* London: Longmans, Green and Co., 1906.

GHISALBERTI, A. M. *Massimo d'Azeglio, un moderate realizzatore.* Rome: Edizioni dell' Ateneo, 1953.

GRIFFITH, G. O. *Mazzini: Prophet of Modern Europe.* London: Hodder and Stoughton, 1932.

HALES, EDWARD E. Y. *Mazzini and the Secret Societies: The Making of a Myth.* New York: Kenedy, 1956.

HALPERIN, S. WILLIAM. *Diplomat under Stress: Viscounti Venosta and the Crisis of July 1870.* Chicago: University of Chicago Press, 1939.

HIGGINSON, THOMAS WENTWORTH. *Margaret Fuller Ossoli.* 10th ed. Boston: Houghton, Mifflin and Co., 1895. She was in Rome during the reformist period of Pio Nono and in Mazzini's Republic as well.

HIMMELFARB, GERTRUDE. *Lord Acton: A Study in Conscience and Politics.* Chicago: University of Chicago Press, 1952.

HOWE, JULIA WARD. *Margaret Fuller (Marchesa Ossoli).* London: W. H. Allen and Co., 1883.

KURTZ, HAROLD. *The Empress Eugenie 1826-1920.* Boston: Houghton Mifflin Co., 1964.

LEETHAM, CLAUDE. *Rosmini: Priest, Philosopher and Patriot.* Helicon Press, Inc., 1957.

LODOLINI, ARMANDO. *Mazzini: Maestro Italiano.* Milan: Dall'Oglio, 1963.

MATHEW, DAVID. *Lord Acton and His Times.* Tuscaloosa: University of Alabama Press, 1968.

MORLEY, JOHN. *The Life of William E. Gladstone.* New York: Macmillan Co., 1904.

OMODEO, ADOLFO. *L'Opera politica del Conte di Cavour.* 2 vols. Florence: La Nuova Italia, 1945.

ORSI, PIETRO. *Cavour and the Making of Modern Italy, 1810-1861.* New York: G. P. Putnam's Sons, 1914.
REDLICH, JOSEPH. *Emperor Francis Joseph of Austria.* New York: Macmillan and Co., 1929.
RODOLICO, NICCOLÒ. *Carlo Alberto.* 3 vols. Florence: Le Monnier, 1936-48.
ROMEO, ROSARIO. *Cavour e il suo tempo. I—1810-1842.* Bari: Laterza, 1969. *II—1842-1854.* Bari: Laterza, 1977. Latest and most comprehensive study of Cavour's career.
SAUVIGNY, G. DE BERBIER DE. *Metternich and His Times.* Translated by Peter Ryde. London: Darton, Longman and Todd, 1962.
THAYER, WILLIAM ROSCOE. *The Life and Times of Cavour.* 2 vols. Boston: Houghton Mifflin Co., 1911.
THOMPSON, J. M. *Louis Napoleon and the Second Empire.* New York: W. W. Norton and Co., 1955.
TREVELYAN, GEORGE MACAULAY. *Garibaldi and the Making of Italy (June-November 1860).* New York: Longmans, Green and Co., 1948.
WARD, WILFRID. *The Life of John Henry Cardinal Newman Based on his Private Journals and Correspondence.* London: Longmans, Green and Co., 1912.

THE RISORGIMENTO

BERSEZIO, V. *Il Regno di Vittorio Emanuele II. Trent'anni vita Italiana.* 8 vols. Turin: Roux e Favale, 1878.
DI NOLFO, ENNIO. *Storia del Risorgimento e dell' Unità d'Italia.* Milan: Rizzoli Editore, 1965.
GAY, H. NELSON. *Scritti sul Risorgimento.* Rome: La Rassegna Italiana, 1937.
GARRONE, ALESSANDRO GALANTE. "Risorgimento e antirisorgimento negli scritti di Luigi Salvatorelli," *Rivista Storica Italiano,* anno LXXVIII (September 1966), 513-43.
GRAMSCI, ANTONIO. *Sul Risorgimento.* Edited by Elsa Fubini with an Introduction by Giorgio Candeloro. Rome: Editori Riuniti, 1967.
GREW, RAYMOND. *A Sterner Plan for Italian Unity: The International Society in the Risorgimento.* Princeton: Princeton University Press, 1963.
HOLT, EDGAR. *The Making of Italy, 1815-1870.* New York: Atheneum, 1971.
KING, BOLTON. *A History of Italian Unity.* 2 vols. 4th ed. London: Nisbet and Co. Ltd., 1934. This remains the most complete survey of the Italian Risorgimento in English and therefore remains useful despite its strong anticlerical bias.
MACK SMITH, DENIS. *Victor Emmanuel, Cavour and the Risorgimento.* New York: Oxford University Press, 1971. Includes fifteen separate articles which provide an overview of developments from 1840 to 1870 and more

specifically concentrate upon the historical roles of Cavour and Vittorio Emanuele in the creation of the Italian Kingdom.

MARTIN, GEORGE. *The Red Shirt and the Cross of Savoy*. New York: Dodd, Mead and Co., 1969.

OMODEO, A. *Difesa del Risorgimento*. Turin: Giulio Einaudi Editore, 1951.

RAMM, AGATA. *The Risorgimento*. London: Routledge and Kegan Paul, 1962.

SALVATORELLI, LUIGI. *Pensiero e azione del Risorgimento*. 2nd ed. Turin: Giulio Einaudi Editore, 1963.

STILLMAN, W. J. *The Union of Italy, 1815-1895*. Cambridge: University Press, 1909.

THAYER, WILLIAM ROSCOE. *The Dawn of Italian Independence*. 2vv. Boston: Houghton-Mifflin, 1892.

WALKER, MACK (ed.). *Plombieres: Secret Diplomacy and the Rebirth of Italy*. New York: Oxford University Press, 1968.

WOOLF, S. J. *The Italian Risorgimento*. New York: Barnes and Noble, 1969.

Index

Aeterni patris, 155
Aldobrandini, Prince, 76
Alsace-Lorraine, 184
Altieri, Cardinal Ludovico, 86, 102
Altieri, Prince, 24
Amat, Cardinal Luigi, 39, 44, 56, 66, 85
American College, 163
Amnesty, 45-47
Ancaiani, Monsignor Mario, 31
Ancona, 19-20, 33, 38, 47, 50, 131-32
Andes, 29
Antonelli, Cardinal Giacomo, 67, 76, 79, 81-83, 90-92, 96, 98, 100-109, 111-14, 116-20, 122, 128-49, 151-53, 155, 157, 160, 163-64, 170, 172, 175, 178-80, 185, 189, 194
Antonelli, Gregorio, 173
Apostolicae Sedis, 148
April Agitation, 115
Ara Caeli, Church of, 164
Armellini, Carlo, 97
Armonia della religione colla civiltà, L', 116
Arnim, Count Harry von, 159, 182, 185
Arrigoni, Monsignor Giulio, Archbishop of Lucca, 161
Artico, Bishop Filippo, 109
Asinari, Ermolao, Count di San Marzano, 66
Aspromonte, 144
Australia, 30
Austria, 37, 40, 42, 47, 49, 52, 79, 81, 85-88, 93, 98-99, 120-22, 125, 128, 130-31, 134-35, 139, 142, 149, 150
Austria-Hungary, 162, 181-82
Austro-Prussian War, 149-50
Avezzana, General Giuseppe, 99
Avignon, 20
Azeglio, Father Luigi Taparelli D', Jesuit brother of Massimo, 55
Azeglio, Massimo D', 41, 45, 47, 49-50, 81, 101, 108-109, 118-19

Bacci, Father, 22
Balbo, Count Cesare, 36, 101, 119
Bandiera, La, 108
Bargagli, Scipione, 104
Bassi, Antonietta, 36
Bavaria, 90-91, 93, 159, 169
Beauharnais, Hortense, daughter of Josephine and wife of Louis Bonaparte, Napoleon's younger brother, and mother of Prince Charles Louis Napoleon, 34
Belgium, 139, 178
Bennigsen, Rudolf von, 183
Berlin, 129, 149, 157, 181
Bernetti, Cardinal Tommaso, 33, 36-38, 44, 46, 57
Berthier, General Louis Alexandre, 21
Beust, Count Friedrich Ferdinand von, 181
Bismarck, Otto von, 159, 169, 182, 184-86, 189
Bofondi, Cardinal Giuseppe, 73
Bologna, 20, 33, 38, 47, 50, 100, 121, 126, 131, 133, 137, 165
Bonaparte, Charles Louis Napoleon, also see Napoleon III, 33, 99, 104-107
Bonaparte, Charles Lucien, Prince of Canino, 48, 90, 96, 125
Bonaparte, Louis, brother of Napoleon and ex King of Holland, 33
Boncompagni, Carlo, 126
Bonnechose, Cardinal, 160
Borgi, Giovanni, 25
Braschi, Giovanni Angelo, Pope, see Pius VI, 20
Brazil, 30
Bread Basket Law, 188
Brinkman, Bishop of Münster, 188
Brougham, Lord, 80
Brunetti, Angelo, known as Ciceruacchio, 62
Brunetti, Luigi, son of Ciceruacchio, 89

Index 261

Buenos Aires, 29
Buol, Count Karl Ferdinand, 125

Cadolini, Cardinal A.M., 51
Cadorna, General Raffaele, 169, 171–72
Caetani, Michelangelo, Duke di Sermoneta and Prince di Teano, 75, 173
Caizzo, 167
Calabria, 138
Camerino, 79
Capogrossi, 25
Cappellari della Colomba, Mauro, see Pope Gregory XVI, 33
Caprera, 138, 152
Carbonari, 37, 51
Carlo Alberto, King of Piedmont-Sardinia, 59, 65, 71–73, 78–80, 82–83, 86, 92, 99, 116
Carlo Emanuele IV, King of Piedmont-Sardinia, 24
Carlotta Maria Amalia, wife of Maximilian and Empress of Mexico, 150
Castel Sant' Angelo, 21, 23, 43, 102, 122, 161
Castiglioni, Cardinal Francesco Saverio, see Pius VIII, 31
Caterini, Cardinal Prospero, 146, 155
Cavaignac, General Eugene, 86, 92
Cavour, Count Camillo di, 38, 69, 73, 108, 110, 116–19, 122–23, 127, 129–30, 132, 134–35, 137–39, 141–42, 150, 195
Cavour, Marquis Gustavo di, 116
Censore, Il, 108
Cesena, 131
Chairamonti, Cardinal Gregorio Luigi Barbara, see Pius VII, 21
Chatrousse, Pierre, Bishop of Valence, 90
Chekib, Effendi, 53
Chile, 27, 29–30
China, 30
Ciacchi, Cardinal Luigi, 63, 85
Ciceruacchio, 62, 71–72, 79, 83, 89
Cincinnati, 115
Cisalpine Republic, 20–21, 37
Cispadane Republic, 20
Civiltà Cattolica, 157–58
Civitavecchia, 91, 99, 169–70, 175–76
Clarendon, George Villiers, Earl of, 125
Claver, Peter, 115

Clerical Abuses Bill, 180
Clotilde, Princess, daughter of Vittorio Emanuele II, 191
Code Napoleon, 105
Collegno, General, 118
Conneau, Dr. Henri, 128
Connubio, 118–19
Consalvi, Cardinal Ercole, 27
Consulta, consultative assembly, 57–58, 66–67
Conti, Abbe, 25
Convents, Law of, 122–23
Corboli Bussi, Monsignor Giovanni, 44, 48, 82, 84, 92, 108
Corsini, Prince Tommaso, 71, 76
Corso, via del, 49, 51, 74, 100
Costantini, Sante, 89
Crimean War, 122, 126, 127
Cristaldi, Monsignor, 26
Cuerta, 28
Cum Catholica Ecclesia, 137
Cum memoranda illa die, 23
Custoza, battle of 1848, 86
Custoza, battle of 1866, 149

Daniel, Father, Chaplain of Papal troops, 172
Daru, Count Napoleon, 163–64
De Angelis, Cardinal F., 50
De Ecclesia Christi, 164–65
De Felici, Antonio, 124
Degli ultimi casi di Romagna, 41
Della Genga, Cardinal, 41, 102, 108
Della Genga, Cardinal Sermattei Gabriele, see Leo XII, 28
Della Minerva, Count Domenico Pes di San Vittorio, 114, 133
Delle speranze d'Italia, 36
Del Primato morale e civile degli Italiani, 36
Destra, 178
Diario di Roma, 48
Directory, 21
Döllinger, Johann Josef Ignatius von, 158–59, 169, 184
Dupanloup, Bishop Felix-Antoine Philibert, 159, 165, 167
Durando, General Giovanni, 73, 79, 80–81
Durando, Giacomo, 123

Eastern Question, 121-22
Ecuador, 172
Elliot, Gilbert, see Minto, 64
Eloisa, 28
Emerson, Ralph Waldo, 54, 68
England, also see Great Britain, 38, 64, 115, 121-22, 129
Esterhazy, Count Mauritius, 96, 103
Eugenia Maria de Montijo, 119, 170
Exequatur, 173

Fabri, Count Edoardo, 86
Faenza, 51, 79, 131
Falconieri, Cardinal Mellini, 41
Falk, Adalbert, 187-88
Fano, 131-32
Fanti, Manfredo, 138
Farini, Luigi Carlo, 45-47, 69, 76, 78
Fausti, Domenico, 145
Ferdinand II, King of the Two Sicilies, 73, 91, 99, 110
Ferdinand VII, King of Spain, 28
Fermo, 50, 61
Ferrara, 20, 33, 35, 62, 79, 86, 121
Ferrari, Colonel Andrea, 79
Ferretti, Cardinal Gabriele, 61-63, 72-73
Fillippani, Benedetto, 91
Fitzgerald, Bishop Edward of Little Rock, 167
Florence, 73, 87, 145, 149, 151, 154, 173
Forli, 33, 35, 39, 41, 131
Fornari, Rafaello, 106
Fossombrone, 131-32
France, 20-21, 23, 40, 87, 90-93, 98-99, 114, 119-22, 129-30, 134-36, 139, 145-46, 153, 158, 162, 167-68, 170
Franco-Austrian War, 130-33
Franco-Prussian War, 167-71, 194
Fransoni, Archbishop Luigi of Turin, 109, 117
Franz Josef, Emperor of Austria, 92, 102, 116, 120, 125, 142, 149, 197
Freiburg, 68
Fulda, conference of German Bishops at, 158
Fuligno, 131
Fuller, Margaret, 54, 68

Gabrielli, Prince Pompeo, 72

Gaeta, 91, 94-96, 99, 101, 103, 105, 106, 112, 154
Galletti, Giuseppe, 76, 85, 90
Garibaldi, Giuseppe, 96, 99, 100, 137-39, 143-44, 151-52, 158, 178
Gaysruck, Archbishop Karl, 42
Gazzetta Ufficiale di Roma, 74, 81, 88
Gazzoli, Cardinal, 89
Genoa, 28-29, 48, 53, 69, 73, 108, 118
German Center Party, 183, 185, 190
Germania, 183, 189
Germany, 158, 162, 168, 178, 182, 197
Gesù, Church of, 53
Gioberti, Vincenzo, 36, 52, 55, 68, 95, 114
Giornale di Roma, 105
Gizzi, Cardinal Pasquale Tommaso, 41, 44-45, 50, 55, 57, 60-61
Goyon, General Charles, 127, 140
Gramont, Antoine Alfred, Duke de, 129, 140
Graziosi, Giuseppe, 25
Great Britain, 23, 37
Gregorovius, Ferdinand, 156
Gregory XVI (Cappellari), Pope, 33-37, 40, 44, 52, 55, 86, 106
Guidi, Cardinal Filippo Maria, Archbishop of Bologna, 165-66
Guizot, François, 63, 87, 120

Harcourt, Duc de, French ambassador at Rome, 91, 100
Hilliers, Baraguay d', 107, 111
Hohenlohe, Cardinal Gustav Adolf zu, 184-85
Hohenlohe, Prince Chlodwig zu, 159, 181, 184
Holland, 115
Holy Office, Supreme Sacred Congregation of the, 146
Hugo, Victor, 158

Iamdudum cernimus, 141
Ignatius of Loyola, Saint, 29
Il gesuita moderno, 55, 114
Immaculate Conception of the Virgin Mary, dogma of, 115, 122, 127, 155, 161
Imola, 21, 34-38, 41-42, 126, 131
Incontri, Monsignor Giuseppe Gaetano, 22

Index

Ineffabilis Deus, Papal Bull, 122
Innocent X (Pamphili), Pope, 30
Ireland, 53, 139, 178
Italy, *passim*
Italy, Kingdom of, 139, 141-44, 148

Janus, pseudonym assumed by Döllinger, 159
Japan, 30
Jesuits, 25, 27, 31, 44, 55, 59, 68-69, 72-73, 78-79, 115, 156-57, 169, 184-86
Jews, 107-108

Kanzler, General Hermann, 148, 153, 171-72
Kenrick, Archbishop Peter Richard, 163
Ketteler, Bishop Baron Wilhelm von, 185
Kulturkampf, 182-90

La Convention du 15 Septembre et l'Encyclique du 8 decembre, 148
La Farina, Giuseppe, 130
La Guéronnière, Viscount Louis de, 130
Lambruschini, Cardinal Luigi, 28, 38, 40, 44, 46, 57, 154
La Moricière, General Christophe Léon Louis, 136, 140
Landtag, 186
Lanza, Giovanni, 173
Lassalle, Ferdinand, 185
Lazarists, 186
Ledóchowski, Johannes Bernhard Brinkmann Graf von, 181, 188, 190
Le mie prigioni, 38
Leo XII (della Genga), Pope, 28, 30-31
Leo XIII (Pecci), Pope, 190
Leonine City, 172
Leopold I of Belgium, originally Georges Chretien Frederic, 94
Le Pape et le Congrès, 134
Lesseps, Ferdinand de, 100
Leziroli, Bishop of Rimini, 35
Ligne, Monsignor de, 42
Lissa, naval battle of, 149
Lombardy, 49, 73, 86, 120, 133
London, 64, 76, 121, 129
Loreto, shrine of, 23, 31, 35, 126
Louis Philippe, King of France, 63, 76
Lucca, 161
Lützow, Count Rudolf von, 49, 193

Macchi, Cardinal Vincente, 44
Macerata, 26
MacMahon, Marie Patrice, 175
Madama, Palazzo, 174
Madrid, 116
Mamiani, Terenzio, 85-86
Mancini, Pasquale S., 179-80
Manning, Henry Edward, Archbishop of Westminster, 165
Mantua, 20, 23
Marches, the, 19, 33, 126, 135, 138
Marchetti, Count Giovanni, 85
Marengo, battle of, 21
Maria Pia of Savoy, daughter of Vittorio Emanuele II, 143
Marinelli, Monsignor Francesco, 191
Martina, Giacomo, 84
Martini, Enrico, Piedmontese envoy at Gaeta, 95
Martini, Giulio, Chamberlain of the Grand Duke of Tuscany, 66
Mastai-Ferretti, Bishop Andrea of Pesaro, uncle of Pius IX, 20, 23, 27
Mastai-Ferretti, Canon Gabriele, uncle of Pius IX, 20
Mastai-Ferretti, Count Gabriele, brother of Pius IX, 133, 156
Mastai-Ferretti, Count Girolamo, father of Pius IX, 19, 35
Mastai-Ferretti, Giovanni Maria, later Pius IX, *passim*
Mastai-Ferretti, Giuseppe, brother of Pius IX, 20
Mastai-Ferretti, Maria Isabella, sister of Pius IX, 20
Mastai-Ferretti, Maria Tecla, sister of Pius IX, 20
Mastai-Ferretti, Maria Teresa, sister of Pius IX, 20
Mastai-Ferretti, Maria Virginia, sister of Pius IX, 20
Mastai-Ferretti, Paolini, uncle of Pius IX, 20, 23, 26
Mattei, Cardinal Mario, 41, 44
Maximilian, Archduke of Austria, later Emperor of Mexico, 150
May Laws, 187-88
Mazzini, Giuseppe, 49, 52, 56, 63, 68, 93, 97, 102, 178
McQuaid, Bishop Bernard J., 164

Meli-Lupi di Soragna, Monsignor, 33
Memorandum of 1831, 37
Menabrea, Luigi Federico, 154, 158, 159
Mentana, 152, 154
Merode, Monsignor François-Xavier de, 126, 136-37, 140, 143-45, 148
Messina, 69
Metternich, Prince Klemens von, 37, 40, 42, 47, 49-50, 61, 63, 78, 193
Mexico, 30
Mezzofanti, Cardinal, 76
Micara, Cardinal, 41
Milan, 69, 73, 78
Minghetti, Marco, 51, 67, 76, 126-27, 145
Minto, second Count of, Gilbert Elliot, 64-65, 77
Modena, 20, 66, 120
Moniteur, Le, 105
Montalembert, Count Charles de, 159, 164
Montecitorio, Palazzo, 174, 179
Monterico, 36
Morichini, Monsignor Carlo Luigi, 76
Morisi, Anna, 129
Mortara Affair, 129
Mortara, Edgardo Levi, 129
Mozley, Thomas, 160
Multiplices inter, 160
Munich, 81, 158
Murat, Joachim, 20, 87
Muzi, Monsignor Giovanni, 27

Naples, 25, 49, 59, 61, 64, 66, 73, 78, 87, 91, 93, 96, 98-99, 101, 105, 135, 137-38, 144, 152, 170, 187
Napoléon Bonaparte, 20-23, 33, 48, 96, 135
Napoléon III, Emperor of France, 117, 119-21, 128-32, 134-36, 137-40, 144-46, 148, 151, 158, 169, 176, 191
Napoléon III et l'Italie, 130
Napoléon, Prince, (Napléon Jermoe Bonaparte), 144, 169, 191
National Liberals, 183, 185, 190
National Society, 130
Newman, John Henry, later Cardinal, 167, 197
New Orleans, 115
New York, 115
Ney, Colonel Edouard, 104-105
Nice, 92, 135

Niel, Colonel Adolphe, 100
Non expedit, 179
Novara, battle of, 99

O'Connell, Daniel, 53-54
Odescalchi, Monsignor Carlo, 26-27
O'Higgins, Bernardo, 29
Old Catholic Movement, 184
Ollivier, Émile, 157
Opere Pie, 176
Opinione, L', 93
Orénoque, 170-71, 175-76
Orsini, Felice, 128
Orvieto, 33
Ostini, Pietro
Oudinot, General Nicolas, 99-100, 104

Palermo, 69, 73
Palestro, 131
Palma de Majorca, 28
Palma, Monsignor, 90
Palmerston, Henry John Temple, Viscount, 42, 64, 77, 121, 128
Panizza, Mario, 152
Pantaleoni, Diomede, 141
Papal Guarantees, Law of, 173-75, 190
Papal Infallibility, dogma of, 160, 162-68, 182, 194
Papal States, *passim*
Pareto, Domenico, 95
Paris, 63, 100-101, 107, 114, 118-21, 127-28, 131, 138, 144-45, 151
Paris, Congress of, 125-26
Paris, Peace of, 128
Parma, 120
Pasolini, Count Giuseppe, 36, 39, 75-76, 126-27
Passaglia, Father Carlo, 122, 141
Patrizi, Cardinal, 175-76
Pecci, Monsignor Giuseppe, 47
Pellico, Silvio, 38
Pentini, Monsignor Francesco, 83
Pepoli, Marquis Gioacchino, 134
Perfetti, Francesco, 72
Perrone, Father Giovanni, 122
Peru, 29-30
Perugia, 39, 131-32
Pesaro, 27, 61
Peter's Pence, 178
Philippines, 30
Piazza del Popolo, 71, 127

Index

Piazza di Spagna, 127
Piedmont-Sardinia, 43, 59, 65, 69, 78–79, 87, 93, 98–99, 101, 110, 114, 116–19, 122, 126, 128, 130–32, 135, 137, 148
Pinelli, Pier Dionigi, 110
Pitti Palace, 173
Pius VI (Braschi), Pope, 20–21
Pius VII (Chairamonti), Pope, 21–26, 28, 42, 90, 135
Pius VIII (Castiglioni), Pope, 31, 33
Placet, 173
Plombières, 128, 134, 191
Ponza di San Martino, Count Gustavo, 170
Popular Club of Rome, 90
Porta del Popolo, 40, 127
Portici, 106, 109, 113, 169
Portugal, 30, 90, 93
Protestants, 157–58
Prussia, 37, 149, 167, 169, 187–90
Pulpit Paragraph, 186

Quanta cura, 145, 147–48, 154
Quay d'Orsay, 148
Qui nuper, 131
Qui pluribus, 52–53
Quirinale Palace, 23, 41, 43, 49, 53, 67, 71, 75, 79, 89–91, 103, 111, 172, 174–75, 191
Quod nunquam, 189

Radetzky, Marshall Josef, 62, 78, 81, 99
Rattazzi, Urbano, 118, 122–23, 127, 144, 151–52
Ravenna, 20, 35, 39, 73, 121, 131
Rayneval, Alphonse, Count d', 101, 104, 117, 119, 121
Recchi, Count Gaetano, 76
Redemptorists, 186
Reichstag, 183–85
Renzi, Pietro, 47
Revel, Count Ottavio Thoan di, 118–19, 123
Ricasoli, Baron Bettino, 150–51
Ricciardi, Count Giuseppe, 158
Riccio, Bishop Luigi, 167
Rieti, 33, 61
Rimini, 35, 47, 131
Ringhetti, Pietro, 89
Risorgimento, Il, Cavour's journal, 73, 93, 108, 110

Rochester, 164
Romagna, 35–39, 127–28, 132–37
Roman Question, 134, 151, 154, 181–82, 193
Roman Republic, 96–100, 106
Romanus Pontifex, 198
Roselli, Colonel Pietro, 99
Rosmini, Reverend Antonio, 87, 95–96, 101–102, 114
Rospigliosi, Prince, 61
Rossi, Count Pellegrino, 42, 52, 67, 87–89, 147
Rossini, Gioacchino, 47, 49
Rostolan L. de, Commander of French troops in Rome, 104–105, 107
Rothschild, Baron James de, 107
Rouher, Eugene, 153
Ruffini, Giovanni, 78
Russell, Lord John, 64–65
Russell, Odo, 130, 135, 138, 144, 147, 155
Russia, 37, 90, 121–22, 125

Sacconi, Carlo, 81, 128–29
Sadowa, battle of, 149
Saint Louis, 115, 163
Saint Michael, School of, 22
Saint Peter, Basilica of, 24, 44, 111, 122, 155, 161, 167, 171
Saint Petersburg, 129
Salasco, armistice of, 98
Saliceti, Aurelio, 97
Sallusti, Don Giovanni, 27
San Carlo, Church of, 51
San Giovanni in Laterano, 23, 51
San Michele, hospice of, 30–32
San Silvestro, 176
Sant' Agnese, accident at, 123–25, 155
Sant' Andrea della Valle, Church of, 53
Santa Maria Maggiore, 23
Santa Scala or Holy Stairs, 19, 171
Santiago, 29
Santucci, Cardinal Vincenzo, 141
Sardinia, see Piedmont-Sardinia
Savelli, Monsignor Domenico, 72
Savoy, 135–36
Schmidt, Colonel Anton, 132
Schwarzenberg, Prince Felix zu, 103
Scolopi, religious order of, 22
Sedan, 170
Senestrey, Bishop Ignaz von, 165
Senigallia, 19–20, 23–26, 30, 32, 36

September Convention, 145–46, 148, 150, 152
Servite order, 22
Sforza, Cardinal Tommaso Riario, 43
Sherlock, John
Siccardi, Count Giuseppe, 109
Siccardi Laws, 110, 118
Sicily, 65, 69, 137–38
Simeoni, Cardinal Giovanni, 179
Sinistra, 178
Sistine Chapel, 142, 160
Soglia, Cardinal Ceroni, 41, 85, 90
Solazzi, Caterina, mother of Pius IX, 19, 21, 23, 27
Sonderbund, 68
South America, 29, 39, 96
Spain, 28, 30, 40, 90–91, 93, 98–99, 142, 169, 178, 197
Spaur, Count, Bavarian Ambassador in Rome, 91
Spielberg, Austrian prison, 38
Spinola, Marquis Ippolito, 114
Spoleto, 31–34, 39
Stanley, Lord, 151
Stellardi, Abbe Vittorio Emanuele, 133, 136
Sterbini, Pietro, 89–90
Stillman, William J., 138
Strambi, Bishop Vincenzo, 26
Strega, La, 108
Sturbinetti, Francesco, 75–76
Subalpine Parliament, 108–10, 114, 116, 122, 130
Suvorov, General Alexander, 21
Syllabus of Errors, 106, 146–48, 154, 158, 161, 185, 194
Switzerland, 64, 68, 182

Talamone, 137
Tata Giovanni, Institution for orphan children in Rome, 25–26, 30
Tauffkirchen, Count Karl von, 185
Testaferrata, Cardinal Fabrizio, 26
Thiers, Adolphe, 182
Thouvenel, Edouard, 134
Tolentino, Treaty of, 20–21
Tonello, Michelangelo, 149–50
Tonkin, 30
Torlonia, Duke Marino, 67
Trent, Council of, 94, 132, 154, 162

Turin, 65, 69, 87, 98, 101, 108–10, 114, 116–20, 127, 129, 131, 137, 139, 141, 143–45, 149
Tuscany, Grand Duchy of, 22, 59, 64–66, 73, 93, 120, 130, 137
Two Sicilies, Kingdom of the, 69, 73, 91, 98

Ubi nos arcano, 174
Ubi primum, 115
Ullathorne, Bishop William Bernard, 161, 163–64, 166
Umbria, 31, 33–34, 38, 135–36, 138
United States, 64, 160, 162
Urbino, 132

Vannicelli, Cardinal, 102
Vaterland, 181
Vatican Council, 30, 154–68, 173, 184, 194
Vatican Palace, 111
Vegezzi, Saverio, 149
Venetia, 49, 120, 129, 133
Venice, 21, 149–50, 169
Ventura, Reverend Gioacchino, 53–54
Vercesi, Ernesto, 41
Viale Prelà, Cardinal Michele, 81, 96
Vienna, 27, 38, 42, 53, 61, 78, 92, 96, 116, 120, 122, 128, 164
Vienna, Congress of, 62
Villafranca, armistice of. 132–33, 135
Virchow, Rudolf, 186
Visconti Venosta, Marquis Emilio, 181
Vittorio Emanuele II, King of Sardinia and after 1861 King of Italy, 99, 101, 108–109, 116, 118–19, 122–23, 126, 129–31, 133, 135, 137, 139, 149–53, 170, 172, 174, 176, 177, 179, 191, 196
Vix dum a Nobis, 182
Volterra, 22

Walewski, Count Alexandre, 125, 134
William I, King of Prussia and German Emperor, 183, 187–88
Windthorst, Ludwig, 190

Young Italy, 49

Zambianchi, Collemico, 137
Zentrumspartei Deutschlands, see German Center Party